Economics of the Pharmaceutical and Medical Device Industry

This book provides a comprehensive examination of the pharmaceutical and medical device industry, including analysis of its current trade and innovation strategies.

Opening with a survey of the global pharmaceutical and medical device industry, Bhardwaj outlines the growing trade and trade interdependence among countries in the global supply chain. He adopts a trade competitiveness approach to analyze patterns of product specialization and examines the drug discovery process and its challenges in translating bioscientific knowledge into lifesaving products. Bhardwaj argues that further economic integration, collaborative R&D, and digital technologies may help accelerate productivity and address global challenges of escalating drug costs, neglected tropical diseases (NTDs), and pandemic risks. The book also considers how the industry may further green its supply chain, and thus contribute to SDG Goals 3 (Good Health and Wellbeing) and 12 (Responsible Consumption and Production), before closing on a review of China and India, major players who have the potential to become drivers of low-cost medical products and innovations.

With its evidence-based analysis, this book will be of great interest to researchers in pharmaceutical studies, supply chain management, global health, and health economics, as well as policymakers and professionals interested in the global issues facing the industry.

Ramesh Bhardwaj is a professor of Business Economics at George Brown College, Toronto, Canada. He has written two books in Health Economics: *Determinants of Mental Health: A Socioeconomic Perspective* and *Protecting Cancer Patients: Controlling Risk Factors, Restraining Cost of Drugs and Preventing Financial Catastrophe*.

Routledge Studies in the Economics of Innovation

The *Routledge Studies in the Economics of Innovation* series is our home for comprehensive yet accessible texts on the current thinking in the field. These cutting-edge, upper-level scholarly studies and edited collections bring together robust theories from a wide range of individual disciplines and provide in-depth studies of existing and emerging approaches to innovation, and the implications of such for the global economy.

Feudal Capitalism and the Innovation Economy
Jon-Arild Johannessen

The Fourth Industrial Revolution and the Labour Market
Future-proofing Work in the Innovation Economy
Jon-Arild Johannessen

Responsible Industry 4.0
A Framework for Human-Centered Artificial Intelligence
David Mhlanga

Deglobalization
China-US Rivalry in the Innovation Economy
Jon-Arild Johannessen

Innovation, Automation and a Sustainable Economy
Tackling the Inequality, Climate and Biodiversity Crises
Jon-Arild Johannessen

Decentralized Autonomous Organizations
Innovation and Vulnerability in the Digital Economy
Edited by Sven Van Kerckhoven and Usman W. Chohan

Economics of the Pharmaceutical and Medical Device Industry
Supply Chain, Trade and Innovation
Ramesh Bhardwaj

For more information about this series, please visit: www.routledge.com/Routledge-Studies-in-the-Economics-of-Innovation/book-series/ECONINN

Economics of the Pharmaceutical and Medical Device Industry

Supply Chain, Trade and Innovation

Ramesh Bhardwaj

Routledge
Taylor & Francis Group
LONDON AND NEW YORK

First published 2025
by Routledge
4 Park Square, Milton Park, Abingdon, Oxon OX14 4RN

and by Routledge

605 Third Avenue, New York, NY 10158

Routledge is an imprint of the Taylor & Francis Group, an informa business

British Library Cataloguing-in-Publication Data
A catalogue record for this book is available from the British Library

ISBN:978-1-032-58195-8 (hbk)
ISBN:978-1-032-58265-8 (pbk)
ISBN:978-1-003-44933-1 (ebk)

DOI: 10.4324/9781003449331

Typeset in in Galliard
by Deanta Global Publishing Services, Chennai, India

Contents

Abbreviations and Acronyms

ANDA: An abbreviated new drug application (ANDA)
APIs: Active Pharmaceutical Ingredients
BERD: Business Expenditure on Research and Development
BOP: Bottom of the Pyramid
BRICS: Brazil, Russia, India, China and South Africa
CAGR: Compound Annual Growth Rate
DDD: Daily Defined Dose
EBP: Emerging Biopharma Companies
EPO: The European Patent Office
EUIPO: The European Union Intellectual Property Office,
FDA: The United States Food and Drug Administration
FICCI: The Federation of Indian Chambers of Commerce & Industry
GERD: Gross Expenditure on Research and Development
GII: Global Innovation Index
GVCs: Global Value Chains
HIIT: Horizontal Intra-industry Trade
HS: The Harmonized Commodity Description and Coding System (HS)
ICT: Information and Communications Technology
IIT: Intra-industry Trade
IFPMA: The International Federation of Pharmaceutical Manufacturers & Associations
INSEAD: Institut Européen d'Administration des Affaires
IQVIA: Formerly Quintiles and IMS Health Inc. The name of the modern company honors the legacy organizations. IQVIA: I (IMS Health), Q (Quintiles), and VIA (by way of).
LDCs: Least Developed Countries
NCDs: Non-Communicable Diseases
NIH: National Institute of Health (US)
NMEs: New Molecular Entities
NSB: National Science Board
NTDs: Neglected Tropical Diseases

OECD: The Organisation for Economic Co-operation and Development
OTC: Over-the-Counter
R&D: Research and Development
RCA: Revealed Comparative Advantage
RTA: Revealed Trade Advantage
SITC: The Standard International Trade Classification
STEM: Science, Technology, Engineering, and Mathematics
UNESCO: The United Nations Educational, Scientific and Cultural Organization
UNIDO: The United Nations Industrial Development Organization
UNTCAD: The United Nations Conference on Trade and Development
USPTO: The United States Patent and Trademark Office
VIIT: Vertical Intra-industry Trade
WHO: World Health Organization
WIPO: World Intellectual Property Organization
WTO: World Trade Organization

1 Global pharmaceutical and medical device industry

Key milestones, global trading environment, and key challenges

Introduction: Global pharmaceutical and medical device industry

The biopharmaceutical industry makes major contributions to the prosperity of the world economy. Medical innovations in diagnostics, medical devices, procedures, and prescription drugs have contributed to significant gains in average life expectancy and quality of life in the past few decades (Buxbaum et al. 2020). In terms of its global economic impact, the industry directly added roughly the GDP of the Netherlands (USD 532 billion) in 2018 (IFMA 2022 a, b). Its total contribution (measured by combining, direct, indirect, and induced effects) to the world's GDP amounted to USD 1,838 billion in 2017 (IFMA 2022a). Indirect effect of USD 791 billion is the effect triggered by the industry's consumption of intermediate inputs from other sectors through its global value chains.[1] The industry's induced effects of USD 515 billion resulted from the additional consumption round triggered by directly and indirectly generated income. The industry directly employed over 5.5 million highly productive persons in 2017, equivalent to Switzerland's total workforce (Ostwald et al. 2020).

Medical products—pharmaceuticals, biologics, vaccines, and devices—are essential tools in the prevention, diagnosis, and treatment of diseases. They are the core segment of the healthcare system which through a host of ground-breaking discoveries and developments have afforded people to live longer and live better-quality lives. Pharmaceuticals and medical devices (hereafter referred to as the medical goods industry)[2] work in conjunction to effectively deliver health services and treatment. Since the mid of the 20th century, the pharmaceutical and medical device industries have experienced many transformative trends and innovations that have rapidly improved the effectiveness of medicines and therapeutic solutions available to patients around the world. Ongoing medical discoveries, novel medical procedures, breakthroughs in fundamental biology (including the landmark sequencing of the human genome), and advances in disease prevention and treatment are resulting in far-reaching salutary effects of reducing the global burden of communicable and age-degenerative chronic diseases (heart and stroke, cancer, Alzheimer's, dementia, Parkinson's, diabetes, etc.).

DOI: 10.4324/9781003449331-1

Pharmaceuticals are chemicals in nature and are designed to actively interact with the body's metabolic or immune system. They are either consumed or injected to produce a biological reaction in the body. A medical device is an instrument, apparatus, implant, machine, tool, in vitro diagnostic procedure, or similar article that is used to diagnose, prevent, mitigate, treat, or cure disease or other conditions. Pharmaceuticals and medical devices are both essential to health. The discovery and development of the next generation of cell and specific gene targeting new vaccines and medicine stand to benefit greatly from medical technologies such as genetic testing, genetic manipulation of living tissue, robotic surgery, and remote patient management (WHO 2010).

The medical goods industry is a high-growth, globalized, and innovation-intensive industry (Gambardella, Orsenigo and Pammoli 2000; WHO 2010). The industry has evolved over time, traversing through weird therapies of the 17th century based upon superstition and pseudo-science of four humors (blood, yellow bile, black bile, and phlegm), to some remarkable developments beginning with the late 18th century. Commonly prescribed drugs as of the 17th century included highly toxic compounds of mercury and arsenic. Primitive practice of "bloodletting" continued to be an accepted medical practice until the mid-18th century. Bloodletting is the withdrawal of blood from a patient to prevent or cure illness and disease, on the presumption that blood, and other bodily fluids (regarded as "humors") had to remain in proper balance to maintain health. Mentally ill were not regarded as "truly" human and were confined with the iron chains (Lambert 2022). During the 18th century, medicine made slow progress, and by 1800, virtually all the strange remedies (such as bloodletting, blowing smoke up a patient's bottom, rabbit's paw, and others) had fallen out of use (Morris T undated). Some noteworthy developments toward the end of the 18th century included vaccination for smallpox, surgical procedure such as tracheotomy (a procedure that provides an air passage to help patient breathe when the usual route for breathing is somehow blocked or reduced), advancements in midwifery on scientific basis, and few others.

Despite some silver linings of the late 18th century, the treatment of diseases was largely based on empirical tradition and folklore, and included herbal preparations, toxins, and other natural substances till at least the mid-19th century (Loscalzo 2012). The industry as we understand it today owes its scientific origin dating back to the middle of the 19th century. During the 1880s, the medicinal effects of dyestuffs and other organic chemicals were discovered (Malerba and Orsenigo 2002). The discipline of pharmacology, one of the cornerstones of the drug discovery process, originated around the middle half of the 19th century (Scheindlin 2001). Pharmacology studies the effects of drugs and how they exert their effects.

Swiss and German chemical companies such as Ciba, Sandoz, Bayer, and Hoechst, with their technical competencies in organic chemistry and dyestuff, began to manufacture drugs (usually based on synthetic dyes) in the late 19th century (Malerba and Orsenigo 2002). The US and UK witnessed the birth of specialized pharmaceutical producers such as Wyeth (later American

Home Products), Eli Lilly, Pfizer, Warner-Lambert, and Burroughs Wellcome (Malerba and Orsenigo 2002). Pfizer was founded in 1849 by two German immigrants in the US. In 1876, Colonel Eli Lilly founded the global research-based company, Lilly Pharmaceuticals, in Indianapolis in the American state of Indiana (Pharmaphorum 2020). In 1856, William R. Warner founded a drug store in Philadelphia. Subsequently, the company expanded through many mergers and acquisitions to become an international competitor in several businesses (Wikipedia). Silas Burroughs and Henry Wellcome, two pharmaceutical salesmen from America, started a new company in London in 1880, called Burroughs Wellcome & Co.

Key milestones and major discoveries since the mid-18th century

Table 1.1 presents a few critical milestones of notable drug discoveries since the mid of the 18th century. The timeline of the drug discoveries can be divided into two broad time periods: from the latter half of the 18th century to the middle of the 20th century and from the middle of the 20th century till recent years. The following subsection presents a brief review of the developments.

From the latter half of the 18th century to the mid-20th century

Developments in chemistry during the latter half of the 18th century led to two types of advances: the synthesis of new drugs as well as the purification of plant extracts used as medicines (Krishnamurti and Rao 2016). William Withering introduced digitalis, an extract from the plant foxglove, with successful experimental treatment of heart conditions in 1776. In 1796, Edward Jenner successfully experimented with smallpox inoculations, which paved the way for the use of vaccination against some infectious diseases in later years. Jenner's work is widely regarded as the foundation of immunology (Riedel 2005). Louis Pasteur (1864) discovered that microorganisms cause diseases, and he devised vaccination against rabies. The isolation of morphine in its pure form was the result of years of research and testing, occurring most prominently between the years 1803 and 1817 (Krishnamurti and Rao 2016). Morphine (also known as opioid analgesic) is one of the world's most ubiquitous and useful pain relievers. It's a natural medicine derived from the opium poppy plant.

Robert Koch, known as the founder of the science of bacteriology, is acknowledged for his discovery in 1882 of the tubercle bacillus that caused tuberculosis and in 1884 the cholera bacillus, *Vibrio cholerae* (CDC 1982). On August 20, 1897, Secunderabad Ross made a landmark discovery by identifying the role of *Anopheles* mosquitoes in the transmission of malaria parasites in humans (CDC 2015 A-Z index).

W.C. Röntgen, a German physicist, reported the discovery of X-rays in December 1895 (Tubiana 1996).[3] Medical X-rays are used to generate images of tissues and structures inside the body. Radiotherapy has its origins in the

Table 1.1 Industry's major milestones

Milestone	*Year or Period*	*Inventor and Remarks*
Digitalis	1776	William Withering introduced digitalis, an extract from the plant foxglove for treatment of cardiac problems
Smallpox vaccination	1796	Edward Jenner replaced the practice of variolation (one of the first methods for controlling smallpox) with small pox vaccination
Morphine	1803	Friedrich Wilhelm Adam Sertürner got a success in isolating an organic alkaloid—a plant compound that has physiological effects on humans—from a resinous gum in the opium poppy plant
Malaria (quinine)	1820	Two French chemists, Pierre Pelletier and Joseph Caventou, isolated quinine from the cinchona bark which became a treatment of reference for intermittent fever throughout the world
Vaccination against Rabies	1864	Louis Pasteur produced an *attenuated vaccine*, and successfully immunized 50 inoculated dogs
Paracetamol	1878	Paracetamol was first made in 1878 by Harmon Northrop Morse
Tuberculosis	1882	Robert Koch discovered the tubercle bacillus that caused tuberculosis
Cholera	1884	Robert Koch discovered the cholera bacillus
X-rays	1895	W.C. Röntgen reported the discovery of X-rays in December 1895. Röntgen received the first Nobel Prize in Physics in 1901
Radiation therapy (radiation)	1895–1896	Victor Despeignes is known as a pioneer in radiation oncology
Aspirin	1897	Felix Hoffman, a chemist working for the Bayer company, was able to modify salicylic acid to create acetylsalicylic acid, which was named aspirin
The electroencephalogram (EEG)	1924	Hans Berger is best known as the inventor of electroencephalography in 1924
Penicillin	1928	Alexander Fleming discovered that penicillin mold was active against *Staphylococcus* bacteria

(*Continued*)

Table 1.1 (Continued)

Milestone	*Year or Period*	*Inventor and Remarks*
Heart pacemaker	1932	Albert *Hyman* created the first artificial *pacing* machine in 1932
Dialysis	1943	Willem Johan was a pioneer of hemodialysis, artificial heart, as well as in the entire field of artificial organs
Virus and Influenza (flu) vaccine	1942	With support from the US Army, the first inactivated flu vaccine was developed by Thomas Francis and Jonas Salk at the University of Michigan. The vaccine was licensed for wider use in 1945
Cochlear prosthesis	1953	Physicist André Djourno and otologist Charles Eyriès implanted a deaf patient in France with the first electrical prosthesis that directly stimulated the hearing nerve
AIDS vaccine	1987	Robert C. Gallo, with his team, co-discovered HIV as the cause of AIDS. Scientists isolated the virus and confirmed that it caused AIDS in 1984
Discovery of DNA	1953	American biologist *James Watson* and English physicist *Francis Crick* discovered DNA in 1953
mRNA (COVID-19 vaccine)	2020	On Dec 11, 2020, the FDA granted an emergency use authorization (EUA) to the Pfizer BioNTech mRNA vaccine for people aged 16 and older. The mRNA vaccines use mRNA created in a laboratory to teach our cells how to make a protein—or even just a piece of a protein—that triggers an immune response inside our bodies. These vaccines do **not** use any live virus

Sources: Various sources were used to compile the above information

aftermath of the discovery of X-rays in 1895 and of radioactivity in 1896 (American Cancer Society 2014). In 1897, Felix Hoffman, a German chemist working for the Bayer company, was able to modify salicylic acid to create acetylsalicylic acid, which was named aspirin (Miner and Hoffhines 2007). The introduction of penicillin in the 1940s, which began the era of antibiotics, has been recognized as one of the greatest advances in therapeutic medicine (American Chemical Society 1999).

Willem Einthoven is known as the founder of modern electrocardiography (ECG). He was awarded the Nobel Prize in 1924 in physiology and medicine, "for the discovery of the mechanism of the electrocardiogram" (Barold 2003). ECG was first used to study arrhythmias (irregular heartbeats) in 1909. The discovery of electroencephalography in 1929 by the German psychiatrist Hans Berger is reckoned as a milestone for the advancement of neuroscience and of neurologic and neurosurgical everyday practice, especially for patients with seizures (Tudor, Tudor and Tudor 2005). In the 1930s, scientists isolated the influenza A virus from animals, proving that influenza is caused by a virus, not a bacterium. In 1942, a bivalent (two-component) vaccine that offers protection against influenza A and influenza B viruses was produced after the discovery of influenza B viruses (CDC 2019). Dr. William Chardack and team invented the first clinically successful cardiac pacemaker, in 1960. They implanted a pacemaker into a 77-year-old man in 1960, who lived for 10 months after the surgery (US Department of Veteran Affairs 2018).

Transformative changes in drug discovery and development since the mid-20th century

The years following the mid-20th century are marked by various watershed and transformative developments in drug investigation, discovery, and development process. Some noteworthy developments underpinning this period are adoption of rigorous scientific approach of "drug development by design" (known as the "rational drug design" approach) to improve effectiveness, increasing application of frontier technologies (characterizing the fourth industrial revolution), integration of rapid advances in basic sciences (including the discovery of the DNA structure and function) into drug exploration, etc. Drug development and approval process had also been subjected to qualifying stringent regulatory standards of safety, starting with the US in the early 1960s. Pharmaceutical companies have been constantly endeavoring to develop new business models of R&D collaboration and product development through competitive global supply chains.

The phase after the mid-20th century is also marked by several other global developments—viz., global dispersal of production activity that led to the emergence of the global supply chain, deeper economic integration of countries at the global scale facilitated by worldwide trade liberalization reforms and innovations in ICT technologies, and growing international demand for medical goods from emerging markets. Emerging markets now represent tremendous growth opportunities for the global pharmaceutical and medical device industry due to the shifting disease pattern (viz., the increasing burden of cardiovascular illnesses, diabetes, and oncologic diseases) (Tannoury and Attieh 2017). The discussion below touches upon the above-mentioned key developments that characterize the modern medical industry as listed below.

Characterizing features of the contemporary drug design process

- Rational drug design and discovery process to develop evidence-based novel products
- Stringent regulation of drugs and devices
- Rapid pace of globalization: expansion of trade and the global value chains (GVCs)
- Role of supranational organizations—WHO, WTO, and WIPO—in facilitating trade of health products and international linkages

Rational drug design approach: Inventive process

Pharmacologists typically distinguish two approaches to the development of pharmaceuticals, one termed "empirical," the other "rational," "deductive," or "a priori." The empirical approach, which was followed before the mid-20th century, proceeded by testing large numbers of random substances for certain desirable effects in biological test systems (Scherer 2000). Typically, drugs emerged from random screening methods without their target (receptor, enzyme, etc.), their mode of action, or the mechanism of disease being understood (Adam 2005). In contrast to this serendipity, the rational method (or "guided" drug discovery) usually involves a theoretical understanding of which protein is targeted by the drug, how the drug acts on it, and which mechanisms lead to the desired therapeutic effects (Adam 2005; Scherer 2000).

Rational drug design is the inventive process of finding new medications based on the knowledge of a biological target (proteins or nucleic acids).[4] Increased knowledge of physiological processes at the molecular level is enabling researchers to develop more selective and potent pharmaceutical targets. Because of these advancements, pharmaceutical industry R&D is now categorized as a "discovery by design" approach, as opposed to the random screening of compounds that was once prevalent (Institute of Medicine (US) Committee on Technological Innovation in Medicine 1991).

In the current modern era, the process of drug development begins with the identification of druggable target followed by subsequent validation to confirm a therapeutic effect, prior to progression into the lead discovery phase (candidate selection) in order to justify a drug discovery effort (Hughes et al. 2011; Matthews, Hanison and Nirmalan 2016). A target is a broad term applied to a range of biological entities which may include proteins, genes, and RNA[5] (Hughes et al. 2011). The idea of druggable targets originates from academia (basic research conducted in universities and public research labs).

The identification of target/molecular lead is a key step in the innovative drug discovery process. A good target needs to be efficacious, safe, meet clinical and commercial needs.

Entry of blockbuster drugs starting 1976

The "rational drug design" method resulted in a number of impressive successful launching of "Blockbuster" drugs such as the development of cholesterol-lowering drugs, anti-inflammatory drugs, libido pills, antidepressants, and others. The first blockbuster drug named Tagamet, for treating ulcers and gastrointestinal problems, hit the market in 1976. Blockbuster drugs are defined as medicines generating global sales of at least $1 billion annually. Three pioneers of this approach, Sir James Black, Gertrude B. Elion, and George H. Hitchings, were awarded the Nobel Prize in 1988. For a few initial decades, the rational drug discovery approach was dominated by a "function-to-gene" approach (Dugger, Platt and Goldstein 2018), meaning that a specific protein associated with or causative of a particular disease was the focus of attention as the potential drug target. This approach basically focused on investigating a specific protein as a potential drug target, associated with or causative of a particular disease.

Shifting focus to new generation of gene and cell-based novel therapies

Since the 1990s, the major advances in both computation and biotechnology, which together cultivated the field of genomics as an innovator for the pharmaceutical industry, led to the widespread and systematic integration of genomics into drug discovery pipelines. High-throughput advances in sequencing, by enabling the identification of thousands of genes, resulted in a paradigm shift to "gene-to-screen" research approach (in contrast to the earlier "function-to-gene" approach) in drug discovery and development (Matthews, Hanison and Nirmalan 2016, Dugger, Platt and Goldstein 2018). The successful completion of the human genome project in 2003 spurred a revolution in biotechnological advances in the umbrella discipline of "Omics." RNA interference and CRISPR-Cas9 are exciting gene editing tools that are arriving on the horizon and will continue to revolutionize medical research (Ngo and Garneau-Tsodikova 2018)

Gene- and cell-based therapies hold a great promise of delivering more precise diagnostics and medicines termed "precision medicine" (WHO, WIPO and WTO 2020). These gene- and cell-based investigations, though contemporarily used widely in cancer research, are paving the way for molecularly defined approaches into immunology, neuroscience, and beyond (Evaluate Pharma 2021 July).

"Precision" medicines: A new paradigm of future health care

The rise of "omics" techniques has resulted in an explosion of molecular data in modern biomedical research. Together with information from medical images and clinical data, analytics advances in the field of omics have driven the implementation of personalized medicine (Tebani et al. 2016, Chen and Snyder 2013, Dugger, Platt and Goldstein 2018). Precision medicine is described as disruptive in its ability to drive down healthcare costs without compromising quality or outcomes (Ginsburg and Phillips 2018).

In contrast with the conventional treatments, which induce therapeutic effects that are transient because they target proteins rather than underlying causes, genetic drugs modulate gene expression to induce therapeutic effects (Kulkarni et al. 2021). These therapeutics can achieve long-lasting or even curative effects via gene inhibition, addition, replacement, or editing (Kaczmarek, Kowalski and Anderson 2017, Kulkarni et al. 2021). It is conjectured that the possibility of defining patient populations genetically may improve outcomes by predicting individual responses to drugs and could improve safety and efficacy in therapeutic areas (Emilien et al. 2000).

Regulation of drugs and medical devices

The thalidomide tragedy in the late 1950s was a watershed moment for pharmaceutical regulation and a key driver of the evolution of evidence standards for drug development and licensing. The thalidomide tragedy, labeled as the biggest man-made medical disaster ever, demonstrated the need for strictly enforced regulation of drug testing, marketing, dispensing, and use. The drug thalidomide caused physical abnormalities in more than 10,000 babies between 1957 and 1962, the world over. The thalidomide scandal prompted an increase in the regulation and testing of drugs before licensing, with a new amendment to U.S. Food and Drug Administration (FDA) rules. Due to thalidomide's effects on fetuses, both nationally and abroad, the US Congress passed the 1962 Kefauver-Harris Amendments to the 1938 Food, Drug, and Cosmetic Act (Tantibanchachai 2014). These amendments imposed guidelines for the process of drug approval in the US and required that a drug be safe as well as effective before it could be approved and marketed (Tantibanchachai 2014).

Regulatory assessment and approval of medicines and devices are essential in every health system to ensure product quality, safety, and efficacy, both before and after market entry. Regulatory agencies issue regulatory exclusivity and supplementary patent protection which extends beyond the market protection that patents afford, providing the industry with additional incentives to invest in R&D.

Most of the industrialized nations, as well as newly emerging developing countries, have created regulatory institutions to ensure that desired safety and efficacy standards are met by new and existing drugs (and also by certain medical devices) (Scherer 2000). Many of the processes to approve drugs in the EU and other countries are similar to those of the FDA. Regulatory bodies provide technical support within regulations to expedite the development and delivery of safe and effective healthcare products to individuals around the world. Drugs are evaluated for safety, efficacy, manufacturing quality, misleading product claims, and illicit inducements to choose a particular drug. Prices are regulated in many countries through their respective healthcare and insurance systems (ITA 2016).

While all medicines and vaccines undergo rigorous testing for safety and efficacy through clinical trials before they are authorized for use, the clinical trial process, however, involves studying these products in a relatively small number of selected individuals for a short period of time (WHO 2002a). Certain side effects may only emerge once these products have been used by a heterogeneous population, including people with other concurrent diseases, and over a long period of time (WHO 2002a). Evidence indicates that adverse drug reactions remain an important cause of morbidity and mortality (Waller, Evans and Beard 2005). A model for excellence in pharmacovigilance has been proposed for enhanced surveillance and reporting of drug-related harms. Pharmacovigilance is the science and activities relating to the detection, assessment, understanding, and prevention of adverse effects or any other medicine/vaccine-related problem (WHO 2002a, b). There is an international guideline that is based on the principles of pharmacovigilance, produced by the International Conference on Harmonization. This guideline is intended to aid in planning pharmacovigilance activities, especially in preparation for the early post-marketing period of a new drug (chemical entities, biotechnology-derived products, and vaccines) (ICH Harmonised Tripartite Guideline 2004). The ICH process is administered by the ICH Steering Committee (ICH SC) and supported by the ICH Secretariat that is run by the International Federation of Pharmaceutical Manufacturers Associations (IFPMA) in Geneva (Bahri 2014). An integrated WHO Pharmacovigilance team was established in 2020, to combine work related to the safety of medicines and vaccines within the Department of Regulation and Prequalification (RPQ) (WHO 2002 a, b).

The regulation of medical devices is a vast and rapidly evolving field. In the 1960s and 1970s, the medical device industry grew tremendously in the US (Stephen 2011). This prompted the FDA to pass amendments that mandated the reporting of adverse reactions to medical devices and post-market monitoring of implants and other devices that pose a serious health risk. The amendments also gave the FDA the authority to recall medical devices (Stephen 2011). The scientific principles upon which a device is based are fundamental to its safety and performance (WHO 2003). Governments need to put in place policies that will address all elements related to medical devices, ranging from access to high-quality, affordable products, through to their safe and appropriate use and disposal. Regulatory controls for medical devices are scarce in the developing world. Table 1.2 presents the list of regulatory bodies in selected countries.

International regulatory agencies and organizations, such as the World Health Organization (WHO), the Pan American Health Organization

Table 1.2 List of selected regulatory agencies worldwide

Country	*Name of the Regulatory Authority*
US	Food and Drug Administration (FDA)
UK	Medicines and Healthcare Products Regulatory Agency (MHRA)
Australia	Therapeutic Goods Administration (TGA)
India	Central Drug Standard Control Organization (CDSCO)
Canada	Health Canada
Europe	European Medicines Agency (EMEA)
New Zealand	Medsafe—Medicines and Medical Devices Safety Authority
Singapore	Centre for Pharmaceutical Administration Health Sciences Authority
China	State Food and Drug Administration
Germany	Federal Institute for Drugs and Medical Devices
Switzerland	Swissmedic, Swiss Agency for Therapeutic Products
Japan	Ministry of Health, Labour and Welfare (MHLW)
Denmark	Danish Medicines Agency
Sweden	Medical Products Agency (MPA)
The Netherlands	Medicines Evaluation Board

(PAHO), the World Trade Organization (WTO), and the World Intellectual Property Organization (WIPO), also play essential roles in enforcing all aspects of pharmaceutical regulations and safety standards.

Global trading environment: Increasing integration of countries though trade

International trade plays a significant and critical role in global access to medicines and medical products. Pharmaceutical products are essentially "universal" in their composition and use (Casadio Tarabusi and Vickery 1998; Helbie and Shephard 2017). International trade in medicinal products has experienced dynamic growth since the adoption of the Pharma Agreement, 1994. The Pharma Agreement, concluded during the Uruguay Round of trade negotiations, eliminated tariffs and other duties and charges on a large number of pharmaceutical products and the substances used to produce them, permanently binding them at duty-free levels.

The global use of medicines has been growing over the past few decades due to the changing demographic factors (longer life expectancy in developed countries, high population growth in developing countries) and the increasing frequency and reach of infectious disease epidemics owing to the increased human mobility across the globe. The growth of trade in health products has surpassed the growth of trade in manufactures over the past two to three decades (World Bank 2022).

With the implementation of the WTO TRIPs Agreement and with the subsequent years of strong trade expansion, the medical goods sector became progressively more globalized (Hakoosson 2009). The process of continuing liberalization of cross-border transactions, rapid advances in production technology and information services, and improvement in transports logistics (e.g. containerization) and services provided increasing motivation to global multinational enterprises to slice up the value chain and perform activities in any location that can help reduce costs (IMF 2008, Nicita, Ognivtsev and Shirotori 2013, Gereffi 2014). This phenomenon of GVC has also been referred to in the literature as international production sharing and vertical integration of production (Seric and Tong 2019). From an economic standpoint, the emergence of GVCs is related to the concept of comparative advantage (Nicita, Ognivtsev and Shirotori 2013). By relocating production processes (i.e., R&D, concept, design, manufacturing, packaging, marketing, logistics, and distribution to support the final customer) in different countries, firms take advantage of the best available human and physical resources in different countries, with a view to maintaining their competitiveness (Nicita, Ognivtsev and Shirotori 2013, OECD 2012a). Firms participating in global supply chains (as exporters, importers, parents, or affiliates of multinationals) do learn better (that is, make more effective use of information to innovate) internally (within the firm) or externally (especially customers and suppliers) (OECD 2012a).

The importance of the multinational activities in the global value chain can be proxied by the Foreign Direct Investment (FDI) intensity indicator, which is constructed as the industry's share in total FDI to share in total trade (UNCTAD WIR 2020, Ch IV). FDI intensity is found to be the highest in the pharmaceutical industry compared to any other industry, as it stood at 2.2 compared to the median intensity of 0.8 in 2015 (UNCTAD WIR 2020, Ch IV) for all industries and services. The relative importance of intellectual property rights, capital intensity, high degree of reliance on tacit knowledge, and high requirement of precise quality control account for the significantly higher degree of FDI (governance) of production networks, rather than by trade in this industry (UNCTAD WIR 2020, Ch IV). MNEs are the lead firms coordinating GVCs, with cross-border trade of inputs and outputs taking place between their affiliates, contractual partners, and arm's-length suppliers (UNCTAD WIR 2020 and Figure 1.2).

With the harmonization of international standards for patents among countries, the globalization of the pharmaceutical industry gained momentum, and its value chain was reorganized into three different strands: a producer-driven strand for branded products, a buyer-driven strand for quality generics, and a strand for low-value generics (off-patents products sold mainly in developing countries at prices negotiated with respective governments) (Haakonsson 2009). In the producer-driven GVC, lead firms (generally MNCs) exert control over their foreign affiliates and contracted suppliers of intermediates (Gereffi 2001; Haakonsson 2009). The lead MNCs increasingly outsource the production of these medicines to players from middle-income or developing countries in order to remain competitive. Firms in developing economies are often concentrated in low-value-added activities. Pharmaceutical supply chains are often very complex, involving multiple steps, with the potential for each step to be undertaken in a different facility, and even in a different country.

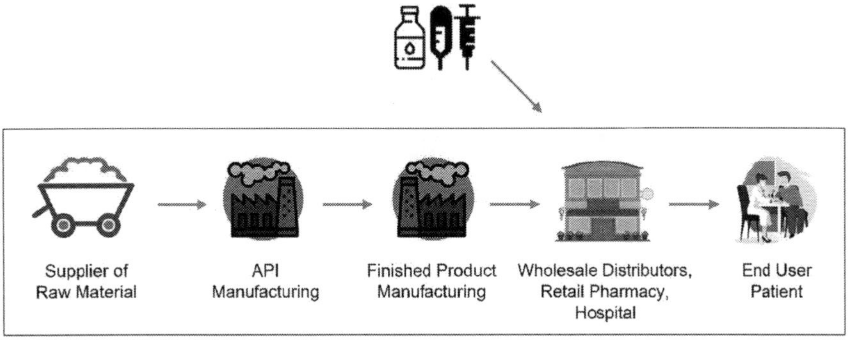

Figure 1.1 A simplified model of global value chain in the pharmaceuticals

Global value chain in the medical industry

Figure 1.1 provides a simplified schematic of the pharmaceutical supply chain of a small molecule (non-biological), in the following broad sequential steps:

- Suppliers of raw materials (solvents, reagents, and other chemicals)
- Primary manufacturers: manufacturers produce the desired APIs (active pharmaceutical ingredients) and intermediates used in medicine (Chapman, Dedet and Lopert (2022); The White House (2021); Aitken (2016))
- Secondary manufacturers: manufacturing of finished pharmaceuticals (such as tablet or liquid) in sterile and secure packaging (The White House (2021); Aitken 2016; Chapman, Dedet and Lopert (2022))
- Distribution and marketing (wholesale distributors, retail pharmacy, hospital, etc.) (Aitken 2016)
- Dispensing to the end-user (that is, providing correct medicine dosage, form, and advice to the right patient) (Aitken 2016)

The following section and Figure 1.2 present a brief discussion of the GVC-related participation modes in the medical goods industry.

Outsourcing and offshoring in the pharmaceutical and medical device industry

In a new global trading environment, firms have expanded geographically and relocated activities abroad to seize the opportunity of differences in costs and resources across countries and achieve a more efficient production process. Falling tariffs and other trade barriers globally, advancements in information and communications technologies, steady improvements in the protection of intellectual property rights, and fast-evolving role of CDMOs (contract development and manufacturing organizations) with knowledge and expertise in R&D and manufacturing are propelling MNEs to outsource to CDMOs certain critical services through collaborative arrangements.

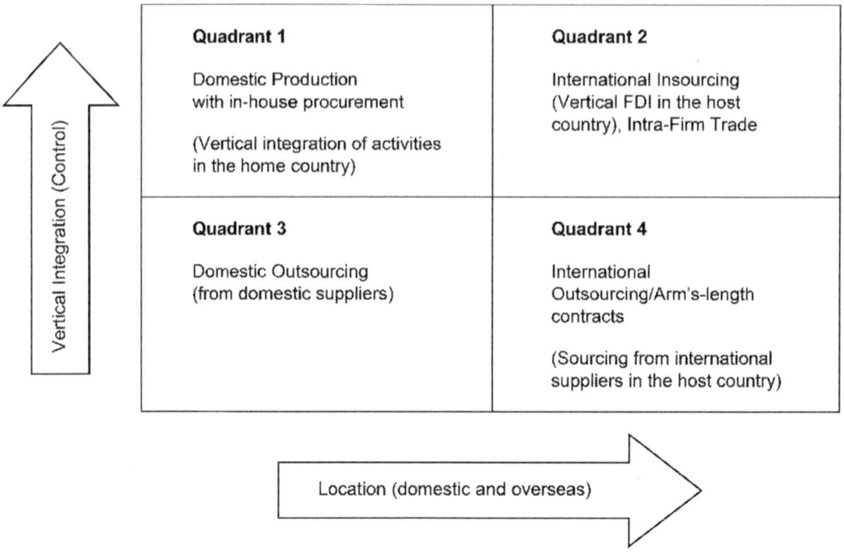

Figure 1.2 Modes of organizing value chains

Regarding making the strategic decision about organizing the global supply, companies have to determine whether the task is to be done in-house (vertical control) or outsourced and of whether it is carried out domestically or across national borders.

Until 1980, the big pharma firms were fully integrated operations performing tasks ranging from drug discovery through marketing in-house, because the "chemistry-based drug discovery process necessitated large labs and significant human capital, financial resources, and expensive technology" (Kapler and Puhala 2010, p 143). The advancements in the field of molecular biology and in drug discovery technology (rapid throughput screening, combinatorial chemistry, bioinformatics, etc.) have increased the possible drug targets by a factor of ten—all of which required big pharma firms to restructure their drug discovery R&D process and use the services of external partners across the globe for sustaining competitiveness (Kapler and Puhala 2010, Schuhmacher, Gassmann and Hinder 2016, Mohs and Greig 2017).

The pharmaceutical industry experienced a series of dramatic changes in the drug discovery and innovation process with the advent of molecular (genetic level) biology and genomic sciences (Drews 2000). The increased complexity of effective translation of scientific knowledge to drugs for human applications is mounting pressure on companies to seek collaboration with multiple contract research organizations, particularly in the areas of molecular biology and bioinformatics across the globe.

There is a growing trend of MNEs to replace their traditional business model of fully integrated pharmaceutical companies by offshoring critical

R&D-related activities either through offshoring to affiliates (through FDI) (quadrant 2, Figure 1.2) or via arm's-length contracts with foreign CROs (quadrant 4, Figure 1.2). Foreign locations (such as India, China, Latin America, Ireland, and Eastern Europe) offer unique advantages of advanced R&D infrastructure, low-cost skilled labor, cost savings in clinical trials and patient recruitment, secured intellectual property rights laws, and growing integrity between western pharma and CROs (Kapler and Puhala 2010).

Offshoring from developing countries started from low-end works such as back-office support, customer service, and data entry, and then rapidly moved to supplying more sophisticated work such as computer coding, medical transcription, medical research, and other high value-added intermediate inputs and services (Kshetri and Dholakia 2010). Standardization of data and procedures, electronic data capture (EDC), ePRO (electronic patient-reported outcomes), eProtocol (for the conduct of clinical trials), and codification resulting from advancements in ICT technologies are speeding up the process of international outsourcing and offshoring of knowledge-intensive services, such as R&D, preclinical testing, conduct of clinical trials, lead optimization,[6] and supply of intermediate chemical inputs (Kapler and Puhala 2010).

International collaborative research and input sourcing in times of pandemics

More significantly, international outsourcing and offshoring of R&D through global research network and collaboration helps to speed up innovations, which has been found to be highly critical in fighting pandemics. Contract development and manufacturing organizations (CDMOs) played a vital role in the development of the COVID-19 vaccine in unprecedented record time (Brown and Bollyky 2022). Firms' strategy of unbundling four critical supply chain stages (R&D, clinical trials, production of the drug substance, and the assembly-line process of putting a vaccine into millions of tiny vials) in overseas locations and input sourcing significantly contributed to the quick response to COVID-19 pandemic (Brown and Bollyky 2022). The scientific community responded with a massive collaborative R&D effort after China shared the genetic sequence of the novel coronavirus. By breaking apart the vaccine production process, firms could specialize in one step, leaving the remainder to be done by other firms through arm's length contracts (Brown and Bollyky 2022). By December 2020, several vaccine candidates had excellent results in large trials, with two vaccines (developed by Pfizer/BionTech and Moderna) receiving emergency use authorization in several countries (Agarwal and Gaule 2021).

Hub-and-spoke pattern of global supply chain in pharmaceuticals

The global value chain of the medical goods sector is akin to the global hub-and-spoke archetype, which means high global integration and low

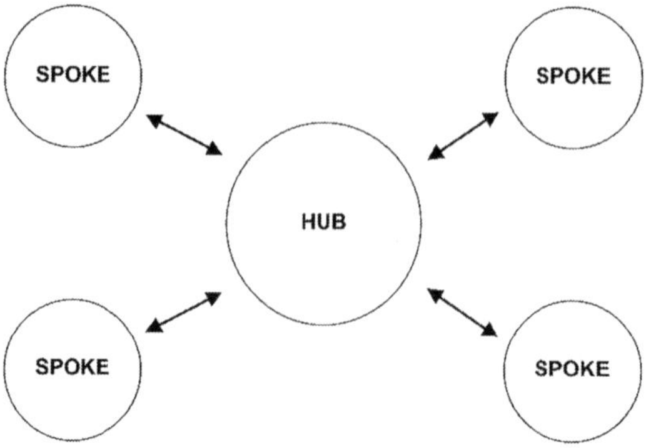

Figure 1.3 Global hub-and-spoke model of GVCs

local responsiveness (WIR 2020; Bruin 2017; Elrod and Fortenberry 2017). This hub-and-spoke relationship is portrayed in Figure 1.3. Global supply spokes are considered as those regions/countries that are important suppliers of the intermediate inputs to the global hubs (Lejour, Rojas-Romagosa and Veenendaal 2017). Global supply hubs are those industry-country pairs that produce output for final use abroad. A well-coordinated production arrangements and cross-border trade are key to ensuring that innovative pharmaceuticals, vaccines, therapies, and diagnostics for the world (IFPMA Oct 2021). Global hub-and-spoke patterns of global supply chains typically exist in the global chain of vaccine manufacturing and supply. In vaccine development, R&D and manufacturing activities are largely undertaken by US and EU firms, because these stages are both complex and require specialized knowledge and production capacity. These production locations (global hubs) draw raw materials and components from over 300 suppliers in 30 countries (spokes). Nearly 100 components and ingredients, ranging from lipids to tubing and single-use reactor bags used in the vaccine production process (Phillips et al. 2022).

The role of international organizations

The global biopharmaceutical industry operates within a wide and interconnected innovation ecosystem and global production network. It is governed and supported by a strong international trading system rooted in core principles of the World Trade Organization (WTO): openness, fairness, and predictability (IFPMA Oct 2021). WTO is a global institution responsible for promoting and ensuring open and rules-based international trade. WHO, WIPO, and the WTO cooperate within the general international framework on issues related to the interface between public health, IP, and trade concerning innovation in, and access to medical technologies (WHO, WIPO and WTO 2020).

The WHO is responsible for providing leadership on global health matters, shaping the health research agenda, setting norms and standards, articulating evidence-based policy options, providing technical support to countries, and monitoring and assessing health trends. WIPO is dedicated to developing a balanced and accessible IP system. WTO operates with the core mission of enforcing trade based on a rules-based, inclusive international trading system. WTO's core functions are to monitor TRIPS Agreement protection and to enforce standards and related policy options. These supranational organizations also collaborate with other international and regional organizations, as well as with civil society and the private sector (WHO, WIPO and WTO 2020).

Key global challenges

The medical goods industry, while yielding significant health benefits for mankind, is also fraught with several challenges. Key formidable concerns that require international attention include the following.

- Escalating drug prices, creating affordability challenges for patients and for the government
- Innovation deficit
- Environmental impact of the production, use, and disposal of drugs and medical devices
- Insufficient availability of essential medicines to poor countries
- Developing countries' concerns with IPRs

The subsequent chapters deal with these global issues for promoting good health of people across the globe (SDG: Goal 3).[7]

Summary

The chapter started with a brief review of the historical evolution of the industry from the mid of the 18th century to the present post-genomic era. The modern pharmaceutical industry has grown out of the growing understanding of organic chemistry and dyestuffs in Europe, UK, and Switzerland. The industry achieved several milestones that saved human lives against deadly bacterial-born and virus-related diseases. The advances in genomic sciences since the 1990s and the innovative applications of new frontier technologies, including the application of data sciences, are revolutionizing drug discovery and drug development. The intent of this chapter is to present the characterizing features of the industry and future dynamics of the industry, which form the subject matter of the ensuing chapters. The chapter has highlighted the following aspects of the medical goods industry.

- The pharmaceutical and medical device industry is highly globalized, with a prominent role played by international trade and global value chains that are requisite to meet the essential health needs of the world population

- The development of novel drugs and devices requires firms and public sectors to engage vigorously in R&D and revolutionize drug discovery and development to achieve the goals of 'precision' therapies
- The advent of molecular biology and genomic sciences has dramatically increased the complexity of drug research, and it cannot be contained within the confines of the pharmaceutical industry (Drews 2000). These advances in biosciences are forcing firms to gain accessibility to global expertise and specialized skills. To speed up the drug discovery process, pharma MNEs are designing global networking (alliances, partnerships) strategies of outsourcing and offshoring activities (R&D, clinical trials, manufacturing, packaging, and distribution) for global operation and value creation
- All the stakeholders—viz., industry, national governments, and supranational organizations—are making efforts in designing policies and strategies to tackle pharmaceuticals-related environmental concerns, improve worldwide accessibility to essential medicines in economically poor countries, accelerate productivity to avoid drug shortages, to help meet the needs of medicines for tropical diseases, and to help developing countries to achieve universal coverage and their indigenous production capabilities

Notes

1 Indirect effect is expenditure on medical inputs by the recipients of direct expenditures. Induced effect is generated when the recipients of direct and indirect revenues in turn spend their newly acquired income on unrelated goods and services, such as housing, transportation, and entertainment. The combination of indirect and induced effects is called spillover effects (Ostwald et al. 2020).

2 The WTO report (2022) includes all products used in the diagnosis, prevention, monitoring, treatment, and alleviation of disease and injury under the definition of medical goods. Medical goods, thus, are pharmaceuticals (such as vitamins, over-the-counter pain relief, prescription cancer medication, and vaccines); medical equipment (such as magnetic resonance imaging apparatus and operating tables); orthopedic equipment (such as wheelchairs and spectacles); personal protective equipment (such as gloves and face masks); and other consumable medical supplies (such as oxygen and syringes).

3 Albert Hyman devised the instrument to apply electrical impulses to stimulate the heart.

4 Nucleic acids are large biomolecules that play essential roles in all cells and viruses. A major function of nucleic acids involves the storage and expression of genomic information (Glossary, National Human Genome Research Institute). Biomolecules are an organic molecule that includes carbohydrates, protein, lipids, and nucleic acids. They are important for the survival of living cells.

5 Ribonucleic acid (abbreviated RNA) is a nucleic acid present in all living cells that has structural similarities to DNA.

6 Lead identification and optimization is the process of discovering a small molecule or large molecule lead compound and progressing it toward a safe and efficacious drug therapy and successful commercialization into the market. www.criver.com

7 Sustainable Development Goal 3(SDG 3) of the United Nations is to ensure healthy lives and well-being at all ages.

References

Adam, Matthias. 2005. "Integrating Research and Development: The Emergence of Rational Drug Design in the Pharmaceutical Industry." *Studies in History & Philosophy of Biological & Biomedical Sciences* 36 (3): 513–537. https://doi.org/10.1016/j.shpsc.2005.07.003.

Agarwal, R., and P. Gaule. 2021. *What Drives Innovation? Lessons from COVID-19 R&D*. International Monetary Fund WP/21/48.

Aitken, M. 2016. "Understanding the Pharmaceutical Value Chain." In *Pharmaceuticals Policy & Law*, edited by J. L. Valverde, and E. Pisani. 18, no. 1–4. IFPMA ORG. https://doi.org/10.3233/PPL-160432.

American Chemical Society. 1999. *The Discovery and Development of Penicillin 1928–1945*. International Historic Chemical Landmark.

American Cancer Society. 2014. *History of Cancer Treatments: Radiation Therapy*, June 12. https://www.cancer.org/cancer/understanding-cancer/history-of-cancer/cancer-treatment-radiation.html.

Bahri, P. 2014. Ch. 5. "Pharmacovigilance-Related Topics at the Level of the International Conference on Harmonisation." In *Book Mann's Pharmacovigilance*, edited by Elizabeth B. Andrews, and Nicholas Moore. John Wiley & Sons, Ltd.

Barold, S. Serge. 2003. "Willem Einthoven and the Birth of Clinical Electrocardiography a Hundred Years Ago." *Cardiac Electrophysiology Review* 7 (1): 99–104. https://doi.org/10.1023/a:1023667812925.

Bown CP and T..J. Bollyky. 2022 "How COVID-19 vaccine supply chains emerged in the midst of a pandemic. *World Economics* 45 (2): 468–522. doi: 10.1111/twec.13183.

Bruin, L. 2017. *International Business Strategy, International Business*, January 27. B2 U (Business-to-You).

Buxbaum, Jason D., Michael E. Chernew, A. Mark Fendrick, and David M. Cutler. 2020. "Contributions of Public Health, Pharmaceuticals, and Other Medical Care to US Life Expectancy Changes, 1990–2015." *Health Affairs (Project Hope)* 39 (9): 1546–1556. https://doi.org/10.1377/hlthaff.2020.00284.

Casadio Tarabusi, C. C., and G. Vickery. 1998. "Globalization in the Pharmaceutical Industry, part I." *International Journal of Health Services: Planning, Administration, Evaluation* 28 (1): 67–105. https://doi.org/10.2190/7JDR-2TFN-2B3X-TYF5.

CDC. 1982. 2015: Ross and the Discovery that Mosquitoes Transmit Malaria Parasites, CDC. "Historical Perspectives Centennial: Koch's Discovery of the Tubercle Bacillus, MMWR Weekly", March 19, 1982. *Globalization & Health: Division of Parasitic Diseases and Malaria* 31 (10): 121–123.

CDC. 2019. "Influenza Historic Timeline". https://www.cdc.gov/flu/pandemic-resources/pandemic-timeline-1930-and-beyond.htm.

Chapman, S., G. Dedet, and R. Lopert. 2022. *Shortages of Medicines in OECD Countries, OECD Health Working Papers, No. 137*. OECD Publishing.

Chen, Rui, and Michael Snyder. 2013. "Promise of Personalized Omics to Precision Medicine." *Wiley Interdisciplinary Reviews. Systems Biology & Medicine* 5 (1): 73–82. https://doi.org/10.1002/wsbm.1198.

Drews, J. 2000. "Drug discovery: A historical perspective." *Science* 287(5460): 1960–4. https://doi.org/10.1126/science.287.5460.1960

Dugger, Sarah A., Adam Platt, and David B. Goldstein. 2018. "Drug Development in the Era of Precision Medicine." *Nature Reviews. Drug Discovery* 17 (3): 183–196. https://doi.org/10.1038/nrd.2017.226.

Elrod, James K., and John L. Fortenberry. 2017. "The Hub-and-Spoke Organization Design: An Avenue for Serving Patients Well." *BMC Health Services Research* 17 (Suppl. 1): 457. https://doi.org/10.1186/s12913-017-2341-x.

Emilien, G., M. Ponchon, C. Caldas, O. Isacson, and J. M. Maloteaux. 2000. "Impact of Genomics on Drug Discovery and Clinical Medicine." *QJM: Monthly Journal of the Association of Physicians* 93 (7): 391–423. https://doi.org/10.1093/qjmed/93.7.391.

Gambardella, A., L. Orsenigo, and F. Pammolli. 2000. *Global Competitiveness in Pharmaceuticals. A European Perspective.* Report Prepared for the Enterprise Directorate-General of the European Commission.

Gereffi, G. 2014. "Global Value Chains in a Post-Washington Consensus World." *Review of International Political Economy* 21 (1): 9–37. https://doi.org/10.1080/09692290.2012.756414.

Gereffi, G. 2021. "Increasing resilience of medical supply chains during the COVID-19 pandemic. Why building future resilience requires a delicate balance between increased flexibility, efficiency, and welfare advantages of GVCs." Industrial Analytics Platform, UNIDO.

Ginsburg, Geoffrey S., and Kathryn A. Phillips. 2018. "Precision Medicine: From Science to Value." *Health Affairs (Project Hope)* 37 (5): 694–701. https://doi.org/10.1377/hlthaff.2017.1624.

Gottschalk, C. W., and S. K. Fellner. 1997. "History of the Science of Dialysis." *American Journal of Nephrology* 17 (3–4): 289–298. https://doi.org/10.1159/000169116.

Haakonsson, A. & He, F. 2009. "R&D Offshoring and Clustering Dynamics in Pharmaceuticals and Biotechnology: Key Features and Insights from the Chinese Case. *Journal of Innovation Economics & Management* 4: 95–117.

Helble, M., & Shepherd, B. 2017. "Trade in Health Products: Reducing Trade Barriers for Better Health." Jan 23, 2017, ADBI Working Paper No. 643, Asian Development Bank Institute, Tokyo

Hughes, J. P., S. Rees, S. B. Kalindjian, and K. L. Philpott. 2011. "Principles of Early Drug Discovery." *British Journal of Pharmacology* 162 (6): 1239–1249. https://doi.org/10.1111/j.1476-5381.2010.01127.x.

ICH Harmonised Tripartite Guideline. 2004. *Pharmacovigilance Planning.* 4th version dated E2e, Current Step.

IFPMA. 2022a. Biopharmaceutical Innovation and Global Public Health, Facts and Figures 2022, Report Sept 20, 2022, International Federation of Pharmaceutical Manufacturers and Associations, Geneva.

IFPMA. 2022b. The Pharmaceutical Industry in Figures Key Data 2022. International Federation of Pharmaceutical Manufacturers and Associations, Geneva.

IMF. 2008. *Globalization: A Brief Overview, by IMF Staff; Issue 02/08.* May Issues Brief - Globalization: A Brief Overview (imf.org).

Institute of Medicine (US) Committee on Technological Innovation in Medicine. 1991. edited by A. C. Gelijns, and E. A. Halm. *The Changing Economics of Medical* Technology Publishing.

ITA. 2016. *Top Markets Report Medical Devices Country Case Study* vol. 2016. US Department of Commerce.

Kaczmarek, James C., Piotr S. Kowalski, and Daniel G. Anderson. 2017. "Advances in the Delivery of RNA Therapeutics: From Concept to Clinical Reality." *Genome Medicine* 9 (1): 60. https://doi.org/10.1186/s13073-017-0450-0.

Kapler, J. K., and K. A. Puhala. 2010. Ch. 5. "Outsourcing, Fragmentation, and Integration: The Pharmaceutical Industry." In *Global Outsourcing and Offshoring: An Integrated Approach to Theory and Corporate Strategy*, edited by F. Contractor, V. Kumar, S. Kundu, and T. Pedersen. Cambridge University Press.

Krishnamurti, Chandrasekhar, and SSC Chakra Rao. 2016. "The Isolation of Morphine by Serturner." *Indian Journal of Anaesthesia* 60 (11): 861–862. https://doi.org/10.4103/0019-5049.193696.

Kshetri, Nir, and Nikhilesh Dholakia. 2010 Ch. 12. "Offshoring of High-Value Functions: A Case Study of U.S.–India Trade in Medical Transcription Services." In *Global Outsourcing and Offshoring: An Integrated Approach to Theory and Corporate Strategy*, edited by F. Contractor, V. Kumar, S. Kundu, and T. Pedersen. Cambridge University Press.

Kulkarni, Jayesh A., Dominik Witzigmann, Sarah B. Thomson, Sam Chen, Blair R. Leavitt, Pieter R. Cullis, and Roy van der Meel. 2021. "The Current Landscape of Nucleic Acid Therapeutics." *Nature Nanotechnology* 16 (6): 630–643. https://doi.org/10.1038/s41565-021-00898-0.

Lambert, T. 2022. "Medicine in the Ancient World, A History of Medicine, Local Histories". https://localhistories.org/a-history-of-medicine/.

Lejour, A., H. Rojas-Romagosa, and P. Veenendaal. 2017. "Identifying Hubs and Spokes in Global Supply Chains Using Redirected Trade in Value Added." *Economic Systems Research* 29 (1): 66–81. https://doi.org/10.1080/09535314.2017.1282436.

Loscalzo, Joseph. 2012. "Personalized Cardiovascular Medicine and Drug Development: Time for a New Paradigm." *Circulation* 125 (4): 638–645. https://doi.org/10.1161/CIRCULATIONAHA.111.089243.

Malerba, F., and L. Orsenigo. 2002. *Innovation and Market Structure in the Dynamics of the Pharmaceutical Industry and Biotechnology: Towards a History-Friendly Model, Industrial and Corporate Change, Oxford University Press* vol. 11, no. 4, August. Open University: 667–703.

Matthews, Holly, James Hanison, and Niroshini Nirmalan. 2016. "Omics"-Informed Drug and Biomarker Discovery: Opportunities, Challenges and Future Perspectives. *Proteomes* 4 (3): 28. https://doi.org/10.3390/proteomes4030028.

Miner, Jonathan, and Adam Hoffhines. 2007. "The Discovery of Aspirin's Antithrombotic Effects." *Texas Heart Institute Journal* 34 (2): 179–186.

Mohs, R. C., and N. H. Greig. 2017. "Drug discovery and development: Role of basic biological research." *Alzheimer's & Dementia* 3 (4): 651–657.

Ngo, Huy X., and Sylvie Garneau-Tsodikova. 2018. "What Are the Drugs of the Future?" *MedChemComm* 9 (5): 757–758. https://doi.org/10.1039/c8md90019a.

Nicita, A., V. Ognivtsev, and M. Shirotori. 2013. *Global Supply Chains: Trade and Economic Policies for Developing Countries*, UNCTAD Blue Series Papers 55. United Nations Conference on Trade and Development.

OECD. 2012. *Trade and Innovation-A Synthesis Report, OECD Trade Policy Working Paper No 135.* OECD.

Ostwald, D., M. Cramer, N. Albu, and J. Tesch. 2020. *The Global Economic Impact of the Pharmaceutical Industry, WifOR*. Research Reports.

Pharmaphorum. 2020. *A History of the Pharmaceutical Industry*, Accessed September 1. https://pharmaphorum.com/r-d/a_history_of_the_pharmaceutical_industry.

Phillips, W., J. K. Roehrich, D. Kapletia, and E. Alexander. 2022. "Global Value Chain Reconfiguration and COVID-19: Investigating the Case for More Resilient Redistributed Models of Production." *California Management Review* 64 (2): 71–96. https://doi.org/10.1177/00081256211068545.

Riedel, Stefan. 2005. "Edward Jenner and the History of Smallpox and Vaccination." *Proceedings* 18 (1): 21–25. https://doi.org/10.1080/08998280.2005.11928028.

Scheindlin, S. 2001. *A Brief History of Pharmacology, MDD (Modern Drug Discovery), Focus: High Throughput Screening* 4 (5): 87–88.

Scherer, F. M. 2000. "The pharmaceutical industry." In *Handbook of Health Economics*, edited by A. J. Culyer, and J. P. Newhouse, 1B, 1297–1338. Elsevier North-Holland, Amsterdam.

Schuhmacher, A., O. Gassmann, and M. Hinder. 2016. "Changing R&D models in research-based pharmaceutical companies". *Journal of Translational Medicine* 14 (105). https://doi.org/10.1186/s12967-016-0838-4

Seric, A., and Y. S. Tong. 2019. *What Are Global Value Chains and Why Do They Matter? Series Putting Resilience at the Heart of Global Production Networks, UNIDO, Industrial Analytics Platform*, UNIDO.

Stephen, Daily. 2011. "A Brief History of the FDA, Cover Stories." *News Editor*, Accessed October 2011. crstoday.com.

Tannoury, Maya, and Zouhair Attieh. 2017. "The Influence of Emerging Markets on the Pharmaceutical Industry." *Current Therapeutic Research, Clinical & Experimental* 86: 19–22. https://doi.org/10.1016/j.curtheres.2017.04.005.

Tantibanchachai, Chanapa. 2004. "US Regulatory Response to Thalidomide (1950–2000)." *Embryo Project Encyclopedia (2014-04-01).*

TebaniA, Carlos Afonso, Stéphane Marret, and Soumeya Bekri. 2016. "Omics-Based Strategies in Precision Medicine: Toward a Paradigm Shift in Inborn Errors of Metabolism Investigations." *International Journal of Molecular Sciences* 17 (9): 1555. https://doi.org/10.3390/ijms17091555.

The White House. 2021. *Building Resilient Supply Chain, Revitalizing American Manufacturing and Fostering Broad Base Growth, June 2021, 100-Day Reviews Under Executive Order* vol. 14017. The White House.

Tubiana, M. 1996. "Wilhelm Conrad Röntgen and the Discovery of X-Rays." *Bulletin de l'Académie Nationale de Médecine* 180 (1): 97–108.

Tudor, Mario, Lorainne Tudor, and Katarina Ivana Tudor. 2005. "Hans Berger (1873–1941)–The History of Electroencephalography." ["Hans Berger (1873–1941)-the History of Electroencephalography."]. *Acta Medica Croatica: Časopis Hravatske Akademije Medicinskih Znanosti* 59 (4): 307–313.

US Department of Veteran Affairs. 2018. "The Invention of the Cardiac Pacemaker, VA Research in Action." Accessed August 2. https://www.research.va.gov/research_in_action/The-invention-of-the-cardiac-pacemaker.cfm

Waller, Patrick C., Stephen J. W. Evans, and Keith Beard. 2005. Jul. 2. "Drug Safety and Regulation." *BMJ* 331 (7507): 4–5. https://doi.org/10.1136/bmj.331.7507.4.

WHO. 2002. *The Importance of Pharmacovigilance. Safety Monitoring of Medicinal Products.* WHO.

WHO. 2003. *Medical Device Regulations: Global Overview and Guiding Principles.* WHO.

WHO. 2010. "Working to overcome the global impact of neglected tropical diseases". "First WHO report on neglected tropical diseases: Working to overcome the global impact of neglected tropical diseases." World Health Organization, Geneva, 2010.

WHO, WIPO and WTO 2020, " *Promoting Access to Medical Technologies and Innovation Intersections Between Public Health, Intellectual Property and Trade*. 2nd ed. World Health Organization, Geneva.

UNCTAD 2020 World Investment Report 2020. "International Production Beyond the Pandemic." *International Production: The Decade of Transformation Ahead*. WIR.

World Bank. 2022. *Trade Therapy Cooperation to Strengthen Pandemic Defenses, A Joint World Bank Group, the WTO Report Launched on 3 June 2022*. World Bank.

WTO. 2022. *Trade Therapy: Deepening Cooperation to Strengthen Pandemic Defenses*. WTO.

2 Evolving product and market structure of the pharmaceuticals and the medical device industry

Introduction: Nature of the industry, changing structure, and pricing of drugs

The pharmaceutical industry is complex, dynamic, highly globalized, and an R&D-intensive industry (U.S. International Trade Commission 1999, Gambardella, Orsenigo, and Fabio 2000). Incredible breakthroughs in therapies are instilling hope of better quality of life for people in the near future.

Growing adoption of scientific advances is shifting the product composition of pharma from small-molecule chemical entities to biologics (large-molecule drugs derived from living cells, which can be grown in vitro) (Makurvet 2021). Another structural change is that biotechnology firms which are spin-offs from research universities (Niosi 2002) and public sector research organizations are becoming key actors in generating new knowledge, tools, and substances for the pharmaceutical industry (OECD 2006). The global pharmerging market is poised for significant growth between 2023 and 2030 and beyond. Increasing merger and acquisition activities since the 1980s have resulted in unprecedented market concentration of production and sales of pharmaceutical products in the hands of a few leading multinationals. Merger and acquisition activity also accounts for the persistence of many of the same multinational firms in the top 20 pharmaceutical companies (Richman et al. 2020; FTC 2022). Standard competitive markets that align prices with value to consumers and costs to producers do not exist in the pharmaceutical industry (Danzon and Taylor 2010). Anti-competitive strategic patenting practices are creating harmful effects on drug prices and pharmaceutical innovation (Gurgula 2018). Drug prices require normalizing by their respective expected health outcomes so that prices correlate with value or clinical benefits (Leighl et al. 2021). Differential pricing that reflects different degrees of willingness to pay across countries with different income levels is also an important challenge for drug manufacturers and policymakers (Danzon, Towse and Mulcahy 2011). This chapter charts the above trends.

DOI: 10.4324/9781003449331-2

Global value-added contribution of major producing nations

The global pharmaceutical and medical instrument industry is characterized as a knowledge- and technology-intensive industry (KTI industry) by the OECD report (2016, NSF 2002). The contribution of countries to the global value-added varies due to the varying strength of innovation capabilities. The analysis of the global value-added by country share can be of immense value for designing policies for accelerating product innovations that matter for reducing the global disease burden.

Globally, the pharmaceutical industry generated 658 billion of value-added contribution to the global GDP in 2019, reflecting a share of 0.8% of the global GDP. Medical and dental instruments contributed another 0.2% to the global GDP.[1] The combined contribution of the medical goods sector amounted to 1% of the global GDP (NSF 2022, Table KTI-3). Global value-added in pharmaceuticals increased from $256,875 million in 2002 to $657,966 million in 2019 in current dollars (NSF 2022), which amounted to an annual compound growth rate of 5.7% per annum.[2] This growth rate is slightly higher compared to the annual compound growth rate of value-added generated by the knowledge and technology-intensive (KTI) manufacturing industries (5.5%) during the same time period (NSF 2022, table SKTI-6). KTI industries include high R&D-intensive and medium-high R&D-intensive industries based on the classification by OECD (NSF 2022).[3]

Table 2.1 presents data of percentage share of major producers in the global value-added generated by the pharmaceutical industry at two different points of time (2002 and 2019). It is observed that the USA accounted for 28% of the global value-added generated by the pharmaceutical industry in 2019. China markedly increased its global contribution from 6% in 2002 to 24% in 2019. The rapid expansion of China's pharmaceutical industry has been fueled by the expanding middle class and healthcare reforms in China. Among the advanced economies, it is observed from the table that Switzerland increased its contribution from 3.74% in 2002 to 5.87 in 2019.

Global value-added generated by the medical and dental instruments increased in current dollars from 74,973 million in 2002 to 175,126 million in 2019, showing an annual compound growth rate of 5.1% from 2002 to 2019. As observed from Table 2.2, the United States accounted for 38% of the global value-added generated by medical and dental instruments. China is observed to have increased its global presence in the production of medical and dental instruments from 8% in 2002 to 21% in 2019. Among G-7 economies, Germany is the exclusive country that increased its share in the global value-added contribution from the medical equipment industry.

Table 2.1 Country share of global value-added of the pharmaceutical industry: 2002 and 2019

Country	*Share in the Global Value-Added in Pharmaceutical Industry 2002*	*Share in the Global Value-Added in Pharmaceutical Industry 2019*
USA	37.93	27.72
Spain	1.53	1.18
Canada	1.14	0.65
China	5.64	24.15
France	4.21	2.18
Germany	4.87	3.77
Italy	3.06	1.57
Japan	8.36	4.10
UK	5.84	2.91
Switzerland	3.74	5.87
Australia	0.61	0.38
Korea Rep	1.03	1.12
India	1.18	3.65
Brazil	1.17	1.20
Singapore	1.06	0.69

Source: NSF 2022

Table 2.2 Country share of global value-added of medical and dental instruments industry: 2002 and 2019

Country	*Share in the Global Value-Added of Medical and Dental Instruments 2002*	*Share in the Global Value-Added of Medical and Dental Instruments 2019*
USA	46.59	37.53
Spain	1.07	0.85
Canada	1.41	1.01
China	7.63	20.64
France	3.18	1.85
Germany	6.81	6.85
Italy	4.11	2.86
Japan	6.79	3.17
UK	4.21	2.19
Switzerland	1.27	1.17
Australia	0.17	0.28
Korea Rep	1.32	1.19
India	0.36	0.99
Brazil	0.71	1.25
Singapore	0.34	1.44

Source: NSF 2022

Evolving market structure: Product composition and organizational developments

Statistics indicate that the drugmakers' revenue composition has been changing profoundly in the past few decades owing to the shift in the product composition. The global industry is populated by very different firms: multinationals, smaller companies which are specialized in the sales of non-R&D-intensive drugs, and research-intensive companies that are specialized in new biotechnologies (called new biotechnology firms (NBFs) or emerging biopharma (EBP) companies (Gambardella, Orsenigo and Pammolli 2000)). These trends are examined below.

Changing product composition

Pharmaceutical products encompass a wide range of products:

1. Innovative chemically derived products
2. Generic products
3. Biologics (biopharmaceuticals)
4. Biosimilars (follow-on biologics)
5. Over the counter (OTC) (no prescription needed)
6. APIs (active pharmaceutical ingredients)

The above categories are broadly classified as active pharmaceutical ingredients (APIs) and finished manufactured forms that are newly branded innovations or generic versions. APIs (also known as bulk drugs) are active chemical substances in powder form—the main ingredient of pharmaceuticals that have therapeutic value and are used to produce pharmaceutical formulations. Major bulk drugs include antibiotics, sulfa drugs, vitamins, steroids, and analgesics. Finished formulations result in the forms in which the drugs are consumed by us. Most finished pharmaceuticals depend almost entirely on the availability of active pharmaceutical ingredients (APIs). Table 2.3 presents the broad structure of the pharmaceutical market.

As observed from Table 2.3, innovator companies primarily focus on finished form manufacturers, which are branded medicines. These companies actively invest in R&D in order to discover new and innovative formulations. Innovative medicine consists of drugs that meet a substantive (i.e., non-trivial) health need and offers enhanced effectiveness (e.g., greater efficacy, reduced toxicity, or both) or another incremental benefit (e.g., a substantive improvement in patient convenience) relative to existing therapeutic alternatives (OECD 2018). Generics[4] are usually produced by a manufacturer who is not the inventor of the original product. They are marketed when intellectual property protection rights are exhausted. Generic pharmaceutical companies manufacture low-cost and low-margin products. Generic companies do not need to incur any research-and-development

Table 2.3 Pharmaceutical market: Innovators, generic, and API manufacturers

Types of Pharmaceutical Companies	*Activities and Costs Involved*	*Value-Added (High or Low)/Competition*
Innovators/originators of new products (chemical based and biologics)	Conducting R&D that identifies new chemicals or biologic entity	High value-added; market exclusivity with patent rights
Generic manufacturers (chemical based and biosimilars)	Bringing the generic version of the original brand to the market	Low value-added due to competition in the market
Manufacturers/suppliers of active pharmaceutical ingredient (API) used in medicine	Producing and supplying the raw ingredients used in medicine	Low value-added due to competition in the market

Source: Adapted from Aitken (2016) and ITA (International Trade Administration, 2016 USA)

costs, although some of the larger companies do undertake process-orientated R&D to introduce more efficient, and lower cost, manufacturing (Taylor 2015). To encourage competition between branded products going off-patent and (generic) drugs, the Hatch-Waxman Act (which came into force in 1984) in the US established the Abbreviated New Drug Application (ANDA), which only required proof that the applicant's product is bioequivalent to the original product but did not require clinical trials from generic producers to demonstrate safety and efficacy (Fiona and Margaret 2011, Grabowski and Vernon 1992).

Shift from chemically synthesized small-molecule medicines to biologics

The molecular biology revolution has tilted pharmaceuticals production away from its fine chemistry path dependence into microbiology and biotechnology (Cooke 2004; Makurvet 2021). Biologics (also known as biopharmaceuticals) are increasingly used in nearly all branches of diseases (Aitken 2020). Biopharmaceuticals that are generated by modern molecular biology are by far the fastest-growing part of the whole pharma industry (Lokko et al. 2018). More and more novel biologic drugs are continuing to emerge, displacing traditional small-molecule-based medicines. Biologics have considerable variability in type and can include vaccines, gene therapies, and monoclonal (man-made proteins) antibodies.[5] The use of biotechnology is estimated to contribute up to 80% of pharmaceuticals and diagnostics production by 2030 (OECD 2009).

Technically, biologics differ from small molecules based on size and manufacturing process (Makurvet 2021). Table 2.4 presents major differences between biologics and small molecules.

Table 2.4 Some key differences between biologics and small molecules

Biologics	*Small Molecules*
Extracted from living cells	Derived by chemical processes
High manufacturing cost; requires highly complex process, biomanufacturing (engineering a cell to produce a specific protein)	Low/variable manufacturing cost: manufactured by chemical synthesis
High molecular weight	Low molecular weight
Protease and heat-sensitive	Mostly stable
Generics: Biosimilar	Generics: Identical
Immunogenic	Non-immunogenic

Sources: Makurvet (2021); Mócsai, Kovács and Gergely (2014)

Table 2.5 Global product market 2014–2018: Net medicine spending by product type

Market Segments of Drugs	*Share in the Medical Spending 2014(%)*	*Share in the Medical Spending 2018(%)*
Small molecules	70	58
Biologics	30	42

Source: Aitken M (2020) Biologics Market Dynamics: Setting the Stage for Biosimilars

Table 2.5 depicts that small molecules have declined by 12% between 2014 and 2018 in their share of medical spending, while biologics share has increased by 50% over the same period Aitken (2020). Since the past few years, antibodies (therapeutic proteins or therapeutic biologics)[6] have become the best-selling drugs in the pharmaceutical market. In 2018, eight of the top ten best-selling drugs worldwide were biologics (Lu et al. 2020). Biotech products—those created through recombinant DNA technology—are expected to represent 35% of global spending by 2027 (IQVIA 2023).[7] The COVID-19 pandemic has demonstrated the vital role of biotechnologies in developing and producing life-saving diagnostics, therapeutics, and vaccines that protect the world (The White House 2022).

Biopharmaceuticals and the future of vaccines

Biopharmaceuticals are produced in living cells, whereas synthetic drugs are the products of chemical processes (Kesik-Brodacka 2018). In contrast to synthetic drugs, biopharmaceuticals are potentially immunogenic (Kesik-Brodacka 2018). Vaccines are biologics that provide active adaptive immunity against specific diseases (Kashte et al. 2021; Pollard and Bijker 2021). Biopharmaceutical developments have great potential to revolutionize the vaccine field[8] (Kesik-Brodacka 2018; Pulendran, Arunachalam and O'Hagan

2021). Several of the COVID-19 vaccines were developed using biotechnology (NSF 2022). Many novel vaccines are at various stages of the drug acceptance process. Some notable vaccines under progress include vaccines against major infectious diseases such as HIV and tuberculosis, a universal flu vaccine, and vaccines against non-infectious diseases (Kesik-Brodacka 2018). New vaccines use mRNA (a type of genetic material) to stimulate some of our own cells to temporarily produce antigens (substances that prompt your body to trigger an immune response against them). (Pardi et al. 2018). Recent advances in immunology, systems biology, genomics, and bioinformatics offer great opportunities to improve our understanding of the induction of immune responses by vaccines and to transform vaccine development through increasingly rational design (Pulendran, Arunachalam and O'Hagan 2021; Pollard and Bijker 2021).

The growing role of small biotech firms

Starting from the mid-1970s, the biotech revolution fueled the growth of specialized small biotech enterprises. These university spin-offs have forced the established large pharma to reconsider their business model from giant vertically integrated firms to greater vertical disintegration, and to seek widespread collaboration with the smaller and younger firms in the early R&D stages of product discovery.

The universe of biopharma companies is diverse and includes a large set of companies that can be classified based on their activities and sales turnover. There is considerable heterogeneity across firms, both in size as well as business strategy (Fiona and Margaret 2011). There are four sets of enterprises in the pharmaceutical market: emerging biopharma (EBP), small pharma, mid-size pharma, and large pharma (Table 2.6). Large pharma multinational companies operate across national borders and set divisions of activities in other countries. Large pharma companies are defined as those with more than $10 billion in annual pharmaceutical sales (Table 2.6). Alongside, there are small- and medium-sized enterprises (SMEs), specializing mainly in manufacturing and commercialization activities, and do not invest in R&D. Specialized biotech firms (also called emerging biopharma (EBP)) are the linchpin of the modern pharmaceutical industry. These EBPs are defined as enterprises that

Table 2.6 Universe of biopharma companies (Sales and R&D in USD)

Emerging biopharma (EBP)	Prescription sales < 500 million, R&D spend < $20 million
Small pharma	Prescription sales between $500 million and <$5 billion
Mid-sized pharma	Prescription sales $5 billion to <$10 billion
Large pharma	Sales >$10 billion

Source: IQVIA (2022c) Emerging Biopharma's Contribution to Innovation, Nov

have less than $500 million in revenue from prescription sales and are estimated to spend less than $200 million annually on R&D (Table 2.6) (IQVIA 2019). These companies have established themselves as the discovery arm of the pharmaceutical industry, and their activities range from the discovery and development of new drug compounds to the development of new drug screening or research tools and technologies in fields like genomics, bioinformatics, etc. (IQVIA 2019; Gambardell, Orsenigo and Pammolli 2000; Drews 2000). These science-based small firms are playing a key role in new product development (Powell and Owen-Smith 1998). There were 2,624 companies defined as emerging biopharma involved in the clinical development of new products at the end of 2021 (IQVIA 2022b). Emerging biopharma (EBP) companies represented two-thirds of the molecules in the R&D pipeline in 2022, up from 51% in 2017 and one-third in 2002 (IQVIA 2023). Large pharma companies, on the other hand, represented just 23% of pipeline activity in 2022, down from 48% in 2002 (IQVIA 2023).

Large companies commonly have the resources and expertise needed to support large-scale clinical trials. These complementarities offer strong incentives for collaborations between traditional large pharma and innovative small biotech firms (Comanor and Scherer 2013). Increasingly, EBP and large pharma companies are collaborating in cell and gene therapies, and RNA- or mRNA-based therapies (IQVIA 2022b). These small biotechnology enterprises often out-license their products to more experienced firms for later-stage drug development, regulatory review, and commercialization (Danzon 2006).

The growing trend of strategic partnership and collaboration in the US has been fostered by the Bayh–Dole Act signed in 1980 in the US (Powell and Owen-Smith 1998; Ezell and Cory 2019). This act gave universities, small businesses, and nonprofit institutions rights to the intellectual property (IP) stemming from research they have undertaken with federal funding in the US (Ezell and Cory 2019).[9] Emerging biopharma (EBP) are rising rapidly, particularly in China also, whose share now exceeds that of Europe (IQVIA 2023a)

Global market size and projected growth pattern

Global medicine use has been increasing over the past few years and is outpacing population growth and economic growth. Increasing consumption has been driven by a growing need for drugs to treat age-related and chronic diseases, and by increasing availability of generics (OECD 2021a). One fast-expanding market is the market for treatments of non-communicable diseases, which kill 41 million people each year, equivalent to 74% of all deaths globally (WHO 2022c). Of all NCD (non-communicable diseases) deaths, 77% are in low- and middle-income countries (WHO 2022c).

Quantification of the pharmaceutical market size (on a global, regional, and country basis, and by therapeutic area) serves as a useful information for corporations, governments, and international health organizations. Statistically, the market size of the medicine use can be quantified and analyzed using two metrics: the invoice spending (using invoice price levels) or the "Defined Daily Dose (DDD)" system, created by the WHO (IQVIA 2021, 2023).

Global market size and growth—using invoice price levels

Overall global medicine spending steadily increased from 2009 to 2019 with a ten-year compound annual growth rate (CAGR) of 4.2%. Spending jumped by 23% from $777 billion in 2014 to $955 billion in 2019 (IQVIA 2020). The global pharmaceutical market is projected to reach $1.9 trillion by 2027 (IQVIA 2023). The therapy areas with the highest forecast spending in 2027 are oncology, immunology, anti-diabetics, and cardiovascular (IQVIA 2023).

In terms of medicine consumption expenditure, developed countries' per capita medicine usage is nearly double that of pharmerging countries and seven times that of lower income countries (IQVIA 2022a). In these developed markets, the use of medicines has remained consistent over the past decade. The market expansion, in recent decades, has largely occurred in pharmerging markets (Table 2.7), defined as countries with per capita income below $30,000 per year and pharmaceutical spending growth above $1 billion over five years (IQVIA 2020).[10] Many of these countries are facing a double burden of increasing non-communicable conditions as well as communicable diseases. Strong growth in pharmerging markets and new brands (such as specialty medicines[11]) in developed markets are projected to lift global spending through 2026 (IQVIA 2022a).

Market size and growth measured by defined drug utilization metric

The above-mentioned projections in Table 2.7 were based on pharmaceutical spending evaluated using invoice prices. Pharmaceutical expenditure, however, might not be an appropriate metric for comparing the contributions of regions/countries to global market growth since the cost of drugs varies widely between regions and countries. To make international comparisons possible, the WHO recommends DDD (Defined Daily Dose) as the unit of comparison.

Table 2.7 Pharmaceutical spending growth (invoice) (constant USD)

	2011–2016 Five-year CAGRs (%)	*2017–2021 CAGRs (%)*	*2021–2026 CAGRs (%)*
Global	6.5	5.1	3.6
Developed	5.3	4.3	2.5
Pharmerging	11.4	7.8	5.8
Lower Income	4.8	0.1	3.6

Source: IQVIA (2022a): The Global Use of Medicines 2022: Outlook to 2026

DDD is the average maintenance dose per day for the medication's main indication for adults (WHO, ATC/DDD Toolkit). DDDs are a fixed measurement unit independent of price, currency, package size, and strength. This enables the researcher to assess trends in drug utilization and to compare countries. The DDD metric and the ATC drug classification help in analyzing patterns of drug utilization and the quality of drug use and health outcomes. As per the WHO methodology, only one DDD is assigned per ATC code[12] and route of administration (e.g., oral, transdermal, and parenteral formulations). The IQVIA institute using the principles of WHO for calculating DDDs has included some additional adjustments (IQVIA 2019).

As is evident from Table 2.8, the global use of medicine, based on the defined daily doze (DDD) assumptions, has been growing for the past decade, driven by the expansion of markets in developing economies, particularly those of Asia Pacific, Latin America, and India (IQVIA 2021, 2023). The change of lifestyle in these countries due to an increase in wealth and longevity is poised to shift their disease patterns. As mentioned earlier, a fast rise in the incidence of non-communicable diseases such as cardiovascular illnesses, diabetes, and oncologic diseases has been observed in emerging markets, mimicking their western counterparts (Tannoury and Attie 2017). The incidence of diabetes and oncologic diseases is expected to grow by 20% or more by 2030 in pharmerging countries (Tannoury and Attie 2017).

Developed economies that accounted for 46% share of global spending (measured in DDDs) in 2012 experienced a decline in the share to 36% in 2022. Their spending is further projected to decline to 34% in 2027 (Table 2.8). Developing countries of Asia and Latin America are predicted to be an important source of expansion of the medicine market in years ahead as well as of the adoption of novel medicines (IQVIA 2023). The medicine use in countries of Africa and the Middle East, however, is likely to decrease from its share of 13.7% to 10.4% in 2027. The region is a significant outlier, despite some countries having robust GDP (IQVIA 2023).

Table 2.8 Global medicine defined daily doses in billions 2012–2027

	2012	*2015*	*2022*	*2027 (Forecast)*
Global	2,318	2,659	3,158	3,422
Developed economies (North America, Western Europe, and Japan)	727	754	773	792
Eastern Europe	292	316	369	378
China	200	244	318	346
India	293	343	443	499
Latin America	175	263	376	424
Asia Pacific	314	369	553	626
Africa and Middle East	317	372	319	357

Source: IQVIA (2023b) The Global use of Medicines 2023: Outlook to 2027

On the supply side of novel medicines, research-and-development pipelines are growing with success rates at historic levels, resulting in more new products launching in the next five years (IQVIA 2019). According to IQVIA (2022a) projections, global new active substances (NAS) launches are projected at an average of 54–63 per year, totaling 290–315 for five years through 2026. There has been an unprecedented record of new launches (79 per year) in both 2020 and 2021. The oncology pipeline is expected to add more than 100 new drugs in the next five years, which includes innovative treatment through cell therapy, RNA therapy, and immuno-oncology treatments—including those that are mutation-specific and thus tumor agnostic (IQVIA 2022a).

Medicine spending pattern: Branded versus generics

Total spending data (Table 2.9) inform that more than 75% of the global spending was on branded (original and non-original) medicines, while the rest 23% of the spending went to generics and other medicines in 2022. The types of medicines driving spending and market growth vary considerably across countries, depending on the level of economic development and the price structure. Medical spending is influenced by the price tags of medicines (branded and generics) as well as by the buying power of people, both of which vary among countries. The data indicate that wealthier countries have higher levels of spending on original branded products, especially earlier in the patented periods of these products. The pharmerging and low-income countries (LICs), on the other hand, have a greater reliance on generics (Aitken 2016).

Within each broad category, there are also variations. For example, branded drugs can either be synthetic, meaning they're made from a chemical process, or biological, which are made from living organisms like yeast, bacteria, or animal or plant cells. Generics are typically smaller chemical compounds, while biosimilars are larger complex biological molecules.

Table 2.9 Medicine spending and growth by product type and by regions (billion US $)

		Original Brands	*Non-original Brands*	*Unbranded Generics*	*Other*	*Total*
Spending 2022 US$	Global	902.1	244.5	150.2	185.5	1,482.3
	Developed	788.8	109.3	101.0	89.3	1,088.3
	Pharmerging	105.7	124.4	47.8	93.0	370.8
	Lower income countries	7.7	10.8	1.5	3.2	23.2
Spending 2027$	Global	1,515–1,185	325	160–190	215–245	1,900–1,930
	Developed	1,000–1,030	150–165	105–115	98–108	1,370–1,400
	Pharmerging	133–153	157–177	62–64	114–134	487–518
	Lower income countries	9–11	12–16	2–3	2.5–5.5	29–33

Source: IQVIA (2023b)

Global market of medical devices

Medical devices are an integral part of the healthcare industry. The medical technology (or medical device) industry produces a broad range of products, including equipment for long-term use, such as imaging and radiology equipment; surgical instruments; in vitro diagnostics; single-use devices, such as syringes and stents; implantable devices, such as hip prostheses; reagents; and sterilization equipment (WTO WHO WIPO 2020). These products are used for preventing, diagnosing, or treating illness or for detecting, measuring, restoring, correcting, or modifying the structure or function of the body for some health purpose.

Medical devices are a much more heterogeneous group of products than drugs in terms of design, use, and purpose. The group consists of approximately 1,700 types of medical devices and 50,000 products (Maresova et al 2020). The four major groups of medical devices, from least to most sophisticated, are (1) disposables (bandages, surgical gloves, and plastic syringes); (2) surgical and medical instruments (devices used in surgeries and cosmetic procedures); (3) therapeutics (including implantable devices like hearing aids and prosthetics and non-implantable devices such as ventilators and infusion pumps); and (4) diagnostic equipment (Torsekar 2018).

Looking at the top 15 medical devices Table 2.10, the global market is projected to increase its sales from $371 billion in 2015 to $595 billion in 2024 (Evaluate MedTech consensus reports 2018 and 2016), for a CAGR of 5.4%.[13] The global medical device market outperformed the prescription drug

Table 2.10 Top 15 categories of medical devices: Market share of each category (%)

	2015	*2017*	*2024(P)*
In vitro diagnostics (IVD)	13.1	13	13.4
Cardiology	11.4	11.6	12.2
Diagnostic imaging	10.5	9.8	8.6
Orthopedics	9.2	9	7.9
Ophthalmic	6.7	6.8	7.1
General and plastic surgery	5.5	6.5	5.8
Endoscopy	4.4	4.6	4.8
Drug delivery	4.8	4.6	4.3
Dental	3.3	3.4	3.6
Wound management	3.3	3.2	3
Diabetic care	3	2.9	3.3
Nephrology	2.8	2.9	2.6
General hospital and healthcare supplies	2.8		
ENT		2.2	2.2
Healthcare IT	2.1	2.9	3
Neurology	1.8	2.1	2.7
Top 15	84.5	84.4	84.4
Other	15.5	15.6	15.6

Source: Evaluate MedTech (2016 and 2018)

market between 2011 and 2018, with a CAGR of 4.4% vs. 2.5%. Part of the trend reflects the COVID-19 pandemic's unprecedented boost to demand for some medical devices.

In vitro diagnostic medical devices that are used for sample collection for the diagnosis of a disease are biotechnology-based (FDA 2019). EvaluateMedTech (2018) reports that the in vitro diagnostics (IVD) market is the largest segment in medical technology, with sales set to reach $55 billion in 2018, growing at a 4.4% CAGR between 2011 and 2018. Per that report, IVD companies will increasingly benefit from the rise of personalized medicine, which is seeing the pharma and medtech sectors become increasingly linked through the introduction of companion diagnostic kits for drugs. In vitro diagnostic medical devices, are used for diagnosing disease, conditions, and infections.

Evolving market structure of medical devices

Medical devices firms devote a high percentage of sales revenue to R&D activities. R&D as a percentage of sales increased from 23.4% in 2011 to 30% in 2018. The percentage is projected to increase to 38.9% in 2024 (Evaluate MedTech 2018). Patents on medical technology grew even faster than patents on pharmaceuticals or biotechnology from 1980 to 2017 (WTO, WHO and WIPO 2020). The scientific and engineering basis for future medical device innovations is expected to center on biomaterials, tissue engineering, genomics, and computing (Chen and Liu 2016).

Table 2.10 presents information on the market share of the top 15 categories of medical devices. In vitro diagnostics is forecast to remain the number one device area in 2024 with sales of $79.6 billion. Diagnostic imaging sales are forecast to reach $51 billion. Neurology is set to be the fastest-growing device area, with a CAGR of 9.1% between 2017 and 2024, while diagnostic imaging and orthopedics will be the slowest, with annual growth of just 3.7%.

Top 50 multinational companies by sales

Evidence indicates that sales of pharmaceutical goods are quite concentrated in the hands of a few large corporations. As a consequence of acquisitions and mergers, the combined market share of the eight largest drug companies climbed from 38% in 1987 to 53 in 2012 (the second merger wave) (Feldman 2021).

There are two methods of measuring the concentration ratio. The Herfindahl–Hirschman Index (HHI) is a common measure of market concentration. Another measure of concentration is the ratio of the sum of annual sales of the leading few firms divided by total sales for the therapeutic market (Vernon 1971). With a data set of 50 largest (see appendix) firms, which represent slightly more than half of the global sales of all companies (OECD/EUIPO 2020), market share of 50 corporations grouped into five size groups is reported in Table 2.11. The table shows that the

Table 2.11 Market share of sales of largest 50 companies: By size group (2021)

Size (Sales Billion USD)	*Number of Companies*	*Percentage of Total Sales*
41–50	9	53.5
31–40	1	4.3
21–30	5	14.6
11–20	8	12.2
1–10	27	15.4
Total	50	100

Sources: Calculations based on the data from 2023 Parm Exec Top 50 Companies

ten largest companies accounted for nearly 58% of sales of these 50 big pharma in 2021.

Geographical concentration of the big pharma

Data show that despite the universal need for medicines, there is a strong concentration of the innovative segment of the pharmaceutical industry in five countries, namely the USA, Germany, Switzerland, the UK, and France (Achilladelis and Antonakis 2001). As observed from Table 2.12, the largest 50 companies were headquartered in selected OECD countries. Among these, 17 were in the United States, and 6 were in Japan in 2022. Close to half of the global sales was controlled by the top 17 US multinationals in 2022. Multinationals from the selected EU countries contributed another 37.5% of sales in 2022 (Table 2.12). A noteworthy development in recent years is the sharp rise of the Chinese MNEs in the pharmaceutical sales to four multinationals among the largest 50 in 2022 compared to nil in 2017 (see for comparison, Table 3.1 in OECD 2020).

The US multinationals also dominate the development of new medicines. Estimates show that 64.4% of sales of new medicines launched during the period 2016 2021 were on the US market, compared with 16.8% on the European market (EFPIA 2022). This is because the USA has an unparalleled strong national system of biotech innovations compared to other countries (Bartholomew 1997). Technology transfer by the research universities to the US corporations play a critical role in developing innovative products (DeVol, Lee and Ratnatunga 2017).

Table 2.13 lists top ten medical devices producers. EvaluateMedTech forecasts that Medtronic will continue to hold onto its big lead in the market in 2024. Johnson & Johnson is forecast to remain close to Medtronics with global medical technology sales of $33.4 billion. Following Abbott Laboratories' acquisition of St. Jude Medical and Alere, and following the sale of its eyecare business to Johnson & Johnson, it is set to remain the third-largest player in 2024 with sales of over $26 billion (Evaluate MedTech 2018). Becton Dickinson is currently the eighth biggest medtech company in the world, but it is expected to move into the top five by 2024 following its acquisition of C.

Table 2.12 Sales of largest 50 pharmaceutical companies, by country of headquarters, 2022

Country	*Total Sales, Including Exports*	*Number of Companies*	
	Billion USD	*% of total*	
United States	441.0	49.3	17
Switzerland	98.0	11.0	2
Japan	64.0	7.2	6
United Kingdom	81.0	9.1	2
Germany	54.0	6.1	5
France	49.0	5.5	3
Denmark	25.0	2.8	1
China	16.0	1.8	4
Australia	13.0	1.5	1
Ireland	13.0	1.5	3
Israel	12.0	1.4	1
Canada	7.0	0.7	1
Belgium	6.0	0.6	1
India	5.0	0.6	1
Spain	5.0	0.6	1
Italy	4.0	0.4	1
Total	893.0	100	50

Source: Calculations based on the data in the appendix table

Table 2.13 Top ten medical device producers with market sales (projected)

	2024 $ Billion
Medtronic (USA)	38.9
Johnson and Johnson (USA)	33.4
Abbott Laboratories (USA)	26.6
Siemens Healthineers (Germany)	20.3
Becton Dickinson (USA)	19.2
Phillips (The Netherlands)	18.7
Stryker (USA)	18.5
Roche (Switzerland)	16.3
Boston Scientific (USA)	14.4
General Electric (USA)	12.9

Source: Evaluate MedTech (2018)

R. Bard, which should boost sales that year to over $19 billion. Both Philips and Stryker are close behind Becton Dickinson, with forecast sales just shy of $19 billion (Evaluate MedTech 2018).

Competition and pricing

Competition is important because it compels the industry to provide higher quality goods and services at lower prices. In the pharmaceutical industry, competition can motivate brand companies to create new and improved medicines and encourage generic companies to offer less expensive alternatives (UNCTAD 2015). Evidence, however, shows pharmaceuticals markets are far from perfectly competitive markets as the industry has several features that significantly depart from the standard models for competitive markets (OECD 2019). Lack of competition results in prices higher than (marginal) cost.

Imperfectly competitive market structure in the pharmaceutical industry

Three types of market structure coexist in the pharmaceutical industry. First, during the patent protection phase, most pharmaceuticals can be viewed as oligopolistic with differentiated competitor products in the short run (Danzon 2011). In the longer run, the appropriate model for a therapeutic class is monopolistic competition, with generic entry on patent-expired older molecules and dynamic competition from newer, improved products (Danzon 2011). Entry by generic pharmaceuticals can enhance competition in the drug market by offering more choices and by lowering drug prices to the benefit of health customers.

The market structure and competition between the originator product and generic producers and between the generic imitators themselves in a particular therapeutic class is influenced by a set of complex demand and supply (drug development and production) forces, discussed below.

Nature of supply and demand in the pharmaceutical industry

The supply of brand drugs is characterized by considerable market power because of the presence of patents (UNCTAD 2015). Patents are generally considered necessary to encourage R&D, particularly in an R&D-intensive industry such as pharmaceuticals (Danzon and Towse 2003). Supply of pharmaceutical goods depends on the following and other multiple factors (Fiona and Margaret 2011):

- Uncertain outcome of R&D spending
- Fluctuations in the government spending on basic research and on drug development, and policies that affect the reward on innovations
- Ongoing market expansion in the developing countries
- Mergers and acquisitions
- Strategic patenting policies of the innovator countries

Demand-side influences

The demand-side forces are rather more complicated due to the participation of multiple parties (such as government agencies, insurance companies, copayment made by the patient in a treatment, physician role in drug prescription) in the pricing and consumption. The research literature has listed the following characteristics of demand of branded medicine in a particular disease area (Grabowski and Vernon 1992; Caves, Whinston and Hurwitz 1991; Fiona and Margaret 2011; UNCTAD 2015):

- Insurance coverage and out-of-pocket expenses for prescription drugs
- Brand loyalty of buyers and the degree of responsiveness to price changes (called elasticity of demand)
- Product promotion policies of the companies
- Physicians' perceptions practices

Due to insurance coverage in many countries, patients do not bear the full brunt of prices (Danzon 2011). Brand loyalty results in less price sensitivity to drug prices. Inelastic demand creates incentives for firms to charge higher prices than they would if consumers were informed decision-makers. Physicians also play a significant role in influencing the drug sales of branded drugs in some countries (UNCTAD 2015).

Demand-side characteristics interact with the presence of monopoly power on the supply side to support prices that commonly exceed drug production costs by a substantial margin (Scherer 2000). Patents, brand loyalty, and product differentiation lead to prices that are well above production costs.

Entry by generic pharmaceuticals is delayed by the incumbent through practices that prolong the exclusivity period. Some of the anti-competitive practices are briefly described below.

Anti-competitive strategic patenting practices of originators

There is a large list of anti-competitive practices. The discussion below, however, focuses on four widely reported practices:

- Mergers and acquisitions
- Evergreening of patents
- Patent thickets (patent clustering)
- Patent settlement (pay for delays)

Mergers and acquisitions and their impact on the market structure

There has been a spate of mergers and acquisitions in the pharmaceutical industry in the past few decades. The literature has cited several potential reasons for mergers and acquisitions. They include: achieving economies of scale and scope, gaining corporate control, acquiring specific assets such as patents, and buying out dying or financially weak companies (Danzon, Epstein and Nicholson 2007; Gagnon and Volesky 2017).

Most consolidation has featured bigger players acquiring smaller start-ups (biotechnology firms) and by large horizontal mergers with other medium and large firms (Danzon 2011). In the past few decades, three waves of mergers have substantially increased concentration in the pharmaceutical industry. These three waves are classified into three time periods: the first wave from approximately 1988 to 1991, with the second following between approximately 1996 and 2002, and the third began in 2010 and remains ongoing

(Feldman 2021). Reduced competition allows prices to drift upward and innovation to wane (Bonaime and Wang 2019).

Anti-competitive effects of M&A

It is argued that the consolidation has enabled drugmakers to directly quell competition through what were known as "killer acquisitions," in which they acquired innovative peers solely to pre-empt future competition (Cunningham, Ederer and Ma 2021). Horizontal mergers between large pharmaceutical companies are found to have resulted in a decline in the rate of pharmaceutical innovation. Horizontal mergers occur when companies of the same industry merge and may result in competition by creating one powerful company instead of two competitors. Evidence shows that the increased concentration brought on by mergers and acquisitions did not contribute to halting the declining rate of productivity (Comanor and Scherer 2013). The review of M&A activities by the US government accountability office (GAO 2017) noted two significant negative outcomes: higher prices, particularly for generic drugs, and negative impact on innovation in case of certain mergers.

Anti-competitive effect of strategic patenting by pharmaceutical companies

Pharmaceutical companies increasingly engage in seeking additional patent protection (called secondary patents and patent thickets) on various aspects of a drug in order prolong to stifle competition from generic companies (Gurgula 2020). Evergreening patents are common in the pharmaceutical sector.

"Evergreening" is the practice of filing for new patents on secondary features of a particular product as earlier patents expire, thereby extending patent exclusivity past the original 20-year term. Such a strategic behavior of originators to recycle and repurpose old ones, rather than creating new medicines, is endemic to the industry (Feldman 2018). An analysis of the ten best-selling drugs of 2019 found that on average these drugs held more than 69 patents to extend the monopoly period with 37.5 years of patent protection, well past the 20 years of patent life intended by Congress (Martin 2021). Feldman (2018) in his analyses, of roughly 1800 drugs on the market between 2005 and 2015, found that 78% of the drugs associated with new patents in the FDA's records were not new drugs coming on the market, but existing drugs.

"Evergreening" tactic has been under heavy debate when India's Supreme Court refused to grant Swiss pharmaceutical company Novartis a patent for a new version of its cancer drug Gleevec (imatinib mesylate). Novartis' plea was that "Gleevec" was an innovation as the refined formulation could more easily be absorbed in the blood to fight leukemia. The Indian court did not accept the claim and it held that drugs did not offer enough of an advantage over generic versions of the original molecules (Collier 2013). The presence of dense patent thickets increases litigation burdens and potentially delays the approval of generics and launch of generics and biosimilars (Nielsen 2021). By filing multiple additional patents on the same drug, brand drug manufacturers extend the exclusivity of their drugs beyond the end of their initial exclusivity period. The presence of dense patent thickets increases litigation burdens and potentially delays the approval of generics and launch of generics and biosimilars (Nielsen 2021).

Pay-for-delay tactics

Brand-name pharmaceutical companies can delay generic competition that lowers prices by agreeing to pay a generic competitor to hold its competing product off the market for a certain period of time. These so-called reverse payments or "pay-for-delay" agreements have arisen as part of patent litigation settlement agreements between brand-name and generic pharmaceutical companies (FTC 2010). Numerous examples have shown how pay-for-delay settlements have increased costs to consumers by billions of dollars (Jones et al. 2016). In many cases, it has been found that they missed out on generic prices that could be as much as 90% less than brand prices (FTC 2010). Such settlements also pose a general dilemma about the proper balance between innovation and consumer access (Hemphill 2006).

Need for reforming the existing patent system and drug pricing mechanism

Critics argue that the patenting practices are being used to keep drug prices high, without any benefit for consumers or innovation (Congressional Research Service 2020). The patent system—not just patent rights but how they are obtained and used—has resulted in an innovation system characterized by a dramatic increase in healthcare costs and decreasing (quantitatively and qualitatively) levels of innovation, especially by dollar spent (Gold et al. 2010).

The present patent system results in two types of inefficiencies: static and dynamic. A patent holder as a monopolist keeps a wide margin between the price and marginal cost, which means a loss of allocative efficiency. Dynamic loss arises because patents impede innovations (Stiglitz 2008, Felman 2018, Gurugula 2020, Paris and Belloni 2013). For the sustained growth of the industry, both pharmaceutical innovation and generic competition need to be duly incentivized and protected (Gurgula 2020, Stiglitz 2008). Current patent legislation may not be optimal for striking the right balance between encouraging innovation and facilitating profiteering (Stanbrook 2013). In the words of Feldman (2018), the "foundational structure of the patent system—one that delicately balances innovation and competition—is not working well." Boldrin and Levine (2013) have argued that the patent laws now do more to hinder innovation than to promote it. And, since there's no way to salvage the system, it is suggested to progressively dismantle the patent system (Plumer 2012; Boldrin and Levine 203). The Commission on Intellectual Property Rights, Innovation and Public Health, in its report in 2006, categorically stated that the system fails to address public health issues, especially in developing countries (WHO 2006). Maintaining a balance between promoting and rewarding innovation and ensuring affordable access to medicines for public benefits is a tough challenge, requiring a prudent search for *alternative means of fostering innovation.* To address the inadequacies of the current system, especially with regard to the management of R&D, Stiglitz and Jaidev (2010) have proposed the following measures:

- Promoting prizes over patents
- Value-based pricing for directing innovation toward socially beneficial outputs
- Publicly funding clinical trials to reduce conflicts of interest while reducing costs
- Actively managing frontier technologies to maximize positive social spillovers

Promoting prizes over patents

A system of prizes is considered to be superior to the existing system of monopolies, because it delinks the financing of R&D from the pricing of end products so that medicines can be sold near the cost of production (Love and Hubbard 2007; Kremer and Williams 2009; Boldrin and Levine 2013, Brunt, Lerner and Nicholas 2011). The policy of de-linking R&D costs from drug prices is one of the effective measures for avoiding conflict between promoting innovations and access to medicines (The report of UN High-Level Panel 2016). Many specific proposals have been put forth in this respect. Some prizes have already been instituted in recent years as governments have acted to foster more high-risk, high reward approaches to solving societal and scientific problems. For example, the United States, in legislation enacted in 2010, granted all US science agencies the authority to conduct prize competitions to spur innovation (OECD 2021b).

A value-based approach to pricing has gained in popularity as it is deemed a cost-effective strategy that appropriately rewards innovation and access to the most valuable innovations is prioritized (EFPIA 2023).

Value-based pricing: Aligning prescription drug prices to their therapeutic value

Value-based pricing is used in conjunction with other pricing policies, such as price negotiation, internal and external reference pricing,[14] and policies to promote the use of quality-assured generic and biosimilar medicines (WHO 2021a, c). In principle, VBP implies that prices are mainly driven by a drug's value (value for money) compared to other available treatments for the same condition and that the impact on budget (sustainability) is a second-order driver of price regulation (Jommi et al. 2020). Value assessments consider factors such as the product's potential to extend life, improve quality of life, and reduce the need for hospitalization or extended treatment (WHO 2021b). Pricing literature suggests that a properly designed value-based pricing policy, besides aligning prices with the drug's value (health benefits), theoretically, may also encourage more research and development into medicines that society and governments value most.

Value-based pricing informed by health technology assessment (HTA) is most commonly used in high-income countries (e.g. Australia, Canada, United Kingdom) that have the resources and capacity to conduct health technology assessment of products on a systematic basis (WHO 2021c). HTA involves systematic evaluation of a product or health intervention including therapeutic, social, economic, organizational, and ethical factors (WHO 2021c). The computation of value-based pricing involves the following steps:

- First, determine the value of one quality-adjusted life year (QALY/quality-adjusted life years/healthy years of life). QALY scores range from 1 (perfect health) to 0 (dead)
- Second, determine what people would be willing to pay for it in the form of an incremental insurance premium based on the epidemiological and cost projections for the treatment of a specific disease (Garrison and Towse 2017)
- Third, compute the "incremental cost-effectiveness ratio" (ICER) comparing a new health technology with the existing healthcare treatment as given under (Garrison and Towse, 2017)

$$ICER = \frac{\textit{Cost of new health technolgy} - \textit{Cost of exiting health technology}}{\textit{QUALYs generated by new health technology} - \textit{QUALYs under existing heath technology}}$$

If this ratio is less than the ceiling willingness-to-pay threshold, then it represents good value for the individual or health plan. For the National Health Service (NHS) in the UK, the threshold used on behalf of the NHS is £20,000/QALY, ranging up to £50,000 for life-threatening conditions (Garrison and Towse, 2017). In a US context, the ratio may vary from \$50K/QALY up to \$150K/QALY or more depending on the individual or disease.

Evidence shows that market prices often exceeded ICER-estimated VBPs by a great margin. Bloudek et al. (2021), on comparing actual estimated net market prices to ICER-estimated VBPs for 102 drugs in the US over the period between November 2007 to October 2020, found that the median change in net price needed to reach the \$150 000 per QALY VBP in the US was a 36% reduction.

Pricing of medicine and developing countries

Current systems of pricing of pharmaceutical drugs and incentive mechanisms for stimulating R&D have come under scrutiny due to their limitations in delivering affordable medicines to people in economically poor nations. It is suggested to adapt drug prices to the purchasing power of consumers in different geographical or socio-economic context (Yadav 2010). As the demand is subject to the ability to pay, the price of products needs to be reduced in lower income countries (Kaló, Annemans and Garrison 2013). In many middle and most low-income countries (LICs), insurance coverage is minimal and patients pay out-of-pocket for drugs. This raises concerns that requiring these countries to adopt standard, 20-year product patents, under the WTO TRIPs provisions, may lead to unaffordable drug prices and suboptimal drug consumption. For globally marketed drugs, price discrimination across countries should enable firms to recoup their R&D investments by pricing above marginal cost in high-income countries while pricing close to marginal cost in LICs (Danzon 2011).

Differential pricing: To improve access to medicines in developing countries

The terms "differential," "tiered," "preferential," and "discounted" pricing, and "market segmentation" are often used to describe the practice of charging lower prices in different markets. Differential pricing refers to a pricing system in which prices in affluent countries are set at a level that could generate sufficient revenue to pay for R&D, whereas prices in developing nations are set only to cover their marginal costs (Danzon 2007). In lower income countries, low per capita income and the absence of universal insurance coverage result in highly price-sensitive markets. The Ramsey optimal pricing solution implies that prices should differ across market segments in inverse relation to their demand elasticities (Danzon and Towse 2003). When customers differ in their price elasticity, static efficiency is improved if charging lower prices to more price-sensitive consumers increases their utilization of drugs, and dynamic efficiency is enhanced if producers face appropriate incentives to invest in R&D (Danzon 2018).

Differential pricing is feasible where there are substantial fixed costs and the variable, or marginal, costs of production are relatively low. In the pharmaceutical industry, R&D is a global joint cost that benefits consumers in high-income, middle-income, and low-income countries, worldwide. Differential pricing requires two conditions to be met: there is no diversion of low-priced products into high-income markets (parallel trade) and no external referencing (see fn. 12). Opportunities for parallel trade and external reference pricing can be avoided if payers in developing countries and pharmaceutical companies negotiate contracts that include confidential rebates (Danzon and Towse 2003). Differential pricing of medicines is used to treat HIV/AIDS, tuberculosis, and malaria in the lowest-income countries (Danzon 2007).

Affordability: A Central issue in developing countries

The differential pricing, it is alleged, does not necessarily result in affordability or equitable access to a product. It is argued that differential or tiered pricing are commercial terms for pricing practices aimed at maximizing the profits of the seller ('t Hoen et al. 2011). Though the differential pricing practices may lead to equitable access to medicines, they do not necessarily mean that even the lowest prices charged will be affordable ('t Hoen 2002, Moon et al. 2011). There is a growing consensus that essential medicines should be priced in developing countries based on the principle of "equity," which means that the poor should pay less for, and have access to, essential medicines ('t Hoen 2002, Rawson 2020, Moon et al. 2020). It is also further contended that no single strategy would, in fact, be sufficient to achieve and sustain equity pricing. Rather, what is needed is a comprehensive system of mutually supportive strategies ('t Hoen et al. 2011). The suggested strategies are:

- Promoting generic competition in developing countries.
- Selling drugs and vaccines in developing countries at prices systematically lower than in industrialized countries.
- Compulsory licensing: adopting TRIPS safeguards into national legislation.
- Creating high volume/high demand through global/regional procurement.
- Encouraging local production through voluntary licensing and technology transfer.

Promoting generic competition in developing markets

Generic competition is one of the most powerful tools that policymakers have to lower drug prices in a sustainable way. Lessons can be learned from Brazil where the price of AIDS drugs fell by 82% over five years as a result of generic competition ('t Hoen et al. 2011). As generic manufacturers in developing countries capture higher market shares in their domestic markets, they achieve better economies of scale to compete in international markets (Yadav 2010).

Compulsory licensing

Countries can counter rising drug prices by building TRIPS-compliant safeguards into their national laws, including compulsory licensing, parallel importation, and measures to accelerate the introduction of generics ('t Hoen et al. 2011). Compulsory licensing is the practice by which a government allows a third party to produce or sell the patented product or process without the patentee's consent. It is one of the flexibilities in patent protection included in the World Trade Organization's (WTO) agreement on intellectual property. The TRIPS Agreement, Section 93 of the International Protection (IP) Code, allows a license to exploit a patented invention even without the consent of the patent owner under circumstances of extreme urgency, such as national emergencies. The DOHA Declaration recognized the inability of poor countries to pay for essential medications for their citizens.

Danzon and Towse (2003) suggest that the "option of compulsory licensing of patented products to generic manufacturers may be important if they truly have lower production costs, or originators charge prices above marginal cost, despite market separation" (p. 183)

Promoting local production capabilities in developing countries

Drugs for diseases that have no market in the developed world will require additional measures at the global and national level (Danzon 2007). Under TRIPS (Article 66.2), developed countries are obligated to transfer technology to least-developed countries ('t Hoen et al. 2011). This theme is covered in more detail in another chapter.

Summary

This chapter has analyzed the evolving structure of the global drugs and pharmaceuticals and medical devices triggered by the expanding knowledge of biosciences and the consequent improvement of medical scientists' ability to understand the underlying causes and development of diseases at a molecular level. The chapter has highlighted the following developments:

- Changing product structure from small molecules-based drugs to gene- and cell-based biologic therapies
- R&D collaboration and strategic partnership between large pharma and innovative small biotech firms (University spin-offs) to develop novel products
- Growing use of medicine owing to the aging population in the western countries and the shifting disease pattern among developing countries
- Mergers and acquisitions leading to high concentration of the innovative segment of the industry in the hands of a few big multinational enterprises headquartered in a handful of OECD countries
- Lack of price competition due to the inherent characteristics of the market (low price elasticity of demand)
- Patenting practices which by extending the period of exclusivity stifle competition and resulting loss of static and dynamic efficiency
- Value-based pricing (VBP) system is considered an effective method of benefiting patients with better health outcomes at a reasonable cost
- Differential pricing approach can increase patient access in developing countries

Notes

1 This industry includes the manufacture of laboratory apparatus, surgical and medical instruments, surgical appliances and supplies, dental equipment and supplies, orthodontic goods, and dentures and orthodontic appliances. Also included is the manufacture of medical, dental, and similar furniture, where the additional specific functions determine the purpose of the product, such as dentist chairs with built-in hydraulic function (NSF 2022).

2 As per the NSF report (2022), the pharmaceutical industry includes the manufacture of basic pharmaceutical products and pharmaceutical preparations. Also included is the manufacture of medicinal chemical and botanical products.

3 High R&D-intensive industries include air and spacecraft and related machinery; pharmaceuticals; computer, electronic, and optical products; scientific research and

development; and software publishing. Medium-high R&D-intensive industries include motor vehicles, trailers, and semi-trailers; medical and dental instruments; machinery and equipment nec; chemicals and chemical products; electrical equipment; railroad, military vehicles, and transport; and information technology and other information services (NSF 2022).

4 A generic medication contains the same active ingredient as the originator medication (i.e., brand-name product).

5 Monoclonal antibody drugs are treatments that enlist the body's germ-fighting immune system against diseases, including cancer.

6 Man-made proteins (known as monoclonal antibodies) act like human antibodies in the immune system. These biologics are improving the quality of life of patients with inflammatory and autoimmune conditions (Johnston 2007; Taylor 2015; Pham-Huy et al. 2021).

7 Recombinant DNA technology involves using enzymes and various laboratory techniques to manipulate and isolate DNA segments of interest. This method can be used to combine (or splice) DNA from different species or to create genes with new functions. The resulting copies are often referred to as recombinant DNA (National Human Genome Research Institute 2023).

8 A vaccine comprises two components: antigens and adjuvants. An adjuvant is a substance that is added to a vaccine to stimulate and enhance the magnitude and durability of the immune response.

9 The Bayh–Dole Act has been criticized for forcing consumers to "pay twice" for patented products—first through the tax system and again when the patentee charges a supercompetitive price (Hemel and Ouellette 2017).

10 These countries are Argentina, Bangladesh, Brazil, Chile, China, Colombia, Egypt, Hungary, India, Indonesia, Mexico, Pakistan, Philippines, Poland, Romania, Russia, Saudi Arabia, South Africa, Taiwan, Turkey, Ukraine, and Vietnam (IQVIA 2022).

11 Specialty medicines as those that treat chronic, complex, or rare diseases, and that have a minimum of four out of seven additional characteristics related to the distribution, care delivery, and/or cost of the medicines (IQVIA 2022).

12 In the ATC classification system, active substances are classified in a hierarchy with five different levels. For example, all plain metformin preparations are given the code A10BA02, which is a subcode of substances targeting the alimentary tract and metabolism (code A).

A	Alimentary tract and metabolism (1st level, anatomical main group)
A10	Drugs used in diabetes (2nd level, therapeutic subgroup)
A10B	Blood glucose lowering drugs, excluding insulin
A10BA	Biguanides (4th level, chemical subgroup)
A10BA02	metformin (5th level, chemical substance)

13 The analysis is based on in-depth forecast models for the top 120 global medtech companies for which data are available in EvaluateMedTech™.

14 External reference pricing is an approach where prices are set according to the benchmark prices for the same or similar medicines in comparable countries (WHO 2021a).

References

Achilladelis, B., and N. Antonakis. 2001. "The Dynamics of Technological Innovation: The Case of the Pharmaceutical Industry." *Research Policy* 30 (4): 535–588.

Aitken, M. 2020. "Biologics Market Dynamics: Setting the Stage for Biosimilars, FD A/F T C Workshop on Competitive Marketplace for Biosimilars", Accessed March 9 2020. https://www.ftc.gov/system/files/documents/public_events/1568297/aitken_-_biologics_market_dynamics_setting_the_stage_for_biosimilars_slides.pdf.

Bartholomew, S. 1997. "National Systems of Biotechnology Innovation: Complex Interdependence in the Global System." *Journal of International Business Studies* 28 (2): 241–266. https://doi.org/10.1057/palgrave.jibs.8490100.

Boldrin, M., and D. K. Levine. 2013. "The Case Against Patents." *Journal of Economic Perspectives* 27 (1): 3–22. https://doi.org/10.1257/jep.27.1.3.

Bonaime, Alice A., and Ye Wang. 2019. *Mergers, Product Prices, and Innovation: Evidence from the Pharmaceutical Industry (March 15, 2019)*. vol. 2019. SSRN 3445753.

Brunt, L., J. Lerner, and T. Nicholas. 2011. *Inducement Prizes and Innovation*. Harvard Business School. http://www.hbs.edu/faculty/Publication%20Files/11-118.pdf.

Caves, R. E., M. D. Whinston, and M. A. Hurwitz. 1991. "Entry, and Competition in the U.S. Pharmaceutical Industry. Brookings Papers on Economic Activity, Economic Studies Program, The Brookings Institution." *Micro. Patent Expiration* 22: 1–66.

Collier, Roger. 2013. "Drug Patents: The Evergreening Problem." *CMAJ: Canadian Medical Association Journal* 185 (9): E385–E386. https://doi.org/10.1503/cmaj.109-4466.

Comanor, William S., and F. M. Scherer. 2013. "Mergers and Innovation in the Pharmaceutical Industry." *Journal of Health Economics* 32 (1): 106–13. https://doi.org/10.1016/j.jhealeco.2012.09.006.

Congressional Research Service. 2020. *Drug Pricing and Pharmaceutical Patenting Practices*. https://crsreports.congress.gov/product/pdf/R/R46221

Cooke, P. 2004 "The Molecular Biology Revolution and the Rise of Bioscience Megacentres in North America and Europe." *Environment & Planning C* 22 (2): 161–177. https://doi.org/10.1068/c0344.

Cunningham, C., F. Ederer, and S. Ma. 2021. "Killer Acquisitions." *Journal of Political Economy* 129 (3): 649–702. https://doi.org/10.1086/712506.

Danzon, Patricia M. 2018. "Differential Pricing of Pharmaceuticals. Theory, Evidence and Emerging Issues." *Pharmacoeconomics* 36 (12): 1395–1405. https://doi.org/10.1007/s40273-018-0696-4.

Danzon, Patricia M., A. Epstein, and S. Nicholson. 2007. "Mergers and Acquisitions in the Pharmaceutical and Biotech Industries." *Managerial & Decision Economics* 28 (4–5): 307–328. https://doi.org/10.1002/mde.1343.

Danzon, Patricia M., and Erin Taylor. 2010. "Drug Pricing and Value in Oncology." *Oncologist* 15(Suppl. 1): 24–31. https://doi.org/10.1634/theoncologist.2010-S1-24.

Danzon, Patricia M., and Adrian Towse. 2003. "Differential Pricing for Pharmaceuticals: Reconciling Access, R&D and Patents." *International Journal of Health Care Finance & Economics* 3 (3): 183–205. https://doi.org/10.1023/a:1025384819575.

Danzon, Patricia M., Adrian Towse, and Andrew W. Mulcahy. 2011. "Setting Cost-Effectiveness Thresholds as a Means to Achieve Appropriate Drug Prices in Rich and Poor Countries." *Health Affairs (Project Hope)* 30 (8): 1529–1538. https://doi.org/10.1377/hlthaff.2010.0902.

DeVol, R., J. Lee, and M. Ratnatunga. 2017. *Concept to Commercialization the Best Universities for Technology Transfer*. Milken Institute.

Drews, J. 2000. "Drug Discovery: A Historical Perspective." *Science* 17 (287): 1960–1964. https://doi.org/10.1126/science.287.5460.1960.

Ezell, S., and N. Cory. 2019. *The Way Forward for Intellectual Property Internationally*. Information Technology and Innovation Foundation. https://www2.itif.org/2019-way-forward-ip.pdf.

FDA. 2019. "In Vitro Diagnostics, US Food and Drug Administration." In *Vitro Diagnostics*, FDA , US Food and Drug Administration . https://www.fda.gov/medical-devices/products-and-medical-procedures/in-vitro-diagnostics

Feldman, R. 2018. "May Your Drug Price Be Evergreen." *Journal of Law & the Biosciences* 5 (3): 590–647. https://doi.org/10.1093/jlb/lsy022.

Feldman, R. 2021. "Drug Companies Keep Merging. Why That's Bad for Consumers and Innovation." *The Washington Post*, April 6.

Fiona, M. S., and K. Margaret. 2011. *Markets for Pharmaceutical Products11The Authors Thank Tom McGuire for Editorial Advice and Improvements and Participants at the Handbook Conference for Helpful Suggestions, Handbook of Health*. Elsevier.

FTC. 2010. "Pay-for-Delay How Drug Company Pay-Off Cost Consumer Billions." *A FTC Study*, Accessed January 2010. https://www.ftc.gov/sites/default/files/documents/reports/pay-delay-how-drug-company-pay-offs-cost-consumers-billions-federal-trade-commission-staff-study/100112payfordelayrpt.pdf.

FTC. 2022. "The Future of Pharmaceuticals: Examining the Analysis of Pharmaceutical Mergers." Accessed June 14–15. https://www.ftc.gov/news-events/events/2022/06/future-pharmaceuticals-examining-analysis-pharmaceutical-mergers.

Gagnon, Marc-André, and Karena D. Volesky. 2017. "Merger Mania: Mergers and Acquisitions in the Generic Drug Sector from 1995 to 2016." *Globalization & Health* 13 (1): 62. https://doi.org/10.1186/s12992-017-0285-x.

Gambardella, A., L. Orsenigo, and F. Pammolli. 2000. *Global Competitiveness in Pharmaceuticals. A European Perspective*. Report Prepared for the Enterprise Directorate-General of the European Commission.

GAO. 2017. *Drug Industry: Profits, Research and Development Spending, and Merger and Acquisition Deals*. US Government Accountability Office, GAO-18-40. Published: November 17, 2017.

Garrison, Louis P., and Adrian Towse. 2017. "Value-Based Pricing and Reimbursement in Personalised Healthcare: Introduction to the Basic Health Economics." *Journal of Personalized Medicine* 7 (3). https://doi.org/10.3390/jpm7030010.

Gold, E. Richard, Warren Kaplan, James Orbinski, Sarah Harland-Logan, and Sevil N-Marandi. 2010. "Are Patents Impeding Medical Care and Innovation?" *PLOS Medicine* 7 (1): e1000208. https://doi.org/10.1371/journal.pmed.1000208.

Grabowski, H. G., and J. M. Vernon. 1992. "Brand Loyalty, Entry, and Price Competition in Pharmaceuticals After the 1984 Drug Act." *Journal of Law & Economics* 35 (2): 331–350. https://doi.org/10.1086/467257.

Gurgula, Olga. 2020. "Strategic Patenting by Pharmaceutical Companies – Should Competition Law Intervene?" *IIC; International Review of Industrial Property & Copyright Law* 51 (9): 1062–1085. https://doi.org/10.1007/s40319-020-00985-0.

Hemel, D. J., and L. L. Ouellette. 2017. "Bayh–Dole Beyond Borders." *Journal of Law & the Biosciences* 4 (2): 282–310. https://doi.org/10.1093/jlb/lsx011.

Hemphill, C. Scott. 2006. Columbia law and economics working Paper No. 306. "Paying for Delay: Pharmaceutical Patent Settlement as a Regulatory Design Problem." *New York University Law Review* 81: 1553.

Nielsen, Hobbs. 2021. "US FDA's [Patent] 'Concerns' Include Thickets, Product Hopping, And Evergreening." *Pink Sheet CITELINE Regulatory*, September 10.

Hughes, J. P., S. Rees, S. B. Kalindjian, and K. L. Philpott. 2011. "Principles of Early Drug Discovery." *British Journal of Pharmacology* 162 (6): 1239–1249. https://doi.org/10.1111/j.1476-5381.2010.01127.x.

International Trade Administration. 2016. *Top Markets Report Pharmaceuticals A Market Assessment Tool for US Exporters* vol. 2016. United States Department of Commerce.

IQVIA. 2019. *The Global Use of Medicine in 2019 and Outlook to 2023 Forecasts and Areas to Watch, Institute for Human Data Science (2019), January 2019 QVIA.* IQVIA.

IQVIA. 2020. *Global Medicine Spending and Usage Trends OUTLOOK TO* vol. 2024. IQVIA.

IQVIA. 2021. *Global Medicine Spending and Usage Trends, Outlook to 2025.* IQVIA.

IQVIA. 2022a. *The Global Use of Medicines 2022, Outlook to 2026, January 2021.* IQVIA.

IQVIA. 2022b. *Emerging Biopharma's Contribution to Innovation, June 2022.* IQVIA.

IQVIA. 2023. *Global Trends in R&D 2023, Activity, Productivity and Enablers.* IQVIA.

Johnston, Sarah L. 2007. "Biologic Therapies: What and When?." *Journal of Clinical Pathology* 60 (1): 8–17. https://doi.org/10.1136/jcp.2005.032300.

Jommi, Claudio, Patrizio Armeni, Francesco Costa, Arianna Bertolani, and Monica Otto. 2020. "Implementation of Value-Based Pricing for Medicines." *Clinical Therapeutics* 42 (1): 15–24. https://doi.org/10.1016/j.clinthera.2019.11.006.

Kaló, Zoltán, Lieven Annemans, and Louis P. Garrison. 2013. "Differential Pricing of New Pharmaceuticals in Lower Income European Countries." *Expert Review of Pharmacoeconomics & Outcomes Research* 13 (6): 735–741. https://doi.org/10.1586/14737167.2013.847367.

Kashte, Shivaji, Arvind Gulbake, Saadiq F. El-Amin 3rd, and Ashim Gupta. 2021. "COVID-19 Vaccines: Rapid Development, Implications, Challenges and Future Prospects." *Human Cell* 34 (3): 711–733. https://doi.org/10.1007/s13577-021-00512-4.

Kesik-Brodacka, Malgorzata. 2018. "Progress in Biopharmaceutical Development." *Biotechnology & Applied Biochemistry* 65 (3): 306–322. https://doi.org/10.1002/bab.1617.

Kremer, M., and H. Williams. 2009. "Incentivizing Innovation: Adding to the Toolkit." In *Innovation Policy & the Economy*, edited by J. Lerner, and S. Stern. Chicago University Press 10: 1–17.

Lokko, Yvonne, Marc Heijde, Karl Schebesta, Philippe Scholtès, Marc Van Montagu, and Mauro Giacca. 2018. "Biotechnology and the Bioeconomy-Towards Inclusive and Sustainable Industrial Development." *New Biotechnology* 40 (A): 5–10. https://doi.org/10.1016/j.nbt.2017.06.005.

Love, J., and T. Hubbard. 2007. "The Big Idea: Prizes to Stimulate R&D for New Medicines." *Chicago-Kent Law Review* 82 (3): 1519–1554.

Lu, Ruei-Min, Yu-Chyi Hwang, I. J. Liu, Chi-Chiu Lee, Han-Zen Tsai, Hsin-Jung Li, and Han-Chung Wu. 2020. "Development of Therapeutic Antibodies for the

Treatment of Diseases." *Journal of Biomedical Science* 27 (1): 1. https://doi.org/10.1186/s12929-019-0592-z.

Makurvet, F. D. 2021. "Biologics vs. Small Molecules: Drug Costs and Patient Access." *Medicine in Drug Discovery* 9: 100075.

Maresova, P., L. Hajek, O. Krejcar, M. Storek, and K. Kuca. 2020. "New Regulations on Medical Devices in Europe: Are They an Opportunity for Growth?" *Administrative Sciences* 10 (1). https://doi.org/10.3390/admsci10010016.

Martin, K. 2021. *Policymakers' Attention Turns to Drug Patents in the Debate on Prices.* Blog Common Wealth Fund. October 7, 2021.

Mócsai, Attila, László Kovács, and Péter Gergely. 2014. "What Is the Future of Targeted Therapy in Rheumatology: Biologics or Small Molecules?" *BMC Medicine* 12: 43. https://doi.org/10.1186/1741-7015-12-43.

Moon, Suerie, Elodie Jambert, Michelle Childs, and Tido von Schoen-Angerer. 2011. "A Win-Win Solution? A Critical Analysis of Tiered Pricing to Improve Access to Medicines in Developing Countries." *Globalization & Health* 7: 39. https://doi.org/10.1186/1744-8603-7-39.

Moon, Suerie, Stephanie Mariat, Isao Kamae, and Hanne Bak Pedersen. 2020. "Defining the Concept of Fair Pricing for Medicines." *BMJ* 368: l4726. https://doi.org/10.1136/bmj.l4726.

National Human Genome Research Institute. 2023. "Recombinant DNA." *Technology.* https://www.genome.gov/genetics-glossary/Recombinant-DNA-Technology.

OECD. 2009. *The Bioeconomy to 2030, Designing a Policy Agenda.* OECD International Future Project, Organization for Economic Co-operation and Development Publishing.

OECD. 2016. *Taxonomy of Economic Activities Based on R&D Intensity, OECD Science, Technology and Industry Working Papers, 2016/4 m Written by Fernando Galindo-Rueda, Fabien Verger.* OECD.

OECD. 2018. *Pharmaceutical Innovation and Access to Medicines, OECD* Health Policy Studies. OECD Publishing.

OECD. 2019. "Analytical Business Enterprise Research and Development (ANBERD)." *Database.* http://oe.cd/anberd.

OECD. 2020, Chapter 3. "Industry Review." In *Trade in Counterfeit Pharmaceutical Products.* OECD.

OECD. 2021a. *Coronavirus (COVID-19) Vaccines for Developing Countries: An Equal Shot at Recovery, Tackling Coronavirus (COVID-19): Contributing to Global Effort.* OECD.

OECD. 2021b. *Health at a Glance 2021: OECD.* Indicators. OECD Publishing.

Pardi, Norbert, Michael J. Hogan, Frederick W. Porter, and Drew Weissman. 2018. "mRNA Vaccines-A New Era in Vaccinology." *Nature Reviews. Drug Discovery* 17 (4): 261–279. https://doi.org/10.1038/nrd.2017.243.

Pham-Huy, Anne, Karina A. Top, Cora Constantinescu, Cynthia H. Seow, and Darine El-Chaâr. 2021. "The Use and Impact of Monoclonal Antibody Biologics During Pregnancy." *CMAJ: Canadian Medical Association Journal* 193 (29): E1129–E1136. https://doi.org/10.1503/cmaj.202391.

Plumer, B. 2012. "The Case Against Patents, Economic Policy." *Washington Post,* October 10.

Pollard, Andrew J., and Else M. Bijker. 2021. "A Guide to Vaccinology: From Basic Principles to New Developments." *Nature Reviews. Immunology* 21 (2): 83–100. https://doi.org/10.1038/s41577-020-00479-7.

Powell, W. W., and J. Owen-Smith. 1998. "Universities and the Market for Intellectual Property in the Life Sciences." *Journal of Policy Analysis & Management* 17 (2): 253–277. https://doi.org/10.1002/(SICI)1520-6688(199821)17:2<253::AID-PAM8>3.0.CO;2-G.

Pulendran, Bali, Prabhu S Arunachalam, and Derek T. O'Hagan. 2021. "Emerging Concepts in the Science of Vaccine Adjuvants." *Nature Reviews. Drug Discovery* 20 (6): 454–475. https://doi.org/10.1038/s41573-021-00163-y.

Rawson, Nigel S. B. 2020. "National Pharmacare in Canada: Equality or Equity, Accessibility or Affordability Comment on "Universal Pharmacare in Canada: A Prescription for Equity in Healthcare." *International Journal of Health Policy & Management* 9 (12): 524–527. https://doi.org/10.15171/ijhpm.2019.146.

Richman, B., W. Mitchell, E. Vidal, and K. Schulman. 2020. "Pharmaceutical M&A Activity: Effects on Prices, Innovation, and Competition," *Loyola University Chicago Law Journal* 48 787–819. https://scholarship.law.duke.edu/faculty_scholarship/3749

Sahin, Ugur, Katalin Karikó, and Özlem Türeci. 2014. "mRNA-Based Therapeutics—Developing a New Class of Drugs." *Nature Reviews. Drug Discovery* 13(10): 759–780. https://doi.org/10.1038/nrd4278.

Scherer, F. M. 2000. Ch. 25. In *Handbook of Health Economics* 1 (B): 1297–1336. Industry: Pharmaceutical Press.

Stanbrook, Matthew B. 2013. "Limiting "Evergreening" for a Better Balance of Drug Innovation Incentives." *CMAJ: Canadian Medical Association Journal* 185 (11): 939. https://doi.org/10.1503/cmaj.130992.

Stiglitz, J. E. 2008. "Economic Foundations of Intellectual Property Rights." *Duke Law Journal* 57: 1693–1724.

Stiglitz, J. E., and A. Jayadev. 2010. "Medicine for Tomorrow: Some Alternative Proposals to Promote Socially Beneficial Research and Development in Pharmaceuticals." *Journal of Generic Medicines: The Business Journal for the Generic Medicines Sector* 7 (3): 217–226. https://doi.org/10.1057/jgm.2010.21.

Tannoury, Maya, and Zouhair Attieh. 2017. "The Influence of Emerging Markets on the Pharmaceutical Industry." *Current Therapeutic Research, Clinical & Experimental* 86: 19–22. https://doi.org/10.1016/j.curtheres.2017.04.005.

Taylor, D. 2015. "The Pharmaceutical Industry and the Future of Drug Development." *Pharmaceuticals in the Environment* 1–33. https://doi.org/10.1039/9781782622345-00001.

The White House. 2022. *Executive Order 14081: Advancing Biotechnology and Biomanufacturing Innovation for a Sustainable, Safe, and Secure American Bioeconomy.* The White House.

Torsekar, M. 2018. "China Climbs the Global Value Chain for Medical Devices." *Journal of International Commerce & Economics.* https://www.usitc.gov/journals.

U.S. International Trade Commission. 1999. "Review of Global Competitiveness, April 1999, Publication 3172." *Office of Industries, Staff Study Research* 25. https://www.usitc.gov/publications/332/pub3172.pdf.

Vernon, J. M. 1971. "Concentration, Promotion, and Market Share Stability in the Pharmaceutical Industry." *Journal of Industrial Economics* 19 (3): 246–266. https://doi.org/10.2307/2097429.

WHO. 2006. *Public Health, Innovation and Intellectual Property Rights, Report of the Commission on Intellectual Property Rights, Innovation and Public Health* vol. 2006. WHO.

WHO. 2021a. *Value Based Pricing: WHO Guideline on Country Pharmaceutical Pricing Policies. A Plain Language Summary.* WHO.

WHO. 2021b. *Ending the Neglect to Attain the Sustainable Development Goals A Road Map for Neglected Tropical Diseases 2021–2030 Overview, 28 January 2021 Executive Summary, WHO Reference Number: WHO/UCN/NTD/2020.01.* WHO.

WHO. 2021c. *WHO Licensing Agreement Can Improve Access to COVID Health Technologies, May 16, Open Access News.* WHO.

Yadav, P. 2010. *Differential Pricing for Pharmaceuticals Review of Current Knowledge, New Findings and Ideas for Action, A Study Conducted for the U.K.* Department for International Development.

3 Trade in health products and trade interdependence

Introduction

International trade is a strong pillar of the growth of the highly globalized and R&D-intensive medical goods industry. Trade is critical in ensuring access to essential medical goods, and in spreading benefits of curing illness and in controlling the spread of deadly diseases. Trade stimulates competition, which, in turn, reduces prices and enables a wider range of suppliers, improving the security and predictability of supply (WHO, WIPO, and WTO 2020).

No country is entirely self-reliant in making the products it needs for its public health system. Trade statistics shows that even among the developed countries, pharmaceutical giants such as the US multinationals, specializing in high-value supply chain tasks such as research and development, patents, clinical trials, and marketing, also offshore the production of other inputs to economies such as China and India. Germany and Switzerland are the largest sources of supply of intermediate goods and services to European nations. Switzerland is particularly active in manufacturing APIs needed in complex pharmaceutical products.

International trade in health-related products has grown significantly since 1995, with annual compound growth rates higher than those for merchandise in general (WHO, WIPO, and WTO 2020). OECD's trade in value-added data (TiVA) reveals that the medical supply chain is extensively multinational in nature, demonstrating complex trade linkages and trade interdependence among countries . Today global competitiveness is about creating value-added gains through specialization in upstream activities within GVCs (Johansson and Olaberria 2014; Szalavetz 2019).

Evidence confirms that trade played a crucial role in ensuring the production and delivery of vaccines, therapeutics, diagnostics, and personal protective equipment in the fight against COVID-19 (OECD 2020, 2021). Trade enabled access to COVID-19 vaccines for many countries that could not produce them, which signifies that trade can be leveraged to improve global health security (OECD 2022). This chapter highlights certain key aspects of global trade: trade in major product categories and the emerging pattern of global trade along the global value chains.

DOI: 10.4324/9781003449331-3

International trade in health-related products: An overview of trade by major product groups

The World Customs Organization has developed a Harmonized System (HS) for reporting and classifying international trade data covering over 98% of the global merchandise trade. The HS classification breaks all trade flows down into 97 chapters and almost 6,000 subheadings. Helble (2012), using the HS classification (2007), identified 207 subheadings containing products that can be directly linked to a health purpose. The list of 207 subheadings has been further classified into three major groups: (A) medicines, (B) chemicals used in the production of pharmaceuticals, and (C) hospital and laboratory inputs and medical equipment (Helble and Shepherd 2017). These three groups are further classified to form six groups and subgroups: A1, A2, A3, B, C1, and C2. The six groups are as follows:[1]

1. A1: Dosified medicines/formulations (HS Headings 3002 and 3004)
2. A2: Bulk medicines (HS Headings 3003 and 3006)
3. A3: Inputs specific to the pharmaceutical industry (HS Headings 2936, 2937, 2939, and 2941)
4. B: Chemical inputs of general purpose (Chapter 29 and HS Headings 2842, 3203, 3204)
5. C1: Hospital and laboratory inputs (HS Headings 3001, 3002, 3005, 3006, 3507, 3822, 4014, 4015, 7017, 9018)
6. C2: Medical technology equipment (HS Headings 8419, 8713, 9006, 9018, 9019, 9021, 9022 and 9402)

Figure 3.1 presents all the groups and subgroups schematically. Group A covers all pharmaceutical-industry products and inputs. A1 and A2 contain products that are finished medicines, while A3 contains pharmaceutical-industry inputs. Goods in groups B and C are produced by other industries. Dosified medicines (medicines for retail sale) (A1) are covered under HS heading 3004, and bulk medicines (A2) fall under HS heading 3003. A1 comprises all subheadings (six-digit HS codes) of HS Code 3004 plus vaccines for humans (HS 300220) while A2 includes all subheadings of HS Code 3003. For example, this heading includes antibiotics, hormones, and vitamins. C includes hospital and laboratory inputs (C1) and medical technology.

Overall trade in health products grew substantially between 1995 and 2018 (Helble 2012, and WHO, WIPO, and WTO 2020).[2] The Pharma Agreement is one of many sectoral initiatives agreed during the Uruguay Round that boosted global trade in health products. The 1994 Agreement on Trade in Pharmaceutical Products (also known as the Pharmaceutical Agreement or the Pharma Agreement) eliminated tariffs and other duties and charges on many pharmaceutical products and the substances used to produce them.

From Table 3.1, it is observed that the global import demand for medical goods grew from 423.9 billion dollars in 2001 to 1917 billion dollars in 2022,

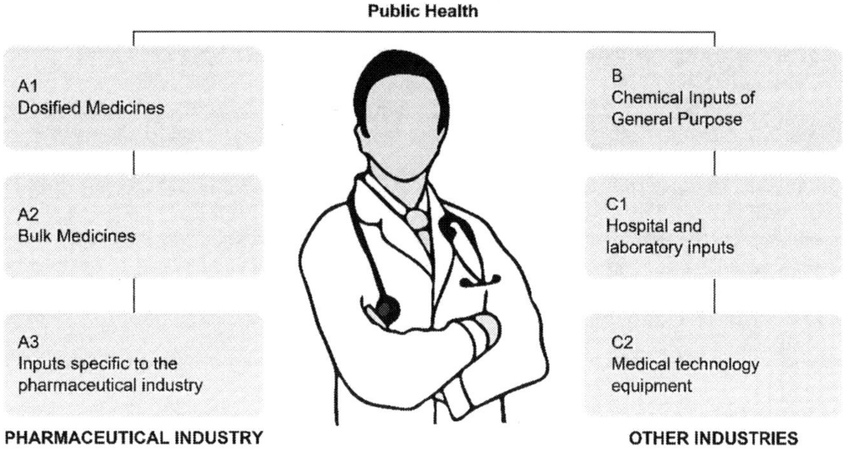

Figure 3.1 Product groups related to public health
Source: Helble (2012)

which amount to a compound growth rate of 13.4% over 2010 and 2022 per annum.[3]

Comparing the trade in the three main commodity groups (A, B, and C), we notice from Table 3.1 that subgroup A_1 (formulations) holds the largest share (in value terms) (45% in 2022) and has exhibited the strongest increase. Trade in hospital and laboratory inputs (C1) accounted for 33% share of trade in health products in 2022. Trade in medical technology has grown steadily over time. Medical technology equipment accounted for 18% share in 2022.

Top exporters and importers

Almost all countries and economies are participating in the global trade in health products, either as exporters or as importers or both (Helble 2012). Developed countries are the largest exporters and importers of medical goods (WHO, WIPO and WTO 2020). Table 3.2 presents the major participants' share in global exports and imports for aggregate health-related products.

While developed countries and territories accounted for just over 66% of all exports of health products in 2018, exports from some developing countries are now gaining a significant share (WHO, WIPO and WTO 2020).

Table 3.3 presents exports of leading exporters in major broad categories of health products. It is observed from this table that only a handful of countries, such as the USA, China, Germany, the Netherlands, Belgium, Switzerland, Japan, and Ireland, are the principal exporters and importers in all areas of the advanced medical goods—particularly formulations (A1) and medical technology equipment (C2). The domination of a few advanced countries can be explained by several factors. First, these countries are typically more integrated

Table 3.1 Trade in health products by major categories: 2010 and 2022

Product Categories (with HS Codes)	*Imports Value (million USD) 2010*	*Imports Value (million USD) 2022*
Dosified medicines/formulations(A1) (3002+3004)	202,703	861,171.4
Bulk medicines (A2) (3003+3006)	9,775	31,272.0
Total medicines	212,478	892,443.4
Inputs specific to (A3) pharmaceutical industry (2936+2937+2939+2941)	26,910	49,207.9
Hospital and laboratory inputs (C1) (3001+3002+3005+3006+3507 +3822+4014+4015+7017+9018)	86,933	632,925.0
Medical technology equipment (C2) (8419+8713+9006+9018+9019 +9020+9021+9022+9402)	97,545	342,454.6
Total: A1, A2, A3, C1, and C2	423,866	1,917,030.9

Sources: Joint Report (2020) for data pertaining to year 2010 and ITC Trade Map (Trade Statistics for International Business) for data pertaining to year 2022

Table 3.2 International trade in health-related products: Percentage share of main importers and exporters 2009 and 2018

	Imports 2009	*Exports 2009*	*Imports 2018*	*Exports 2018*
United States	23.2	21.06	22.5	33.4
European Union	24.33	38.08	18.5	15.3
China	3.55	5.31	11.1	12.2
Japan	6.24	3.17	5.8	4
Switzerland	5.82	14.07	4.7	10.9
Canada	4.21	1.9	2.8	1.7
Korea, Republic of	1.75	0.75	2.7	3
Mexico	1.98	1.56	2.1	1.6
India	1.4	2.4	2.1	3
Russian Federation			2	
Brazil	2.3	0.52	2	
Australia	2.7	1.05	1.7	
Singapore	1.15	0.75	1.6	
Chinese Taipei	0.97	0.52	1.3	1.5
Hong Kong, China	0.89	0.83	1.3	1.5
Turkey	1.58	0.88	1.1	

Source: Helble (2012), WHO WIPO and WTO 2020

into the world economy and thus participate very actively in supply chains (Helble 2012; Joint Report of WHO, WIPO and WTO 2020). Second, developed countries spend a substantially higher share of their public and private expenditures on health products compared to developing countries. Third, the production of most health products requires technological sophistication, which is still predominantly the preserve of developed countries (Helble 2012), with the recent exception of China. Fourth, major trading countries undertake most of the research and development efforts in the health sector (Helble 2012).

Developing countries are emerging as important international players in several categories of medical products. China now represents more than one-quarter of all exports in some categories, such as pharmaceutical inputs (category A3), chemical inputs (category B), and medical technology equipment (category C2) (WHO, WIPO and WTO 2020 and Table 3.3). It ranks as one of the leading exporters (after Germany and USA) of laboratory, hygienic, or pharmaceutical glassware for hospital use. Israel, the Republic of Korea, and Singapore have grown to become significant exporters of bulk medicines (category A2). India is emerging as a major exporter of pharmaceutical inputs (category A3). Malaysia, Thailand along with China are at present the world's top exporters of articles of apparel and clothing accessories (including gloves, mittens, mitts) as hospital consumables. Malaysia, Chinese Taipei, and Thailand are also appearing as important exporters of chemical inputs (Category B), some of which are used to manufacture health-related products (Joint Report of WHO, WIPO and WTO 2020, p 266). Similarly, Costa Rica, Mexico, Singapore, Chinese Taipei, and Thailand are important exporters of orthopedic equipment (WHO, WIPO and WTO 2020). Of the 197 countries and territories reviewed by the Joint Report (WHO, WIPO and WTO 2020), the vast majority of countries and territories are net importers of health products and, in particular, of pharmaceutical products (categories A1, A2, and A3).

Trade interdependence: Significance of intra-industry (two-way) trade

Evidence shows considerable overlap in top suppliers' imports and exports of medical products, as measured by indicators of intra-industry trade (IIT) (OECD 2020, UNCTAD 2021a, b). In other words, countries tend to be both importers and exporters of medical goods, which highlights a high degree of interdependence among countries in the supply of medical devices and medicines.

Intra-industry trade: Concept and measurement

Intra-industry trade (IIT) arises if a country simultaneously imports and exports similar types of goods or services. Intra-industry trade can be divided into two parts: horizontal intra-industry trade (HIIT) and vertical intra-industry trade (VIIT) (Wakasugi 2007; OECD 2002). HIIT means the technological levels of imports and exports are similar. In other words, trade in final goods belonging to the same industry category but with different brands and quality (Wakasugi 2007). It enables countries with similar factor endowments to benefit from economies of scale by specialization.

Table 3.3 Trade in health-related product (by broad categories): Country's share in global exports/imports, 2022

Countries	*A1 Formulations (e.g., Immunological Products, Vaccines, Medicaments for Retail Sales)* %	*A2 Bulk Medicines (e.g., Pharmaceutical Goods, Medicaments Not in Measured Dozes)* %	*A3 Pharmaceutical Inputs (e.g., Antibiotics, Hormones, and Vitamins)* %	*C1 Hospital Inputs (e.g., Masks, Gloves Diagnostic or Laboratory Reagents, Test Kits, Bandages, Syringes, Laboratory Glassware, etc.)* %	*C2 Medical Equipment (e.g., Devices Used in Diagnostics, Treatment Covering Furniture, X-rays, Ventilators, Machinery, etc.)* %
Australia	0.3/1.5	0.35/1.04	1.11/0.50	0.37/1.73	0.62/1.69
Belgium	12.8/9.42	6.7/4.5	5.18/10.44	12.12/9.09	3.36/3.18
Brazil	0.14/1.14	0.44/1.18	0.153/2.09	0.15/1.37	0.18/0.81
Canada	1.32/2.20	0.93/4.41	0.13/1.77	0.53/2.43	1.03/2.89
China	1.0/4.56	6.32/4.73	14.73/4.8	5.13/5.66	9.87/7.10
Denmark	2.46/0.64	1.22/0.96	5.05/0.54	1.13/0.55	0.85/0.62
France	4.54/3.56	2.51/3.56	1.95/5.38	2.90/3.86	2.72/3.99
Germany	15.03/8.98	12.42/5.74	3.63/6.96	12.30/10.00	11.1/6.95
India	2.4/0.27	2.0/0.91	4.1/4.52	0.59/0.78	0.87/1.43
Ireland	9.0/1.16	13.04/5.77	17.85/0.66	10.10/0.98	4.85/1.0
Italy	5.9/4.01	3.11/2.45	3.5/9.16	2.70/3.38	2.76/2.32
Japan	0.85/4.58	1.21/3.25	0.77/1.67	1.62/5.13	3.03/4.05
Korea, Republic of	0.78/1.22	0.76/1.29	0.64/1.22	1.89/1.44	1.97/1.73
Mexico	0.2/0.62	0.31/0.94	0.02/1.09	1.86/1.16	4.55/2.3
The Netherlands	2.94/2.33	5.89/7.46	3.46/1.78	5.00/4.06	9.83/7.39
Poland	0.52/0.95	0.88/1.01	0.17/0.58	0.54/0.65	1.5/0.99
Singapore	1.05/0.49	2.16/1.09	1.59/0.72	1.43/1.00	2.64/1.48
Spain	3.37/2.64	4.13/2.98	1.57/1.88	2.95/2.25	0.78/1.89
Switzerland	12.26/5.8	3.62/2.56	9.0/1.72	9.0/3.22	4.1/1.75
UK	3.39/3.69	1.7/5.86	3.79/1.32	2.05/3.38	2.48/3.56
USA	9.87/18.96	11.73/17.28	9.28/20.34	15.38/19.23	17.24/21.47

Source: Compiled from ITC Trade Map, Trade Statistics for International Business for 2022

Vertical intra-industry trade (VIIT) means that trade in goods belonging to the same industrial category, but with different factor intensities (labor-capital ratio and technological sophistication level) (Wakasugi 2007). Theoretically, VIIT takes place between developed countries and developing countries (Hellvin 1996). International fragmentation creates opportunities for vertical intra-industry trade of components and unfinished products along the global value chains (Andreff 2009).

The most often used method for determining the extent of intra-industry trade is due to Grubel and Lloyd (1975). Bilateral intra-industry trade between two countries is expressed as follows:

$$IIT_{jk} = 1 - \left(\frac{|X_{jk} - M_{jk}|}{X_{jk} + M_{jk}}\right) \qquad \text{......... } 3.1$$

where X_{jk} *and* M_{jk} are country j's exports and imports, respectively, of medical devices or pharmaceuticals in trade with the kth country. Higher index values are associated with greater IIT as a proportion of total trade. If IIT is close to 1, it means the level of intra-industry trade is high. Conversely, if the index is close to zero, the country in consideration either exports or imports good *j*—not both.

Intra-industry trade in pharmaceuticals and medical devices are computed here using COMMTRADE data from the UN website. The following subsections present evidence on two-way trade among selected leading countries.

IIT in pharmaceuticals

Data in Table 3.4 highlights a strong bilateral interdependence in trade among leading producers in pharmaceuticals. The green-shaded cells indicate significant trade overlap in pharmaceutical and medicine among trading partners. Trade flows are computed using SITC (Rev 3) division 541(Medicinal and pharmaceutical products, excluding 542). As seen below, the intra-industry trade in medicinal and pharmaceutical products (SITC 541) between Switzerland and partner countries is, however, below 0.5, excepting few European partners. This is because Switzerland's overall exports in SITC 541 are found to be more than seven times of exports to UK, USA, and China than its imports from these trade partner countries.

IIT in medical devices

Medical devices range from relatively homogeneous, commodity-type items (such as syringes, intravenous and blood administration apparatus, and other general hospital supplies) to more advanced and technology-intensive items (such as cardiac pacemakers, defibrillators, and stents; electromedical

Table 3.4 Intra-industry trade in pharmaceutical products SITC 541(Rev 3) 2022

	Intra-Industry Trade Pharmaceuticals SITC 541 2022										
	Belgium	*France*	*Germany*	*Italy*	*The Netherlands*	*Switzerland*	*UK*	*USA*	*China*	*Japan*	*India*
Belgium											
France	0.93										
Germany	0.35	0.90									
Italy	0.90	0.71	0.43								
The Netherlands	0.93	0.48	0.52	0.45							
Switzerland	0.80	0.27	0.70	0.28	0.98						
UK	0.17	0.60	0.34	0.76	0.81	0.23					
USA	0.30	0.49	0.84	0.85	0.48	0.24	0.46				
China	0.65	0.73	0.15	0.38	0.31	0.24	0.72	0.57			
Japan	0.02	0.22	0.21	0.82	0.69	0.47	0.54	0.36	0.83		
India	0.002	0.62	0.64	0.72	0.87	0.38	0.94	0.71	0.12	0.72	

Source: Computed from COMMODITY Trade Statistics, UN

therapeutic, monitoring, and imaging devices and apparatus; in vitro diagnostics). As such, medical devices offer tremendous trade opportunities of participation, both for horizontal IIT and vertical IIT. To analyze intra-industry trade in medical devices, the chapter has limited its focus on HS category 9018 (Medical and Surgical Instruments),[4] since this category is found to be the largest proportion (48%) of the medical devices traded in 2022.

Table 3.5 reveals a significant phenomenon of "trade overlap" indicating that large exporters are also among the large importers of health products. This trade interdependence is growing with the expansion of the demand for health products and the resulting opportunities to participate in the global network of supply chain through task specialization.

Intra-industry trade in COVID-19-related medical devices

The medical devices market has been significantly impacted by the COVID-19 pandemic which resulted in an increased demand for devices to diagnose and treat COVID-19. COVID-19 goods largely include the following medical devices and hospital consumables (OECD 2020):

- Test kits/instruments and apparatus in diagnostic testing
- Protective garments
- Oxygen therapy equipment (medical ventilators, etc.)
- Other Medical devices (ultrasound machines, infusion pumps, electrocardiograph, etc.)
- Medical consumables (medical oxygen, wadding, gauzes, syringes, soap, etc.)
- Vehicles and mobile equipment (wheelchair, mobile clinics vehicles, etc.)
- Medical and surgical furniture, oxygen cylinders, etc

The OECD report (2020) also indicates that the global exports of COVID-19-related goods are concentrated in a few, mostly OECD, countries. As per the report, the top 5 global exporters, which together account for 49% of trade, are Germany, the United States, Switzerland, the People's Republic of China, and Ireland. Similar patterns emerge for imports. Evidence also shows that the developing and low-income countries do not engage in trade in these products with each other, or either import or export COVID-19 goods but do not do both (OECD 2020).

Intra-industry trade in vaccine for COVID-19: A glimpse of international vaccine supply chain

Production and global trade in vaccines[5] played a very critical role in controlling the devastating health and economic consequences of the COVID-19 pandemic. Global trade in vaccines offers a valuable insight into the global value chain and trade interdependence. The goods needed to vaccinate,

Table 3.5 IIT in medical devices

	Intra-Industry Trade Medical Devices (9018 HS) 2022									
	Belgium	*France*	*Germany*	*Italy*	*The Netherlands*	*Switzerland*	*UK*	*USA*	*China*	*Japan*
Belgium										
France	0.78									
Germany	0.76	0.59								
Italy	0.40	0.90	0.53							
The Netherlands	0.56	0.43	0.86	0.26						
Switzerland	0.61	0.95	0.98	0.97	0.78					
UK	0.44	0.41	0.97	0.99	0.28	0.53				
USA	0.10	0.71	0.75	0.98	0.35	0.47	0.56			
China	0.81	0.79	0.58	0.75	0.69	0.17	0.64	0.77		
Japan	0.24	0.97	0.83	0.38	0.75	0.13	0.88	0.79	0.76	

protect, and test during the COVID-19 pandemic are produced across many different countries (OECD 2022). The global trade data shows that the vaccine producers sourced 88.3% of key ingredients from other vaccine producers during 2017–2019 period (Evenett et al. 2021). The share of imports of key ingredients from other vaccine producers as a group ranged from a low of 76.4% (India) to 98.7% (United Kingdom) (Evenett et al. 2021). Besides the active ingredients needed to produce vaccines, distribution and administration requires access to goods produced across a range of countries: vials to move the vaccines, syringes to administer, cold boxes to transport, dry ice to maintain cold temperatures, and freezers to store (OECD 2021).

Table 3.6 presents the contribution of a selected few countries in meeting the global needs of vaccines. The vaccine supply chain contains a range of common ingredients that originate from specialized locations—e.g., (i) preservatives to prevent contamination of the vaccine; (ii) stabilizers used to prevent further chemical reactions from occurring, and keeping the vaccine potency stable as it is being transported; (iii) surfactants are required to ensure that ingredients remain blended, avoiding the clumping of elements that are in liquid form; (iv) adjuvants are sometimes used to enhance the immune response; (v) other substances, including antibiotics to prevent contamination; and (vi) diluents to temper the concentration of vaccines before use (OECD 2021).

COVID-19 will not be the last disease with the potential to grow into a pandemic. Innovation in vaccinology and immunology are critical to the future preparedness against more pandemics.

Table 3.6 Selected global suppliers of ingredients for vaccine production and distribution

Core Ingredients	*Exporters (Percentage Share in Global Exports)*
Adjutants (e.g., aluminum salts)	Mexico (11.4), China (11.1), Turkey (9.1)
Preservatives (e.g., thimerosal)	Germany (17.2), Argentina (13), India (12)
Stabilizers (e.g., sorbitol)	France (23.1), China 13.3) Germany (12.5)
Antibiotics (e.g., neomycin)	China (23.1), Switzerland (17), Italy (9)
Needles	USA (21.4), Ireland (13.5), Mexico (11.3)
Syringes	USA (14.5), China (11.2), Germany (9.6)
Vials	China (17), Germany (13), Italy (8.7)
Stoppers	Germany (17), China (11.1), Poland (6.7)
Freezers	China (67), Italy (3.5), Romania (3.5)
Vaccine carriers	USA (17.7), Germany (14.2), Mexico (11.9)
Cold boxes	China (14.7), Germany (12.6), France (6.9)
Dry ice	The Netherlands (15.4), Israel (12), USA (8.8)

Source: OECD (2021b)

Analyzing trade competitiveness in health products

In today's global trading environment, the competitive performance of a country is reflected in its ability to enhance the domestic value-added contents of its exports and capture a larger slice of the global value chain from global participation. Trade data shows that supply chains are a system of value-added sources and destinations, and as such offer profitable opportunities for countries that upgrade their specialization (Koopman, Wang and Wei 2014).

Domestic value-added as a metric of export performance

Domestic value-added in exports has become a key measure of a country's global competitiveness with the emergence of global value chains (Vrh 2018). The domestic value-added (DVA) in exports indicates the gains realized by a country from participation in the global supply chain (Koopman, Wang and Wei 2014). Value-added exports measure the amount of domestic value added embodied in the final expenditure in each destination (Johnson 2014).

The growing use of imports by exporters in their exports results in intermediate inputs crossing borders many times (Beltramello, De Backer and Moussiegt 2012; Johnson 2014; Kee and Tang 2016). As official trade statistics are measured in gross terms, they include both "intermediate" and "final" products. The official records of trade suffer from substantial double counting, since the value of intermediate inputs recorded each time they cross international borders along the value chain (Johnson 2014; Koopman, Wang and Wei 2014). Exporters in the contemporary business world focus on maximizing the net value-added gains by specializing in tasks (Amador and Cabral 2016; Banga 2014).

Decomposing *gross exports* into different *value-added* terms allows to remove the *double counting* of intermediate inputs (Miroudot and Ming 2017). Algebraically, gross exports in value-added terms are expressed as:

$$\begin{aligned} Gross\ Exports = {} & Domestic\ Valued - Added\left(DVA\right) \\ & + Foreign\ Value - Added\left(FVA\right) \end{aligned} \tag{3.2}$$

Domestic value-added (DVA) in exports comprise of the following four channels of trade (see Figure 3.2):

(a) Domestic value-added exported as a final good
(b) Domestic value-added embodied in intermediates (goods and services) that is directly consumed by the importing economy
(c) Domestic value-added contained in intermediates (goods or services) exported to a partner economy that re-exports them to a third economy
(d) Domestic value-added in intermediate exports used by the direct importer to produce goods shipped back to the home/source country (Koopman et al. 2011)[6]

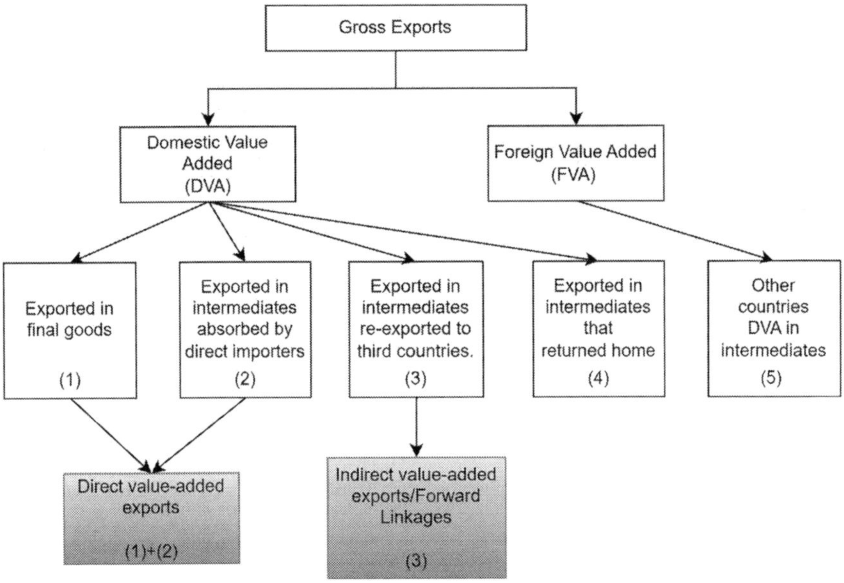

Figure 3.2 Decomposition of gross exports and linkages from participation

Source: Koopman et al, 2011

Foreign value-added (FVA) corresponds to the value-added of inputs that were imported in order to produce intermediate or final goods/services to be exported. FVA is termed as "Backward GVC participation". It is also referred to as "vertical specialization" when expressed as a percentage of gross exports (WTO 2014, WTO 2022).

If we express FVA and DVA in equation (3.2) as percent of gross exports, we get following two measures GVC participation:

$$GVC_{Participation} = \frac{DVA}{Gross\ Exports} + \frac{FVA}{Gross\ Exports} \tag{3.3}$$

$$= \text{Forward Participation} + \text{Backward Participation} \tag{3.4}$$

"Forward participation" measures exports of intermediate goods that are used as inputs for the production of exports of other countries. "Backward participation" measures imported intermediate inputs that used to generate output for export.

Domestic value-added and foreign value-added in gross exports of the pharmaceuticals sector

The availability of global input-output tables enables us to trace the value-added embodied in sectors and countries, and hence enables us to trace the value-added embodied in final goods back to its source. Using the OECD TiVA (trade in value-added) database, Table 3.7 presents the information on the above two components of GVC for the pharmaceutical sector for 2000 and 2018.

It is observed from Table 3.7 that most countries are experiencing a growing reliance on foreign value-added contents in their gross exports over time (col 2). Similar results have been reported by Hummels, Ishii and Yi 2001 in their analysis of total world exports during 1970–1995. Using input-output tables from the OECD and emerging market countries, Hummels, Ishii and Yi (2001) found that vertical specialization accounted for up to 30% of world

Table 3.7 Domestic value-added and foreign value-added in gross exports: Pharmaceuticals, medicinal chemicals, and botanical products (2000–2018)

Region and Countries	*Domestic Value-Added*	*Foreign Value-Added*
USA 2000	94.9	5.1
USA 2018	89.2	10.8
Switzerland 2000	69.0	31.0
Switzerland 2018	74.2	25.8
UK 2000	90.6	9.4
UK 2018	81.5	18.5
Germany 2000	87.5	12.6
Germany 2018	80.3	19.7
Japan 2000	95	5.0
Japan 2018	86.2	13.8
China 2000	91.2	8.8
China 2018	88.6	11.4
France 2000	85.1	14.9
France 2018	79.6	20.4
The Netherlands 2000	78.8	21.2
The Netherlands 2018	72.1	27.9
Denmark 2000	83.6	16.4
Denmark 2018	86.3	13.7
Ireland 2000	73.4	26.7
Ireland 2018	55.3	44.7
Canada 2000	70.9	29.1
Canada 2018	74.4	25.6
India 2000		13.7
India 2018	85.0	15.0
Australia 2000	85.8	2.5
Australia 2018	95.6	4.4
Korea (Rep) 2000	81.4	18.6
Korea (Rep) 2018	78.5	21.5
Brazil 2000	88.4	11.6
Brazil 2018	89.6	10.5
Israel 2000	86	14.0
Israel 2018	80.8	19.2

Sources: OECD Stat Trade in Value Added (TiVA) 2021 ed: Principal indicators

exports in the 1960s, which had subsequently grown as much as 40% in the last 25 years (1970 and 1995).

The foreign content of countries' exports, either as a final product or as a good-in-process, is a measure of vertical specialization (Hummels, Ishii and Yi 2001). Formally, vertical specialization for country *k* and sector *i* is defined as the following ratio:

$$VS_{ki} = \left(\frac{Imported\,intermediates}{Gross\,output}\right) \text{x exports} \tag{3.5}$$

$$= \left(\frac{exports}{Gross\,output}\right) \text{x imported intermediates} \tag{3.6}$$

In simple terms, VS_{ki} is the imported input content of exports, or equivalently, foreign value-added embodied in exports of country k in sector i. This measure takes value zero, if the country uses no imported input content of a country's exports in a given sector (Hummels, Ishii and Yi 2001). Evidence shows that greater *backward* GVC participation is significantly associated with higher growth of domestic value-added eventually, since "sourcing inputs from abroad is associated with technology transfer and technology know-how" (van der Marel 2015, p 4).

The GVC participation index, however, alone does not shed light on the relative sharing of gains by participating countries. Higher participation in GVCs may not ensure higher gains (Banga 2014). Value is distributed unevenly across supply chains (Gereffi 2020). Capturing an increasingly bigger slice of the GVC pie depends upon a country's position on upstream production activities (Cheng et al. 2015).

Upstream and downstream positioning

To get insight into the sharing of gains from GVC, Koopman et al. (2014) also suggest considering a position index that helps us to gauge whether a country is likely to be in the upstream or downstream of the global value chain (GVC) in any particular sector. Evidence shows that "upstream" specialization enables countries to reap a larger share of GVC pie than the "downstream specialization." Koopman et al. (2011) have suggested the following index to represent whether a country is likely to be in the upstream or downstream of the global value chain (GVC) in any particular sector:

$$GVCPosition_{ir} = Ln\left(1 + \frac{DVA}{Gross\ Exports}\right) - Ln\left(1 + \frac{FVA}{Gross\ Exports}\right) \tag{3.7}$$

In the above equation, the subscripts i and r denote a country and sector respectively.

Countries with a larger position index (high forward linkages) are relatively more upstream in GVC, i.e., they contribute more value-added to other countries' exports than other countries contribute to theirs (Koopman, Powers and Zhang 2011, Ignatenko et al. 2019).

The position of firms/countries in GVCs can graphically be mapped as a "Smile curve" with a Y-axis representing value-added ratio and X-axis representing production stages. "Smile curve" of value creation postulates a hypothetical relation between the production stages and value-added along the GVC. The shape of this curve suggests that most value-added in a GVC accrues to firms at the two ends of the production line, such as R&D in the upstream and marketing in the downstream, with a smaller share of value-added captured by assembling in the midstream (Cheng et al. 2015). Figure 3.3 depicts the hypothesized relationship in case of a medical goods sector where the production stages range from the initial phase of R&D and product design and product development to the delivery of the final product to hospitals, retailers, and medical practitioners.

Both the analysis of GVC participation and position indices indicate the significance of a country's ability to enhance domestic value-added contents in exports (forward linkages) for reaping a larger share of the GVC pie in an industry (Banga 2014). Analyzing export competitiveness in terms of value-added contributions in a highly technology and knowledge-intensive industry informs us about the leading role played by firms/countries that specialize in upstream activities. These countries provide critical inputs for

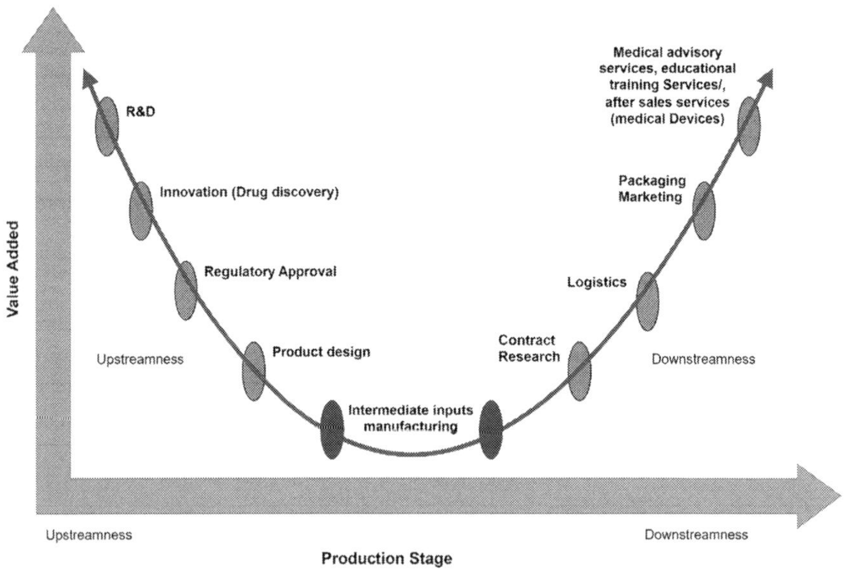

Figure 3.3 A hypothesized "smiley-shaped" relationship between value-added and GVC position

others and transfer technology and product know-how to the importing countries.

A comparative analysis export competitiveness: Domestic value-added in exports

One widely used, export measure of competitiveness is the Revealed Comparative Advantage (RCA) measure, which is due to Balassa (1965). Researchers have used Balassa's RCA index based on gross export data. Now with the availability of data on domestic value-added in exports, the value-added decomposition of exports provides a way to remove the distortion of multiple counting by focusing on domestic value-added in exports (Koopman et al. 2011).

The Balassa index of export competitiveness identifies whether a country has a "revealed" comparative advantage rather than determining the underlying sources of comparative advantage. Balassa's measure of relative export performance by country *i* and industry *j* is calculated as follows:

$$RCA_{ij} = \frac{\left(\dfrac{X_{ij}}{X_{wj}}\right)}{\left(\dfrac{X_i}{X_w}\right)} \tag{3.8}$$

where X_{ij} refers to a country *i*'s exports of product *j* (pharmaceuticals), X_{wj} stands for the world exports of pharmaceuticals, X_i represents the total exports of country *i* to the world, and X_w equals total world exports. In our computations, we use data on domestic value-added in exports, rather than gross exports data. Total exports refer to exports from the manufacturing sector. The results are presented in Table 3.8 for two time periods. When the RCA exceeds 1, a country is said to have a revealed comparative advantage in the pharmaceutical sector; when the RCA is below 1, the country is said to have a revealed comparative disadvantage in that sector (Koopman et al. 2011). Overtime comparison reveals that a few countries that have improved their relative competitiveness include Australia, Belgium, Denmark, Germany, Norway, USA, and India. Among these, USA is a forerunner in medical innovations.

Empirical evidence from research studies demonstrates that a firm's ability to generate higher domestically added in exports is facilitated by a combination of several factors, including investments in intangible capital, in particular, investments in research and development (Vrh 2018), and active substitution of more competitive domestically produced intermediate inputs for imported materials (Koopman, Wang and Wei 2014).

Table 3.8 Exports in value-added terms 2010–2020: Pharmaceuticals, medicinal chemicals, and botanical products

Countries	*RCA (Domestic Value-Added in Exports) 2010*	*RCA (Domestic Value-Added in Exports) 2020*
Australia	1.3	1.59
Belgium	3.85	7.27
Canada	0.7	0.83
Denmark	7.7	9.65
France	2.26	1.88
Germany	1.39	1.66
Ireland	14.38	8.21
Israel	5.44	3.58
Italy	1.58	1.24
Japan	0.41	0.9
Korea Rep	0.12	0.22
The Netherlands	1.66	0.76
Norway	1.08	1.19
Spain	1.97	1.64
Sweden	3.92	3.13
Switzerland	10.88	10.47
UK	4.07	2.42
USA	1.84	2.31
Brazil	0.30	0.27
China Rep	0.36	0.34
India	1.81	2.07
Singapore	2.4	1.76
South Africa	0.23	0.78

Data Source: OECD Stat TiVA 2022

Maintaining a competitive position in the R&D-intensive medical goods industry requires firms to continually enhance domestic capabilities through catching up with advances in scientific knowledge and investing in supporting technologies for furthering innovative strength. Strengthening of competitive advantage would require companies to tap external resources through active participation in open innovation networks. National innovation system (discussed later) plays a critical role in supporting innovation capabilities and technological upgrading of firms. Product innovations in the pharmaceutical sector involve, directly or indirectly, a large variety of actors, including: firms, other research organizations, such as universities and other research centers; financial institutions; regulatory authorities; and medical community (McKelvey, Orsenigo and Pammolli 2004).

Promoting the participation of developing countries

Many developing countries are overly reliant on international supply chains for essential medical products. Several innovative approaches, based on partnerships, intellectual property, and technology transfer, can be used to stimulate innovation, promote healthcare delivery, and reduce global health disparities (Stevens and Huys 2017).

Public health is inherently a global challenge and thus assumes high priority for international cooperation (WHO, WIPO and WTO 2020). Supranational organizations have a vital role to play in promoting innovation, access to medicines, and health technologies. There is a strong rationale for the cooperation and coordination between the WHO and other international organizations such as the World Intellectual Property Organization (WIPO) and the World Trade Organization (WTO) on matters of health issues and other policy domains—human rights, development policy, intellectual property (IP), and international trade (WHO, WIPO and WTO 2020).

Summary

This chapter has analyzed trade flows by major product categories and discussed the emerging pattern of trade in medical goods. Product categories considered here fall under three classes: medicines (formulations and bulk medicines), hospital and laboratory inputs, and medical instruments (used for diagnostics and treatment). As most modern medicines (including vaccines) comprise ingredients sourced from multiple countries, an entirely self-sufficient pharmaceutical model would be difficult for any one country to sustain. World trade and production are increasingly organized around global value chains (GVCs). Using the available international data from the UN and OECD databases, the chapter has arrived at following broad conclusions about the trade in health products and export competitiveness.

- Trade data supports a high degree of interdependence (two-way trade) of countries on trade linkages.
- Decomposing gross exports into different value-added terms allows to remove the double counting of intermediate inputs.
- Depending on a country's comparative advantage in a value chain, firms can participate as upstream suppliers of inputs to foreign firms through forward linkage, and/or as downstream producers using foreign inputs in their own production and exports through backward linkage.
- Analysis of revealed comparative advantage, based on value-added exports, reveals that developing and maintaining a competitive edge in the medical goods industry requires firms and countries to respond proactively to the new modes of global competition.

Notes

1 The following discussion on trade in health-related goods draws heavily on Helble (2012) and the joint report of WHO, WIPO, and WTO 2020).
2 Hereafter, the joint report of WHO, WIPO, and WTO (2020) will be referred to as Joint Report (2020).

3 Annual compound growth rate is computed as: $\left(\frac{V_n}{V_0}\right)^{\frac{1}{n}}-1$, where v_n is the trade value in 2022 and v_0 is the trade value in 2010.
4 These are the instruments and appliances used in medical, surgical, dental, or veterinary sciences, including scintigraphy apparatus, other electromedical apparatus, and sight testing instruments.
5 For trade purposes, vaccines (for human use) are classified under a single harmonized system (HS) code (300220) (OECD 2021).
6 This, (d), part of domestic value-added plus FVA equals the portion of trade that is "double counted' in official trade statistics (Koopman et al. 2011).

References

Amador, João, and Sonia Cabral. 2016. "Global Value Chains: A Survey of Drivers and Measures." *Journal of Economic Surveys* 30 (2): 278–301. https://doi.org/10.1111/joes.12097.

Andreff, W. 2009. "Outsourcing in the New Strategy of Multinational Companies: Foreign Investment, International Subcontracting and Production Relocation." *Papeles de Europa* 18: 5–34.

Balassa, B. 1965. "Trade Liberalization and "Revealed" Comparative Advantage." *Manchester School* 33: 99123.

Banga, R. 2014. "Linking into Global Value Chains Is Not Sufficient: Do You Export Domestic Value Added Contents?" *Journal of Economic Integration* 29 (2): 267–297. https://doi.org/10.11130/jei.2014.29.2.267.

Beltramello, A., K. De Backer, and L. Moussiegt. 2012. *The Export Performance of Countries Within Global Value Chains (GVCs) OECD Science, Technology and Industry, Working Paper 2012/2.* OECD.

Cheng, K. C., S. Rehman, D. Seneviratne, and S. Zhang. 2015. "Reaping the Benefits from Global Value Chains." *IMF Working Papers* 15 (204): 1–23. https://doi.org/10.5089/9781513516738.001.

Evenett, S. J., B. Hoekman, N. Rocha, and M. Ruta. 2021. "The Covid-19 Vaccine Production Club: Will Value Chains Temper Nationalism?" [Policy research working paper]. *SSRN Electronic Journal* 9565. https://doi.org/10.2139/ssrn.3800058.

Gereffi, G. 2020. "What Does the COVID-19 Pandemic Teach Us About Global Value Chains? The Case of Medical Supplies." *Journal of International Business Policy* 3 (3): 287–301. https://doi.org/10.1057/s42214-020-00062-w.

Grubel, H. G., and P. J. Lloyd. 1975. *Intra-industry Trade.* Macmillan.

Helble, M. C. 2012. "More Trade for Better Health? – International Trade and Tariffs on Health Products." WTO Staff Working Paper. *SSRN Electronic Journal.* World Trade Organization: ERSD-2012–ERSD-17. https://doi.org/10.2139/ssrn.2165734.

Helble, Matthias and Shepherd, Ben, Trade in Health Products: Reducing Trade Barriers for Better Health. January 23, 2017. ADBI Working Paper No. 643.

Hellvin, L. 1996. *Vertical Intra-industry Trade Between China and OECD Countries, OCDE/GD* (96). 54, Working Paper No. 114 OECD Publishing, Paris.

Hummels, David, Dana Rapoport, and Kei-Mu Yi. 2001. "Vertical Specialization and the Changing Nature of World Trade." *FRBNY Economic Policy Review* 4 (2): 79–99.

Ignatenko, A., F. Raei, and B. Mircheva. 2019. "Global Value Chains: What Are the Benefits and Why Do Countries Participate?" IMF Working: paper WP/19/18.

Johansson, A. "Olaberria." 2014. *Global Trade and Specialisation Patterns over the Next 50 Years.* OECD Economic Policy Paper no. 10. OECD Publishing Paris.

Kee, H. L., and H. Tang. 2016. "Domestic Value Added in Exports: Theory and Firm Evidence from China." *American Economic Review* 106 (6): 1402–1436. https://doi.org/10.1257/aer.20131687.

Koopman, R., W. Powers, Z. Wang, and S.-J. Wei. 2011. "Give Credit Where Credit Is Due: Tracing Value Added in Global Production Chains". NBER Working Paper No. 16426. *SSRN Electronic Journal.* https://doi.org/10.2139/ssrn.1949669.

Koopman, R., Z. Wang, and S.-J. Wei. 2014. "Tracing Value-Added and Double Counting in Gross Exports." *American Economic Review* 104 (2): 459–494. https://doi.org/10.1257/aer.104.2.459.

McKelvey, M., L. Orsenigo, and F. Pammolli. 2004. Ch. 3. "Pharmaceuticals Analyzed Through the Lens of a Sectoral Innovation System." In *Sectoral Systems of Innovation: Concepts, Issues and Analyses of Six Major Sectors in Europe*, edited by F. Malerba: 73–120. Cambridge University Press.

Miroudot, S., and Ye Ming. 2017. *Decomposition of Value-Added in Gross Exports: Unresolved Issues and Possible Solutions*, MPRA Paper 83273. University Library of Munich.

OECD. 2020. *Trade Inter Dependence in COVID-19 Goods, Tackling Coronavirus(COVID-19), Contributing to Global Effort* May 5. OECD.

OECD. 2021. *Using Trade to Fight COVID-19: Manufacturing and Distributing Vaccines* February 11. OECD.

OECD. 2022. *Global Supply Chains at Work: A Tale of Three Products to Fight COVID-19 OECD Policy Responses to Coronavirus (COVID-19).* OECD, Paris.

Stevens, H., and I. Huys. 2017. "Innovative Approaches to Increase Access to Medicines in Developing Countries." *Frontiers in Medicine* 4. https://doi.org/10.3389/fmed.2017.00218.

Szalavetz, A. 2019 "Digitalisation, Automation and Upgrading in Global Value Chains – Factory Economy Actors versus Lead Companies." *Post-Communist Economies* 31 (5): 646–70. doi.10.1080/14631377.2019.1578584.

UNCTAD. 2021a. Improving access to medical products through trade: What can regional trade agreements do in times of crisis?

UNCTAD. 2021b. Technology and Innovation Report 2021: Catching technological waves - Innovation with equity. United nations.

Van der Marel, E. 2015. "Positioning on the global value chain map: Where do you want to be?" ECIPE Occasional Paper, 01/2015, European Centre for International Political Economy (ECIPE), Brussels.

Vrh, N. 2018. "What Drives the Differences in Domestic Value Added in Exports Between Old & New E.U. Member States?" *Economic Research-Ekonomska Istraživanja, Taylor & Francis Journals*, 31 (1): 645–663.

Wakasugi, R. 2007. *Vertical Intra-industry Trade and Economic Integration in East Asia, Asian Economic Papers, 2007 The Earth Institute at Columbia University and the Massachusetts Institute of Technology.* MIT Press, 6 (1): 26–39.

WHO, WIPO, and WTO 2020. *Promoting Access to Medical Technologies and Innovation Intersections Between Public Health, Intellectual Property and Trade.* 2nd ed. World Health Organization, Geneva.

WTO 2014 "World Trade Report 2014. Trade and development: Recent trends and the role of the WTO" WTO Secretariat, https://www.wto.org/english/res_e/booksp_e/world_trade_report14_e.pdf

WTO 2022 "Trade in value-added and global value chains: Statistical profiles, Global Value Chains, 2022 Edition, Country Data." WTO Secretariat.

4 The innovation challenge and cross-country comparison of innovation capabilities

Introduction: Innovation challenge

Innovation has always been the backbone and underlying strength of the pharmaceutical industry. According to the OECD classification of industries by R&D intensity (measured as the ratio of global R&D to global value-added output), the pharmaceutical industry, with its R&D intensity of 27.98 in 2011 (reference year), ranked third just after (i) air and spacecraft and (ii) computer, electronic, and optical products (OECD 2016).

During the past decades, the industry has delivered multiple life-saving medicines, several blockbuster drugs, and record-setting approval of new molecular entities (NMEs) and new biopharmaceutical entities (NBEs) by the US FDA (Khanna 2012). Medical innovations have not only eliminated certain diseases and improved human survival rates and the quality of life for many patients, but have also demonstrated their ability to fight the global scale pandemics (Roy 2011). Pharmaceutical innovation, with its novelty and effectiveness, meets otherwise unmet or inadequately met healthcare needs. The competitive growth of the global pharmaceutical industry can play a vital supporting role in developing and delivering cost-effective innovative therapies to society.

The global medical industry is currently facing a tough challenge of grappling with the innovation deficit/gap that is steadily widening since the past few decades. Innovation deficit is reflected in two ways: increasing gap between the growth of scientific knowledge and the development of new molecular entities (NMEs) that effectively address the changing global health needs; and sustaining sufficient innovation to replace the loss of revenue due to patent expiration for 'blockbuster' drugs of the past decades.

With the advances in the scientific knowledge base, the rift between basic research (bench) and clinical research and patients (bed) is widening and getting deeper (Seyhan 2019). The basic biomedical knowledge is increasing exponentially, but the gap between it and bedside application appears to be expanding (FDA 2004). This critical issue of translation innovation gap remains to be

DOI: 10.4324/9781003449331-4

addressed (van Gool et al. 2017). The complex process that spans the generation of ideas, their translation into products, and the commercialization of products rests on the innovation ecosystem of a country (WEF 2020). There are multiple factors that determine the successful progression of scientific ideas into new therapeutics. This chapter deals with this innovation challenge and evaluates the relative performance of countries in developing their innovation system.

Element of an innovation system

In the innovation literature, a country's innovation system is described in two ways. One way of describing the innovation system is to think of it as a set of inputs and outputs as shown in Figure 4.1 (Galli and Teubal 1997). The Global Innovation Index (GII), constructed by the World Intellectual Property Organization and INSEAD, is based on five input subindices and two output subindices. The inputs include human capital and research, institutions (political, business, and regulatory environment), infrastructure, market sophistication (trade openness, competition, credit), and business sophistication. Innovation output includes knowledge and technology outputs, and creative output (see Figure 4.1).

The other route of analyzing the process of innovation is to think about the elements of the innovation system, as depicted in Table 4.1 (Edquist 2005). The innovation system of a country comprises its organizations and supporting institutions. A country's organizations include actors like firms, universities, financial institutions, and government agencies. Firms participating in the innovation interact with many other organizations (e.g. research institutes, customers, authorities, financial organizations) and institutions (e.g. IPR, regulations, culture) (Mowery and Oxley 1995; Gambradella et al. 2003; Klein Woolthuis et al. 2005; Edquist 2006). Firms' interactions, reciprocity, and feedback mechanisms determine the success of innovation (Galli and Teubal 1997; Klei Woolthuis et al. 2005).

The government and public research organizations play vital roles in basic research, making infrastructure available, nurturing academia-industry

Figure 4.1 The innovation function: innovation inputs, innovation output, and outcomes.

Source: Adapted from Cirera and Maloney (2017)

Table 4.1 System of innovations: Determinants of the innovation process

Organizations are actors that include political bodies, such as ministries or national councils for science and technology (S&T); bureaucratic bodies, such as public agencies and offices implementing innovation policy; regulatory bodies, such as those involved in setting standards and norms and in certification; social bodies, like academies and professional associations; educational bodies, like universities and schools; knowledge-oriented bodies without economic goals, such as government laboratories researching in the field of defense or health; non-profit organizations with economic goals, such as technical centers and experimental stations of industrial associations; profit-oriented firms, including R&D companies, joint ventures, and consortia; and bodies—such as innovation centers associated with chambers of commerce or industrial associations, or the industrial liaison units of universities—connecting S&T with the needs of business firms.
Institutions can be formal or informal components of an innovation system. Formal institutions refer to provisions such as patent laws, formal criteria for allocating resources to science, peer-review procedures, technical standards and norms, and rules of the game. Informal institutions refer to common habits, norms of behavior, conventions, routines, established practices, codes of conduct, etc.

Source: Edquist and Johnson (1997)

collaboration across cross-cutting disciplines, and mobilizing development funding for new risky ventures as well as in directing the R&D resources (through procurement policy) to meet the desired societal goals. Institutions play the role of shaping the interactions between organizations (Edquist 2005; WHO, WIPO, and WTO 2020). Institutions consist of formal (written rules, technical standards, procedures, and regulations) and informal (norms, values, culture, ideology, and practices) rules and the mechanisms forcing individuals to comply with these rules. Institutions such as tax rules, government subsidies, and allocation of resources to universities channel resources to innovation activities (Johnson 2001). Klein Woolthuis et al. (2005) distinguish between hard and soft institutions. Hard institutions concern formal, written laws and regulations: technical standards, labor law, risk management rules, health and safety regulations, and the general legal system relating to contracts, employment, and IPR within which actors (not only firms but also knowledge institutes and the government) operate. Soft, or informal, institutions concern such things as social norms and values; culture; willingness to share resources with other actors; the entrepreneurial spirit within organizations, industries, regions, or countries; and tendencies to trust or risk averseness. Soft institutions form the implicit rules of the game that can stimulate or hinder innovation.

The role of the organizations and institutions in stimulating innovation activities is outlined below.

(i) Universities supply trained manpower and for conducting cutting-edge research (Mowery and Sampat 2005; Mansfield 1998)
(ii) Firms generate commercial innovations through experimentation, R&D, and product improvement (Patel and Pavitt 1994; Mowery and Oxley 1995)
(iii) Public research labs and universities generate new knowledge in fundamental sciences (Narin et al. 1997)
(iv) Governments and public agencies support innovation through regulation, standard setting, public-private partnerships, and funding of basic research (Patel and Pavitt 1994; Mowery and Oxley 1995)
(v) Legal framework of patent rights reward innovations and facilitate diffusion of new technologies
(vi) Availability of seed capital (Angel investment for early-stage technology development) and venture capital (later stage than angel investment) finance to facilitate product development and commercialization.

Translational research challenge—bridging gap between basic science and launching of new molecular entities

The path from conceiving a new idea to translation into new products with improved health outcomes compared to the existing products is termed the critical path. The path can be divided into discovery and development segments. Figure 4.2 presents the path of biomedical research from the idea (basic research/drug discovery phase) to the market approval phase which can briefly be summarized into the following five sequential development stages.

First, in the basic and applied research phase, the research for a new drug begins in the laboratory, and the knowledge is translated from basic science into the new treatment. Researchers first identify targets that might be a new drug. These targets are proteins and the genes that define how those proteins are structured. Once researchers have identified a target, they determine whether the target is relevant to the disease that they are studying. Once a single compound is selected, preclinical studies are performed.

Second, in the preclinical research phase, drugs undergo laboratory and animal testing to answer basic questions about safety, efficacy, and potential toxicity in animal models.

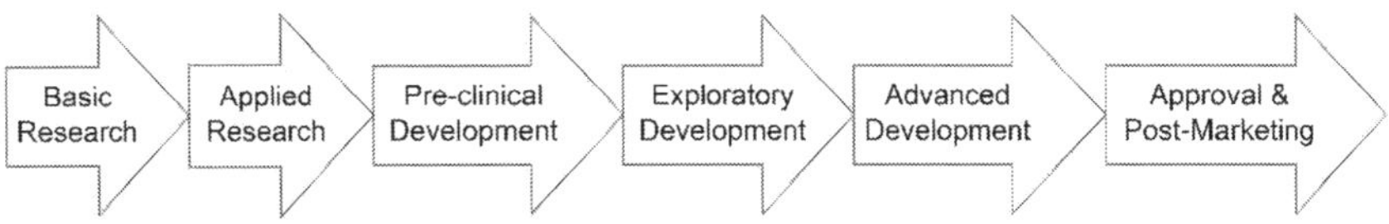

Figure 4.2 Classification of R&D stages in pharmaceutical products.

Source: Adapted from Institute of Medicine, US (2009)

Third, in the clinical research phase, drugs are tested on people to make sure they are safe and effective. This phase is also called the "Exploratory Development" phase, which is also labeled as "Proof of Concept" stage. The proof of concept (POC) demonstrates that the drug does what it is intended to do—that is, it interacts correctly with its molecular target and, in turn, counters the disease. POC is a key milestone in the development of a new drug. This phase includes developing a full conceptual model of the proposed new drug mechanism: specific biological targets, bioavailability, toxicity, and the like (Tassey 2014). At this stage, the translational gap poses a significant risk of failure. This is the most critical challenge in medical research. The translational research is very risky in outcome. The translational gap is also termed as the "Valley of Death" (Seyhan 2019).

Fourth, the advanced development phase requires "Regulatory Proof." FDA review teams thoroughly examine all of the submitted data related to the drug or device and make a decision to approve or not to approve it.

Fifth is the marketing stage. FDA continues to monitor all drug and device safety once products are available for use by the public.

On an average, it takes ten to fourteen years from basic research to the NDA (new drug application).

Innovation challenge in medical devices

Regulatory agencies also oversee the development of medical devices. For medical devices, the regulatory process is more complex than for pharmaceuticals since device manufacturers must seek premarket clearance, which generally does not require clinical data (Institute of Medicine (US) 2009). Devices are classified into three groups by the FDA: Class I, or devices with "low risk of illness or injury" (e.g., surgical gauze); Class II, or devices with "moderate risk" (e.g., suture); and Class III, devices which "support or sustain human life, are of substantial importance in preventing impairment of human health or present a potential, unreasonable risk of illness or injury" (e.g., pacemakers). For class III devices, the research team may include physicists, materials scientists, engineers, and mathematicians as well as biologists and physiologists. Such devices require clinical evidence to support the application for approval. Physicians often play a critical role in identifying consumer needs for medical devices in general and in the initial testing of prototypes in human clinical trials (Institute of Medicine (US) 2009). As with new drugs, the Food and Drug Administration's approval process is intended to provide consumers with assurance that, once it reaches the marketplace, a medical device is safe and effective. Bringing a device to market takes an average of three to seven years, compared with an average of twelve years for drugs (Van Norman 2016).

Cross-country comparisons of innovation capabilities and performance

Evidence indicates a great deal of variation in R&D activities—from idea generation to commercialization of innovative products—exists across countries. Depending upon the availability of the comparative data, the following discussion focuses on the broad input indicators for which the secondary data are published. It also discusses two types of innovation outputs: patents and new molecular entities.

Business expenditure on R&D (BERD) in the pharmaceutical industry

Most biomedical R&D, including pharmaceutical R&D, takes place in OECD countries (OECD 2018). More than half (61.7%) of global spending on pharmaceuticals occurred in the United States in 2019 (as seen in Table 4.2), rising from $56 billion in 2015 to $88.6 billion in 2019 (OECD Online Data Base). China, Japan, and Germany ranked next to the USA with their global share amounting to 10.08%, 8.94%, and 5.19%, respectively. The industry accounted for 33.4% and 25.9% of total BERD in Switzerland and Belgium, respectively, and for 20.58% and 17.62% of BERD in Denmark and the USA. Most BERD in the USA is found to be focused on biotechnology sciences

Table 4.2 BERD (business expenditure on R&D) in pharmaceutical 2019

	Percentage of BERD Performed in the Pharmaceutical Industry (%)	*Country's Share in Global BERD in Pharmaceuticals (%) (2019)*
Australia	3.23	0.26
Belgium	25.91	2.69
Canada	2.25	0.28
Denmark	20.48	0.91
France	2.51	0.75
Germany	7.17	5.19
Italy	3.96	0.7
Japan	9.42	8.94
The Netherlands	2.94	0.22
Sweden	5.69	0.56
Switzerland	33.41	3.12
United Kingdom		
United States	17.62	61.70
China	3.6	10.8
India		

Source: OECD Online Data Base (Main Science and Technology Indicators). Note: country's share is calculated using data of 34 countries. Data for UK is missing. For France, the Netherlands, and Slovenia, nearest available data is used.

(Shackelford and Wolfe 2020). The United States performs the most business sector biotechnology R&D ($63 billion, or 70%) among the 25 countries for which data are available (NSB 2022, Figure KTI-27, OECD e). This is almost 16 times that of France ($3.9 billion), the next largest.

OECD countries host more than three-quarters of all registered clinical trials worldwide (OECD 2018). The vast majority (approximately 90%) of patients recruited for industry-sponsored trials registered with the US National Institutes of Health (NIH) come from OECD countries (OECD 2018).

Research publications in health sciences

Formulating a research idea and its envisaged applications in health sciences is an essential step in the preclinical drug development phase. The output of research publications is an indicator, albeit crude, of research capabilities. According to the NSF report (2022), health sciences is the largest field of science globally (25% of the publications in 2020). Tables 4.3 and 4.4 present the fractional count (meaning that a co-authored publication is assigned fractionally to each of the co-authors) of research publications respectively in health sciences, and in the combined field of biotechnology and biomedical sciences. As seen from Table 4.3, USA has produced the largest number of publications in health sciences, followed by China, Japan, Germany, and others. China has increased its research publications by more than six times of the publications in 2000.[1] India and Brazil have more than doubled their publications over 20 years period, from 2000 to 2020.

Table 4.3 Research publications in health sciences, 2020

Country/Region	*Global Share 2020 (%)*
USA	22.4
Canada	2.95
China	14.0
Japan	4.42
India	3.27
Europe (EU 27)	21.41
UK	4.77
Italy	3.62
Spain	2.51
France	2.55
Germany	4.0
Korea (Rep)	2.46
Switzerland	1.03
Australia	2.74
Brazil	2.71

Source: NSF 2022

Table 4.4 Research publications in biological and biomedical sciences, 2020

Country/Region	*Global Share 2020 (%)*
USA	17.42
Canada	2.18
China	19.66
Japan	3.62
India	4.69
Europe (EU 27)	20.10
UK	3.49
Italy	3.16
Spain	2.54
France	2.50
Germany	3.67
Korea (Rep)	2.48
Switzerland	0.90
Australia	2.21
Brazil	3.57

Source: NSF 2022

In regard to the publications in biotechnology and biomedical sciences (Table 4.4), a similar pattern of research performance and capabilities can be observed. Biomedical science focuses on how cells, organs, and systems function in the human body. Two countries that are producing the most publications in medical fields are the United States and China.

According to the National Science Foundation (2016, 2022), the US, EU-27, UK, and Japanese health sciences publication output far exceeds that of any other field. In China, health sciences are the second largest area of research after engineering. Table 4.5 presents the specialization index of research publications in health sciences. UNESCO (2021) defines specialization as the proportion of output by a given country on a given topic, divided by the global proportion. For example, if a country devotes 2% of its output to a research topic and that output represents 1% of global output on the topic, it will score 2.00, meaning it outperforms the global average. High-income economies are observed to outperform the global average specialization index. Developing nations, including India and China, are trailing behind by a wide margin.

Investment in human capital

Investment in human capital is critical for innovation (Cirera and Maloney 2017). Educational attainment, measured as the proportion of a population that has reached a specific level of education, is often used as a proxy for human capital and skill levels (OECD 2016). It is observed that countries with strong education systems[2] also tend to have strong R&D sectors and high levels of innovation (IFPMA 2012a). Investment in education and the

Table 4.5 Specialization in health science publications

	2011–2019
World	1.00
High-income economies	1.18
Canada	1.27
United States of America	1.42
Brazil	1.13
European Union	1.13
Belgium	1.21
Denmark	1.44
Italy	1.16
The Netherlands	1.56
Sweden	1.28
United Kingdom	1.37
Norway	1.15
Switzerland	1.24
Russian Federation	0.48
China	0.54
China, Hong Kong SAR	0.87
Japan	1.10
Singapore	0.73
Thailand	0.85
India	0.64
Australia	1.29
France	1.07
Germany	1.10

Source: UNESCO Science Report 2021

capacity to carry out research have become particularly important in view of the fast-changing frontiers of biopharmaceutical R&D.

Innovative biopharmaceutical enterprises—from discovery and development to manufacturing and delivery of new medicines—require well-educated, highly skilled, and talented individuals, particularly in the fields of science, technology, engineering, and mathematics (STEM) (Pharma 2017). STEM occupations—both middle and highly skilled—include math and computer science jobs, architecture and engineering occupations, and life and physical scientists (Pharma 2017). In 2015, there were nearly 7.8 million STEM workers in the US, or almost 6% of all workers. Around 12% of STEM workers were employed in life- and physical-science occupations (Pharma 2017). STEM jobs represented 27% of all biopharmaceutical manufacturing jobs in the US, which amounted to more than four times their (STEM) share of all jobs (Pharma 2017).

The STEM-focused curriculum is emphasized in many countries beyond the United States. UNESCO (2021) reports that India, with almost 32% of students majoring in STEM fields, produced the most graduates in 2018—almost

Table 4.6 Total tertiary graduates and tertiary STEM graduates 2018

	Total Tertiary Graduates ('000) 2018	*STEM Graduates (Tertiary) ('000) 2018*	*Ratio of STEM to Total Tertiary Graduates 2018*
Canada	420.35	89.58	21.3
USA	3,903.54	699.52	17.9
Brazil	1,284.43	222.77	17.3
Belgium	115.387	19.35	16.7
Denmark	82.58	17.32	21.0
France	772.78	197.53	25.6
Germany	569.15	202.35	53.6
Italy	373.78	87	23.3
Sweden	73.51	20.22	27.5
UK	754.3	198.53	26.3
Switzerland	88.7	22.04	24.8
Russia Fed	1,657.48	496.61	30.0
China	1,2915.5		
Japan	985.43		
Korea Rep	628.74	184.5	29.3
Singapore	65.31	22.81	34.9
Australia	373	68.74	18.4
India	8,441.26	2,678.78	31.7
South Africa	232.6	43.2	18.6

Source: UNESCO 2021

2.7 million (see Table 4.6). In 2016, according to the World Economic Forum (2016), China reported a staggering 4.7 million STEM graduates (Buchholz 2020). Yet, according to the National Science Foundation, China defines STEM quite broadly, making its data incomparable with other countries' (Buchholz 2020). As another measure, the US government agency counted 1.6 million Chinese science and engineering graduates in 2014 (Buchholz 2020). Other countries with a high share of STEM graduates out of all tertiary degree graduates include Germany, Singapore, and Russia (see Table 4.6).

Venture capital (VC) financing

Financing is essential for both new and growing firms to translate inventions into innovations. Greater availability of early-stage VC financing, and an increasing number of incubators/accelerators, has helped researchers and early-stage biotech firms to cross the Valley of Death (CPHL 2019). As seen in Table 4.7, USA received the highest share of global VC (62.13%) in 2020 in the biotech sector. This is followed by China (19% global share) and Europe (15% global share).

The availability of venture capital financing is one of the key characteristics of a high-quality innovation ecosystem for commercializing biopharmaceutical

Table 4.7 Venture capital raised in biotechnology sector: Global share of selected countries and regions: 2020

Country/Region	*Global Share 2020 (%)*
North America	63.16
USA	62.13
Canada	1.0
Asia	21.24
China	18.88
Japan	0.43
India	0.02
Europe	14.54
Central America	NA
South America	0.0
Africa	0.04
Middle East	0.80
Oceania	0.23

Source: NSF 2022

innovations (Teconomy 2017). It is not only the quality of the research advances but also the ability to form proven management and scientific teams to lead new companies that attract venture capital investment (Teconomy 2017). In the US, the supply of venture capital funded much of the biotech boom during the 1980s and 1990s, resulting in a rise in the number of small biotech companies producing NMEs. Venture capital data show China's increasing presence in biotechnology (NSF 2022). In China, VC investments are significantly backed and influenced by the government.

An important indicator of venture funds' performance is the existence of a well-functioning exit mechanism, particularly in the form of initial public offerings (IPOs) on second-tier stock exchanges. Without a second-tier stock exchange, venture capital is harder to attract. Venture capital exits are the most important aspect of the venture-financed industry's survival and growth (Gompers and Lerner 2001) because venture capitalists only provide early-stage financing to generate a return through such actions as selling shares to the public in an initial public offering (IPO) or disposing of shares via a merger, via a sale to another entity such as a private equity firm in a secondary market, or via a sale to a trading company such as a competitor. The NASDAQ secondary stock market, established in 1971, is one source of profitable exit options for venture capitalists in the US. Investments by individuals (business angels) and corporations are also substantial there. Other OECD countries have less successful venture capital industries. In addition to benefiting from public and private venture capital, small and start-up companies have benefited from the federal government's SBIR program in the US, which provides early-stage financing to help commercialize technology originating in federally funded R&D (NSF 2014, 2020). The exit mechanism is not well-developed in other countries.

Innovation output: Patents

R&D increases the stock of knowledge, which enables invention and product innovations. Patents grant inventors of novel, useful, and non-obvious inventions legal ownership rights for a specified period (NSF 2020). Patenting is an intermediate step toward innovation, so patent data provide indirect indicators of innovation (NSF 2014 Ch 6).[3]

Patent statistics are available from various databases. Major databases include patent applications filed at the European Patent Office (EPO), the United States Patent and Trademark Office (UPSTO), the Japanese Patent Office (JPO), and the OECD Triadic Patent Family (TPF) database. "Triadic Patent Families" comprise the sets of patents covering a single invention, filed altogether in Europe, Japan, and the US.[4]

Patents in pharmaceuticals: Cross-country performance

In pharmaceuticals, USA's share of Triadic Patent Families stood at 42.24%, between 2015 and 2018 (Table 4.8). The next highest-ranking countries were Japan (11.4%), China (6.79%), Germany (5.54%), and UK (4.7%). China holds a dominant (and increasing) share among non-OECD countries.

Table 4.8 Patents in pharmaceuticals

Patent Office and Patent Families	Triadic Patent Families
Technology domains and IPC	Pharmaceuticals
Reference country	Inventor(s)'s country(ies) of residence
Reference date	Priority date
Unit	Percentage Share in World Patents
Country	2015–2018
Australia	1.24
Belgium	1.67
Canada	1.4
China Republic	6.79
Denmark	1.2
France	3.48
Germany	5.54
Italy	1.13
Japan	11.48
Korea	4.07
The Netherlands	1.24
Sweden	1.27
Switzerland	3.7
UK	4.7
USA	42.24
India	0.98

Source: OECD, Main Science and Technology Indicators(online), Data Set Patents by Technology

Patents in biotechnology

Pharmaceutical firms are increasingly dependent upon the biotechnology industry for the key innovations that are necessary to effectively compete in the marketplace against cheaper generic alternatives. "Biotech" includes the disciplines of genetics, molecular biology, biochemistry, embryology, and cell biology and is linked to biomaterials, cell therapy, gene therapy, immunotherapy/vaccines, protein therapeutics, and some specialty pharmaceuticals and small molecule therapeutics (Cummings et al. 2018). The number of patents in the biotechnology sector has been increasing over the years (Raghupathi and Raghupathi 2019). Important examples of biotechnology-related patented products and methods include insulin, blood transfusions, anti-cancer drugs, autoimmune drugs, and pasteurization (Klein 2019).

Table 4.9 reports cross-country evidence on Triadic Patent Families in biotechnology from 2015 to 2018. It is observed from the table that the USA leads other countries with its global share of 42.58. Japan ranked next with its global share 16.52%. Among developing and non-OECD countries, China ranked quite high with its share of 3.97%.

Table 4.9 Patents in biotechnology

Patent office and patent families	Triadic Patent Families
Technology domains & IPC	Biotechnology
Reference country	Inventor(s)'s country(ies) of residence
Reference date	Priority date
Unit	Percentage share in world patents
Country	2015–2018
Australia	1.25
Belgium	1.34
Canada	1.29
China Republic	3.97
Denmark	1.38
France	3.84
Germany	5.26
Italy	0.79
Japan	16.52
Korea	4.31
The Netherlands	1.83
Sweden	1.12
Switzerland	3.02
UK	4.2
USA	42.58
India	0.45

Source: OECD, Main Science and Technology Indicators (Online), Data Set Patents by Technology

As mentioned in the earlier chapters, small, dedicated biotechnology companies have been overwhelmingly active in driving innovations in the pharmaceutical industry, and they have been playing a key role in transferring knowledge from university laboratories to the marketplace. These firms often use intellectual property rights (IPR) strategy as most of their assets are knowledge assets (Veugelers and Schneider 2018). The biotechnology firms routinely form collaborative ties with diverse types of partners, thereby generating inter-organizational networks for product innovation (Powell et al. 1996). The number of active biotechnology firms in a country is one of the critical indicators of industry's innovation potential in biologics.

Number of firms active in biotechnology: International comparisons

OECD, based on their surveys of biotechnology indicators, has compiled international data, part of which is presented in Table 4.9. USA is a pioneering country where, starting from the early 1980s, small biotechnology companies (New Biotechnology Firms or NBFs) have driven innovation through the introduction of new drugs, using living cells. The United States is home to the lion's share of the world's biotechnology firms as seen from Table 4.10.

Table 4.10 Number of firms active in biotechnology 2020 (or the nearest year)

Country	*2020*
Austria	200
Belgium	327
Canada	683
China Republic	
Denmark	119
France	2,239
Germany	877
Italy	777
Japan	
Korea	998
The Netherlands	
Sweden	
Switzerland	345
UK	
USA	2,910
India	

Source: OECD, Key Biotech Indicators (KBI), https://www.oecd.org/innovation/inno/keybiotechnologyindicators.htm

Table 4.11 Number of dedicated firms active in biotechnology 2020 (or the nearest year)

Country	*2020*
Austria	151
Belgium	176
Canada	
China Republic	
Denmark	55
France	1,510
Germany	736
Italy	486
Japan	
Korea	666
The Netherlands	
Sweden	
Switzerland	233
UK	
USA	1,500
India	

Source: OECD, Key Biotech Indicators (KBI), https://www.oecd.org/innovation/inno/keybiotechnologyindicators.htm

Dedicated biotechnology firms (DBFs) emerged in the US to capitalize on the extraordinary development of molecular biology, genetics, and biochemistry (Niosi 2002). OECD defines "dedicated" biotechnology firms as those that devote at least 75% of their production of goods and services, or R&D, to biotechnology. Table 4.11 presents the information on dedicated firms active in the biotech sector. Dedicated biotech firms usually develop upstream and downstream ties with large pharmaceutical companies in order to perform their new product development process (Quintana-García and Benavides-Velasco 2004). These dedicated biotech firms have proved to be critical to drug development and US competitiveness.

Patents in medical technology

Medical technology here includes medical devices such as computed tomography scanners, Gamma Cameras, mammography, radiation therapy, etc. (OECD online databases on Health Care Resources). EPO statistics show that with 2.6% of all patents in technical fields, medical technology is the leading technical field for inventions after surpassing digital communication in 2020 (Geulette 2021). The US held over 34% of Triadic Patent Families in medical technology during 2015–2018 (Table 4.12). Japan attained the next highest share at 21%. Germany came in third at 6.5%. China increased its share from

Table 4.12 Patents in medical technology

Patent office and patent families	*Triadic Patent Families*
Technology domains and IPC	Medical technology
Reference country	Inventor(s)'s country(ies) of residence
Reference date	Priority date
Unit	Percentage share in world patents
Country	2015–2018
Australia	1.0
Belgium	0.5
Canada	1.1
China Republic	2.3
Denmark	1.1
France	3.6
Germany	6.5
Italy	1.2
Japan	20.7
Korea	2.6
The Netherlands	7.4
Sweden	1.3
Switzerland	4.2
UK	3.0
USA	34.3
India	0.3

Source: OECD, Main Science and Technology Indicators (Online), Data Set Patents by Technology

a meager 0.6% in 2005 to 2.3% during 2015–2018. The USA, Japan, and Europe are the regions with the most patents in medical goods, demonstrating their great capacity to generate innovation in the sector and to dictate competitive dynamics (Akkari et al. 2016).

Innovation output: Development of new molecular entity drugs

In the pharmaceutical industry, measuring innovative output is a complex task since drugs vary significantly in their scientific significance, health impact, and economic value. This heterogeneity means that simple counts of NMEs may seriously mismeasure R&D performance (Cockburn 2006). To address the problem, Lanthier et al. (2013) has distinguished three subcategories of NMEs: first-in-class, advance-in-class, and addition-to-class. First-in-class drugs reflect major advances in therapeutic innovations because each drug represents a new pathway for treating a disease (Lanthier et al. 2013). Advance-in-class drugs are drugs that were not first-in-class but received a priority review designation, which is reserved for medicines that potentially offer major advances in treatment (Lanthier et al. 2013). Addition-to-class, or "me too," drugs do not entail genuine therapeutic progress; they are developed as a result of a great deal of emulation of successful drugs undertaken by rival companies (Correa 2004).

The US dominates in the global development of New Molecular Entity (NME) drugs. Zeukeng et al. (2018) found that of the 134 new drugs approved between 2007 and 2016, 66.4% were first approved by the FDA (Food and Drug Administration), 30.6% by the EMA (The European Medicines Agency), and 3.0% by SMC (Swissmedic). The EMA and the FDA had high concordance (91–98%) in decisions on marketing approvals (Kashoki et al. 2020). Both authorities have robust scientific and technical collaborations.

As of 2022, The US share of the global R&D pipeline has remained relatively stable, at above 40% over the past 15 years (IQVIA 2023). Europe's share has declined from 31% to 23% over the same 15 years (IQVIA 2023). Products from China-headquartered companies represented 15% of the R&D pipeline in 2022, up from 6% five years ago and 2% in 2007 (IQVIA 2023).

Concluding remarks

From the above international evidence, it is clear that innovation capabilities are highly concentrated across the globe; there are selected few countries that have developed technological capabilities to contribute to the global health sector. There is vital need for strengthening the innovation system in other countries across the globe through international initiatives.

Despite the spectacular advances in innovative drugs and devices, the global health industry is facing several challenges that need to be redressed. These include:

- Lack-luster R&D productivity
- Escalating costs and affordability concerns
- Inadequate drugs for tropical diseases and shortage of essential medicines
- Eco-innovations concerns

These issues are covered in subsequent chapters.

Summary

This chapter has analyzed certain key determinants of medical innovations. In identifying the critical factors, an empirical analysis of linear innovation models is conducted of countries that are the leading providers and partners in developing innovative medical products. The following factors are found to be of great significance:

- BERD in the pharmaceutical industry
- Research publications in health science
- Availability of skilled scientific manpower
- Venture capital financing
- Patents in pharmaceuticals, biotechnology, and medical technology
- Number of dedicated biotechnology firms

Countries greatly vary in the innovation performance as revealed from the empirical findings on the factors.

Notes

1 Data for 2000 is not shown here.

2 Education systems differ widely across the world. To ensure that international statistics and indicators are comparable, most countries collect and report their education data under the United Nations Educational, Scientific and Cultural Organization (UNESCO) International Standard Classification of Education (ISCED), developed in collaboration with different countries and international organizations. Mapping a country's educational programs into the ISCED structure helps ensure that the international comparisons are more transparent and consistent. Data include degrees at International Standard Classification of Education (ISCED) 7 (master's or equivalent) and 8 (doctorate or equivalent).

3 Patent statistics are available from various databases, including those of the European Patent Office (EPO), United States Patent and Trademark Office (USPTO), and the Japanese Patent Office (JPO) as well as the OECD Triadic Patent Family (TPF) database.

4 Triadic Patent Families' database consolidates raw patent data from the EPO (and the WIPO DOCDB database it maintains), JPO, and the USPTO.
http://www.olis.oecd.org/olis/2002doc.nsf/43bb6130e5e86e5fc12569fa005d004c/db7182d5e0c8f2efc1256c b0005b00ce/$FILE/JT00137753.DOC.

References

Akkari, Alessandra Cristina Santos, et al. 2016. "Pharmaceutical Innovation: Differences Between Europe, USA and "Pharmerging" Countries" *Gest. Prod., São Carlos* 23 (2): 365–380. https://doi.org/10.1590/0104-530X1626

Buchholz, K. 2020. *Where Most Students Choose STEM Degrees, STEM EDUCATION.* Statista.

Cirera, X., and W. F. Maloney. 2017. *Paradox-Developing Country Capabilities and the Unrealised Promise of Technological Catch-Up.* World Bank Publications, ISBN: 9781464811609.

Cockburn, I. M. 2006. "Is the Pharmaceutical Industry in a Productivity Crisis?" In *Innovation Policy & the Economy* 7: 1–32. NBER. "Chapters." In Innovation Policy & the Economy. National Bureau of Economic Research, Inc 7: 1–32. https://doi.org/10.1086/ipe.7.25056188.

Cockburn, I. M., and R. M. Henderson. 2001. "Publicly funded science and the productivity of the pharmaceutical industry." In *Innovation Policy and the Economy,* 1: 1–34. National Bureau of Economic Research, Inc.

Correa, Carlos María. 2004. "Ownership of Knowledge – The Role of Patents in Pharmaceutical R&D." *Bulletin of the World Health Organization* 82 (10): 784–787; discussion 787–790.

CPHL. 2019. *Global Business Report, Industry Explorations United States, Biopharmaceuticals.*United States Biopharmaceuticals.

Cummings, Jeffrey, Carl Reiber, and Parvesh Kumar. 2018. "The Price of Progress: Funding and Financing Alzheimer's Disease Drug Development." *Alzheimer's & Dementia* 4: 330–343. https://doi.org/10.1016/j.trci.2018.04.008.

Drews, J. 2000. "Drug Discovery: A Historical Perspective." *Science* 17 (287): 1960–1964. https://doi.org/10.1126/science.287.5460.1960.

Edquist, C. 2005. Systems of Innovation: Perspectives and Challenges. In *Oxford Handbook of Innovation*, edited by J. Fagerberg, D. Mowery, and R. Nelson, (pp. 181–208). Oxford University Press.

FDA. 2004. *Challenge and Opportunity on the Critical Path to New Medical Technologies, Innovation Stagnation.* FDA.

Galli, R., and M. Teubal. 1997. "Paradigmatic Shifts in National Innovation Systems." In *Systems of Innovation*, edited by C. Edquist. Pinter Publishers.

Godin, B. 2005. "The Linear Model of Innovation: the Historical Construction of an Analytical Framework", Project on the History and Sociology of S&T Statistics Working Paper No. 30. *Science, Technology, & Human Values* 31 (6): 639–667. https://doi.org/10.1177/0162243906291865.

Gompers, P., and J. Lerner. 2001. "The Venture Capital Revolution." *Journal of Economic Perspectives* 15 (2): 145–168. https://doi.org/10.1257/jep.15.2.145.

Geulette, M. 2021. "Pandemic spurs growth of patents in pharmaceuticals and biotech, bringing together industry, Research and Policy." March 18. Science Business Publishing International Belgium.

IFPMA. 2022 New Frontiers of Biopharmaceutical Innovation and Global Public Health, Facts and Figures 2022. International Federation of Pharmaceutical Manufacturers and Associations., IFPMA Geneva.

Institute of Medicine (US) Committee on Conflict of Interest in Medical Research. 2009. "Education, and Practice." In *Conflict of Interest in Medical Research, Education, and Practice*, edited by B. Lo, and M. J. Field. National Academies Press. US. E, The Pathway from Idea to Regulatory Approval: Examples for Drug Development.

IQVIA. 2023. *Global Use of Medicines 2023 OUTLOOK TO* vol. 2027. IQVIA.

Johnson, A. 2001. "Functions in Innovation System Approaches". Electronic paper at the Nelson and Winter Conference, Aalborg.

Kashoki, Mwango, Zahra Hanaizi, Stella Yordanova, Richard Veselý, Christelle Bouygues, Jordi Llinares, and Sandra L. Kweder. 2020. "A Comparison of EMA and FDA Decisions for New Drug Marketing Applications 2014–2016: Concordance, Discordance, and Why." *Clinical Pharmacology & Therapeutics* 107 (1): 195–202. https://doi.org/10.1002/cpt.1565.

Khanna, Ish. 2012. "Drug Discovery in Pharmaceutical Industry: Productivity Challenges and Trends." *Drug Discovery Today* 17 (19–20): 1088–1102. https://doi.org/10.1016/j.drudis.2012.05.007.

Kiriyama, N. 2011. *Trade and Innovation: Pharmaceuticals OECD, OECD Trade Policy Working Paper No. 113.* Working Party of the Trade Committee.

Klein, C. 2019. *The Biotechnology Patent Landscape*. BioSpace.

Lanthier, Michael, Kathleen L. Miller, Clark Nardinelli, and Janet Woodcock. 2013. "An Improved Approach to Measuring Drug Innovation Finds Steady Rates of First-in-Class Pharmaceuticals, 1987–2011." *Health Affairs* 32 (8): 1433–1439. https://doi.org/10.1377/hlthaff.2012.0541.

Ledford, Heidi. 2011. "Translational Research: 4 Ways to Fix the Clinical Trial." *Nature* 477 (7366): 526–528. https://doi.org/10.1038/477526a.

Mansfield, E. 1998. "Academic Research and Industrial Innovation: An Update of the Empirical Findings." *Research Policy* 26 (7–8): 773–776. https://doi.org/10.1016/S0048-7333(97)00043-7.

Mohs, Richard C., and Nigel H. Greig. 2017. "Drug Discovery and Development: Role of Basic Biological Research." *Alzheimer's & Dementia* 3 (4): 651–657. https://doi.org/10.1016/j.trci.2017.10.005.

Mowery, D. C., and B. N. Sampat. 2005. "The Bayh-Dole Act of 1980 and University? Industry Technology Transfer: A Model for Other OECD Governments?" *Journal of Technology Transfer* 30 (1–2): 115–127. https://doi.org/10.1007/s10961-004-4361-z.

Mowery, D. C., and J. E. Oxley. 1995. "Inward Technology Transfer and Competitiveness: The Role of National Innovation Systems." *Cambridge Journal of Economics* 19 (1): 67–93.

Narin, F., K. S. Hamilton, and D. Olivastro. 1997. "The Increasing Linkage between U.S. Technology and Public Science." *Research Policy* 26 (3): 317–330. https://doi.org/10.1016/S0048-7333(97)00013-9.

Nelson, R.R. 1993 *National Innovation Systems: A Comparative Analysis*. Oxford University Press, Oxford.

NSF. 2014. *Science and Engineering Indicators*. NSB.

NSF. 2016. *Taxonomy of Economic Activities Based on R&D Intensity, OECD Science, Technology and Industry Working Papers, 2016/4 m Written by Fernando Galindo-Rueda, Fabien Verger*. NSB.

NSF. 2020. *Science and Engineering Indicators, Production and Trade of Knowledge-and Technology Intensive Industries*. NSB.

NSF. 2022. The State of U.S. Science and Engineering 2022, Science and Engineering Indicators, https://ncses.nsf.gov/pubs/nsb20221/. National Science Board US.

OECD. 2016. "G20 Innovation Report, Report prepared for the G20 Science", Technology and Innovation Ministers Meeting: OECD: The Innovation Imperative: Contributing to Productivity, Growth and Well-Being.

OECD. 2018. *Pharmaceutical Innovation and Access to Medicines, OECD*. Health Policy Studies. OECD Publishing.

OECD/IDRC. 2010a. "Ch. 3. By Erika Kraemer-Mbula and Watu, Wamae." In *The Relevance of Innovation Systems to Developing Countries*, edited by Erika Kraemer-Mbula, and Watu Wamae. Innovation and the Development Agenda.

OECD/IDRC. 2010b. *Innovation Strategies in Developing Countries (Chapter 7 by Rasigan Maharajh Erika Kraemer-Mbula) in Innovation and the Development Agenda*, edited by Erika Kraemer-Mbula, and Watu Wamae. OECD/IDRC.

Patel, P., and K. Pavitt. 1994. "National Innovation Systems: Why They Are Important, and How They Might Be Measured and Compared." *Economics of Innovation & New Technology* 3 (1): 77–95. https://doi.org/10.1080/10438599400000004.

Pharma. 2017. *Enhancing Today's STEM Workforce to Ensure Tomorrow's New Medicines: Biopharmaceutical Industry Partnerships with U.S. Colleges and Universities.* Teconomy Partners. LLC.

Powell, W. W., W.K. Kenneth, and L. Smith-Doerr. 1996. "Interorganizational Collaboration and the Locus of Innovation: Networks of Learning in Biotechnology." *Administrative Science Quarterly* 41 (1): 116–45.

Quintana-García, C., and C. A. Benavides-Velasco. 2004. "Cooperation, Competition, and Innovative Capability: A Panel Data of European Dedicated Biotechnology Firms." *Technovation* 24 (12): 927–938. https://doi.org/10.1016/S0166-4972(03)00060-9.

Raghupathi, V., and W. Raghupathi. 2019. "Exploring Science-and-Technology-Led Innovation: A Cross-Country Study." *Journal of Innovation & Entrepreneurship* 8 (1): 5. https://doi.org/10.1186/s13731-018-0097-0.

Roy, J. 2011. *Future Prospects for the Pharmaceutical Industry. An Introduction to Pharmaceutical Sciences.* National Library: 357–84. https://doi.org/10.1533/9781908818041.357.

Seyhan, A. A. 2019. "Lost in Translation: The Valley of Death Across Preclinical and Clinical Divide – Identification of Problems and Overcoming Obstacles." *Translational Medicine Communications* 4 (1): 18. https://doi.org/10.1186/s41231-019-0050-7.

Shackelford B., and R. Wolfe. 2020. National Center for Science and Engineering Statistics (NCSES) Businesses Performed 60% of Their U.S. R&D in 10 Metropolitan Areas in 2018. NSF 21-331. National Science Foundation, Alexandria, VA. Available at https://ncses.nsf.gov/pubs/nsf21331.

Tassey, G. 2014. "Competing in Advanced Manufacturing: The Need for Improved Growth Models and Policies." *Journal of Economic Perspectives* 28 (1): 27–48. https://doi.org/10.1257/jep.28.1.27.

van Gool, A.J., F. Bietrix, E. Caldenhoven, K. Zatloukal, A. Scherer, J.E. Litton, G. Meijer, N. Blomberg, A. Smith, B. Mons, J. Heringa, W.J. Koot, M.J. Smit, M. Hajduch, T. Rijnders, and A. Ussi. 2017. "Bridging the translational innovation gap through good biomarker practice." Nature Reviews Drug Discovery 16 (9): 587–588.

Van Norman, Gail A. 2016. "Drugs, Devices, and the FDA: Part 1: An Overview of Approval Processes for Drugs." *JACC. Basic to Translational Science* 1 (3): 170–179. https://doi.org/10.1016/j.jacbts.2016.03.002.

Veugelers, R., and C. Schneider. 2018. "Which IP Strategies Do Young Highly Innovative Firms Choose?" *Small Business Economics* 50 (1): 113–129. https://doi.org/10.1007/s11187-017-9898-y.

WEF (World Economic Forum) 2020. Technology Pioneers 2020, https://www.weforum.org/agenda/2020/11/heres-how-technology-has-changed-and-changed-us-over-the-past-20-years/

WHO, WIPO, & WTO. 2020. "Promoting Access to Medical Technologies and Innovation: Intersections between public health, intellectual property, and trade, 2nd Edition."

Woolthuis, K. R. K., M. Lankhuizen, and V. Gilsing. 2005. "A System Failure Framework for Innovation Policy Design." *Technovation* 25 (6): 609–619. https://doi.org/10.1016/j.technovation.2003.11.002.

Zeukeng, Minette-Joëlle, Enrique Seoane-Vazquez, and Pascal Bonnabry. 2018. "A Comparison of New Drugs Approved by the FDA, the EMA, and Swissmedic: An Assessment of the International Harmonization of Drugs." *European Journal of Clinical Pharmacology* 74 (6): 811–818. https://doi.org/10.1007/s00228-018-2431-7.

5 Tackling the grand challenge of productivity slowdown

Innovation strategies and the power of frontier technologies

Introduction: R&D productivity and its key dimensions

In simple terms, R&D productivity can be defined as the "relationship between the value (medical and commercial) created by a new medicine (considered here to be an NME) and the cost(investments) required to generate that medicine" (Paul et al. 2010, p 204). Sagging R&D productivity in the biopharmaceutical industry has been a topic of concern among analysts over the last ten to 15 years (Roland and Baker 2023). Paul et al. (2010) have stressed the need to substantially increase the number and quality of innovative, cost-effective new medicines, without incurring unsustainable R&D costs.

To provide insight into the productivity puzzle, Paul et al. (2010) have considered analyzing two dimensions of R&D: R&D efficiency and R&D effectiveness as depicted in Figure 5.1.

R&D efficiency refers to improving the ability of the R&D system to translate inputs (for example, scientific ideas, investments, effort) into clinically useful products and applications over a defined time period per dollar spent on R&D. Efficiency can be accomplished by reducing the time gap in the drug discovery process (particularly the duration of clinical trials) and attrition rates in the later phases of development with a positive contribution to productivity (Kola and Landis 2004; Paul et al. 2010; Pammolli et al. 2020). Improving R&D effectiveness means that the pharmaceutical industry makes a transition from an era of "me-too" or "slightly me-better"[1] drugs to one of highly innovative medicines that result in markedly improved health outcomes (Paul et al. 2010). Both aspects of productivity improvement call for remedial measures and new business strategies.

Measure to improve R&D efficiency

Innovation literature suggests that R&D efficiency can be enhanced by concerted efforts to implement at least the following interrelated R&D activities:

- Promoting public research support (and participation) in research consortia[2]
- Forging greater research collaboration between industry-academia and specialized biotech firms

DOI: 10.4324/9781003449331-5

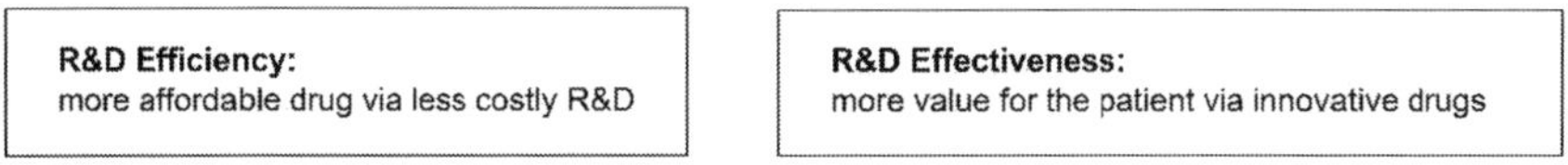

Figure 5.1 Two dimensions of R&D productivity strategy

Source: Paul et al. 2010

- Supplementing in-house R&D efforts with external sources of innovation including open-sourcing, crowdsourcing, public-private partnerships, etc.
- Strengthening the translational capabilities (Cockburn 2007; Khanna 2012; Schuhmacher et al. 2016)
- Tapping the potential of frontier technologies
- Improving clinical efficiency through adaptive clinical trial design

The above-mentioned measures for raising R&D efficiency in the medical industry are examined below.

Boosting public-funded research to foster innovations and diffusion of knowledge

Drug discovery and development process requires tremendous investments in state-of-the-art technology platforms and infrastructure (Gassmann and Reepmeyer 2005). Public-funded (academic and industry) research is noted to have a substantial impact on the technological and productivity performance of the pharmaceutical industry (Cockburn and Henderson 2001). Public sector science provides important inputs (new knowledge, new tools to private sector research, highly trained researchers) to private sector research for product development (Cockburn and Henderson 2001; Toole 2007). Using panel data over 18 years, Toole (2007) found strong evidence that public basic and clinical research are complementary to pharmaceutical R&D investment and thereby stimulate private industry investment.

In the pharmaceutical and medical devices industry, knowledge spillovers (externalities) play a major role in increasing research productivity (Henderson and Cockburn 1996). The presence of spillovers prevents profit-maximizing private firms from investing at the socially optimal level of R&D. To overcome this market failure, Stiglitz and Wallsten (1999) have advocated a model of public-private technology partnership to mitigate the underinvestment problem. As per these authors, the technology partnership comes in two forms: (i) direct government funding of private R&D and (ii) direct collaboration between government and industry scientists. Both constitute vital positive elements of public policy and help to address major challenges and opportunities at the nexus of science, technology, and economic growth.

Research in publicly funded labs has a long history of creating a new scientific knowledge base and contributing to the global pool of knowledge that ushered in several technological and biomedical revolutions. The revolution in molecular biology began in publicly funded scientific research (Cockburn and Henderson 2001). Artificial intelligence, genomics, and personalized medicine are other examples of innovations that came about due to scientific and technological developments enabled by entrepreneurial public research (Mazzucato 2013, OECD 2015, 2016a, 2016b). Public research funding and support in genomics, pharmacogenomics,[3] and proteomics are having far-reaching impacts on drug discovery and development (Vogenberg et al. 2010).

Collaborative research model: Industry-academia and specialized biotech firms

Meeting the challenge of high risk of attrition rates requires pharmaceutical enterprises to forge strategic alliances within and across national borders to supply high-quality products, deliver fast responses, and make their dynamic competencies sustainable (Askariazad et al. 2009; Mohs and Greig 2017; Henderson et al. 1999).

Fully integrated biopharmaceutical companies with in-house R&D are facing tough challenges of sustaining the flow of innovations needed to compensate for the loss of revenue from the "patent cliff," with more than $200 billion in annual revenue at risk through 2030 (Ural 2023). Drug producers that partner with virtually all elements of R&D through a coordinated and global network are likely to "substantially improve R&D productivity by affordably enhancing the pipeline from early discovery through to launch" (Paul et al. 2010 p. 208). Danzon et al. (2005) found that the products developed in an alliance tend to have a higher probability of success, at least for the more complex phase 2 and phase 3 trials, particularly if the licensee is a large firm.

To compete in the global markets and to improve R&D efficiency, large pharma companies are increasingly partnering and networking with smaller emerging biopharma (EBP) companies,[4] which are playing a critical role in the innovation process (IQVIA 2019a, 2019b). Empirical evidence on successful innovations suggests that innovation is increasingly dependent on knowledge exchange and collaboration (Pénin and Neicu 2018). Such partnerships are further being abetted by digital technologies and computer-information technologies (Baldwin and Hippel 2009). With the power of massive computing and networking, it is now possible for informal collaboration to occur around targeted discovery efforts across dispersed geographical regions (Shaw 2017).

Open science platform—the wave of the future

Open science (or open innovation) is an umbrella term for strategies that seek external input and public engagement. Such strategies—like collaboration, crowdsourcing, data sharing, and open-sourcing—aim to tackle some of the most pressing problems in medicine (Shaw 2017, Schuhmacher et al. 2018). Open innovation models are purported to have the following advantages:

- Help corporations to improve the R&D process by sharing broad as well as deep scientific knowledge (Seyhan 2019)
- Enable organizations to gain access to worldwide innovations and solutions via inter-organizational network relationships (Perkmann and Walsh 2007; Talaga 2010)[5]
- Facilitate recruitment of world-class experts, distribute R&D costs across firms, and reduce research redundancies (IFPMA 2012)
- Offset domestic skill shortages, even in the most advanced economies (Lee & Haupt 2021)
- Sharing of a big database relating to clinical, genomic, and proteomic data across a large population with diverse demographic character

The Human Genome Project is a pioneering open-source biomedical project. The Human Genome Project demonstrates the global aspects of genomic knowledge as it involves research teams in 20 different countries and arose from the belief that taking a global view of genomics was required to tackle this complex subject and to accelerate biomedical research (Smith et al. 2004).

In discussing modes of foreign collaboration, Bianchi et al. (2011) distinguish between "Inbound Open Innovation" and "Outbound Open Innovation." In their view, "Inbound Open Innovation" is the practice of leveraging the technologies and discoveries of others, and it requires an organization to establish relationships with external organizations to exploit their technical and scientific competencies (P24). "Outbound Open Innovation," on the other hand, refers to the practice of establishing relationships with external organizations to which an organization transfers its proprietary technologies to be exploited commercially (Bianchi et al. 2011). Based on their longitudinal study, Bianchi et al. found evidence of such widespread organizational modes for "Inbound Open Innovation" as in-licensing, minority equity investments, acquisitions, joint ventures, R&D contracts, purchase of technical and scientific services, and non-equity alliances. Typical organizational modes for "Outbound Open Innovation" included licensing out, spinning off new ventures, selling innovation projects, engaging in joint ventures for technology commercialization, supplying technical and scientific services, and corporate venturing investments and non-equity alliances (Bianchi et al. 2011, p. 24).

International research collaboration during the COVID-19 crisis

International research collaboration and joint publications during the global health crisis have been labeled as the "engine of global science" that brings together the best minds and available data from different countries for the benefit of all (Kituyi 2020; Lee and Haupt 2021). COVID-19 led to a stronger push for the open science model and mobilized scientific efforts at an unprecedented scale (Haghani and Bliemer 2020). Global information sharing and collaboration of research data reached an unprecedented level with the onset of the pandemic. The researchers published the full genome of COVID-19 as an open-access publication in the *Lancet* (January 30, 2020, issue), barely a month after the first patient was admitted into Wuhan hospital (OECD 2020). After that there has been a high engagement in international research collaborations of several countries, including the USA, China, the United Kingdom, Germany, France, Italy, Australia, Canada, and India (OECD 2021). It is estimated that around 75,000 scientific publications on COVID-19 were published in 11 months, of which more than 75% were open-source access (OECD 2021). Engagement of more than 330 partnerships—public-private, private-private, private-academic, and others—bolstered manufacturing capacity, facilitated technology and knowledge transfer, and drove historically rapid R&D (IFPMA 2023). Strong international scientific and regulatory collaboration facilitated the rapid production of new vaccines (in less than a year's time), testing kits, and treatments for COVID-19 (OECD 2021). Models of knowledge exchange, open-source innovations, and collective investments are warranted to safeguard human and planetary health and sustainability (Hensher et al. 2020).

Crowdsourcing

Crowdsourcing is "a form of sourcing in which individuals or organizations solicit contributions from Internet users to obtain desired services or ideas," and it has been described as a new business practice (Schuhmacher et al. 2018). Crowdsourcing has two essential elements (Tucker et al. 2019): (i) a large group of individuals, including those with skills and those without skills, propose potential solutions; (ii) organizations share those solutions. The public domain knowledge can thus be a central force in contributing to formative, preclinical, and clinical research.

Crowdsourcing research, which is related to open innovation, contrasts with conventional, closed innovation research (Tucker et al. 2019). Crowdsourcing has shifted medical research from a closed environment to an open collaboration between the public and researchers (Tucker et al. 2019). The website InnoCentive, for example, was established by drug giant Eli Lilly and then spun off as a company for crowdsourcing science (Shaw 2017).

Clinical trial design

Adaptive clinical trial design is considered to have an impact on R&D costs and productivity. In this type of clinical trials, the accumulating data is used to modify the trial's course (Berry et al. 2012). Adaptive approaches make each research phase a learning tool to improve the next phase in a flexible process that can accelerate timelines, reduce costs, and generate the most knowledge from the smallest number of patients. The Bayesian approach is an example of adaptive designs (Berry et al. 2012). Bayesian uses both evidence that accumulates over time (e.g., interim clinical trial data) and prior information (literature or previous relevant studies). This combination of evidence provides a posterior probability (a term for the probability of an event that is conditional on the prior information and current data), which is analyzed to draw conclusions (Berry et al. 2012, National Pharmaceutical Council 2012).

Improving R&D effectiveness: Enhancing health benefit-to-risk ratio

There is no standard definition of effectiveness of R&D. Following Paul et al. (2010), R&D effectiveness can be construed as cost-effective innovative output with valued outcomes for patients. R&D effectiveness would require comparing intended benefits with cost and risks. R&D effectiveness can be quantified as the patient benefit-to-risk ratio (Paul et al. 2010). Benefits can be measured objectively in various ways: decreased mortality, morbidity, and reduced hospitalization (Paul et al. 2010). Two types of risks that can arise from new drug treatment include financial cost and health risk. High cost of medicines results in considerable financial hardship for patients and their families in case of non-communicable diseases (Narang and Nicholas 2017; Tran and Zafar 2018). Regarding the health risks, tailored therapy (Personalized therapy) can avoid exposing patients to the risk of a serious adverse effect (Paul et al. 2010). The financial burden of medicine costs can appropriately be proxied by value-based prices estimated using the cost-effectiveness criteria (Gregson et al. 2005, WHO 2018 Technical Report). Thus, in overall terms, the effectiveness of pharmaceutical R&D can, therefore, be improved through implementing appropriately designed cost-effective pricing and tailor-based therapies. These are discussed below.

Precision medicine and improved health outcomes

Precision medicine, the next generation of therapeutics, is predicted to revolutionize the clinical practice of medicine and provide personalized treatment (Landry et al. 2018). Precision medicine seeks to use genomic data to help provide the right treatment to the right patient at the right time, thereby leading to better outcomes for patients (EFPIA 2023a). Every person has a unique variation of the human genome, the knowledge of which can be leveraged to provide sophisticated personalized medicine. Precision medicine methods identify phenotypes[6] of patients with less-common responses to treatment or unique healthcare needs (Johnson et al. 2021). These medicines, by stratifying patients and diseases into molecular subtypes and treating with subtype-specific drugs, help to improve drug efficacy and effectiveness (Li and Jones 2012).

While the discovery of disease-causing and drug-response genetic variants has accelerated, adoption into clinical medicine is in progress (Ginsburg and Phillips 2018). Lack of diversity in genomic databases is currently a barrier to translating precision research into practice (Ginsburg and Phillips 2018). Genomic databases, covering all human races, are in progress for sharing knowledge related to the impact of genetics on human health, as well as a basic understanding of genetic differences between human beings (Landry et al. 2018).

Cost-effective pricing

Cost-effectiveness analysis can provide a measure of health outcomes relative to cost of a new molecular entity. Under the present system of less competitive markets, resources are being frittered in developing "me-too" drugs for the market that offer no additional therapeutic benefits over the existing drugs, despite carrying a higher price tag. Evidence indicates that many highly priced new drugs lack meaningful synchronicity with benefits or outcomes in terms of additional years of life gained.

There is a consensus that prices be proportional to the benefits, such as survival prolongation, or improved quality of life, etc. It is, however, observed that the pharmaceutical companies often set prices according to their income expectations, and not according to the value of medicines (WHO Technical Report 2018, P21).

The most widely accepted outcomes-adjusted price metric is the cost per quality-adjusted life year gained (cost/QALY). Comparison of cost/QALY provides a reasonable measure of the value gained per dollar spent across different drugs or health interventions, provided a standardized and comprehensive methodology is used to measure costs and outcomes (Danzon and Taylor 2010). The quality-adjusted life year (QALY) metric has served as a fundamental component of cost-effectiveness analyses in the US and around the world. Cost-effectiveness analysis is similar to value-based pricing (VBP see Chapter 2) in which the prices of medicines and medical devices are set at a level where the ICER is below the cost/QALY threshold (Shiroiwa 2020). The mechanism of setting value-based pricing is also discussed in an earlier chapter. It is claimed that value-based pricing would encourage research into health conditions that are historically unresearched and underserved (WHO 2021 a, b).

Strengthening the translational research network

Efficiently translating scientific ideas into novel medicines is recognized as an important driver to facilitate increased biomedical productivity (Zerhouni 2003; Fishburn 2013). The challenge of bridging the translational research gap was also highlighted in Chapter 4. Translational research refers to the "bench-to-bedside" process that harnesses knowledge from basic scientific research into clinical research to create novel treatments and treatment options devices, medical procedures, preventions, and diagnostics essentially forming a bridge between basic research and clinical research (Seyhan 2019). Ideally, translational science helps companies prioritize among their early development candidates more effectively and reach the correct go/no-go decision without much financial burden (Bandali and Scott 2018). The interaction of several disciplines is required to translate knowledge from basic science discovery to the bedside (Rubio et al. 2010).

There are two "translational roadblocks" in the clinical research enterprise. The first roadblock (Phase 1 clinical trials, that aims to establish the proof of safety in volunteer human subjects) is "the transfer of new understandings of disease mechanisms gained in the laboratory into the development of new methods for diagnosis, therapy, and prevention and their first testing in humans." The second roadblock (Phase 2 clinicals trials necessary to test the proof of efficacy) is "the translation of results from clinical studies into everyday clinical practice and health decision making" (Woolf 2008). Both Phase 1 and Phase 2 of clinical trials are vital for clinical outcomes. Since drug discovery takes place in academic institutions, biotech companies, and large pharmaceutical corporations, the critical importance of collaboration between industry (including biotech and large firms) and academia in translational research has been highlighted in several research studies (O'Connell and Roblin 2006; Fishburn 2013; Rosenblatt 2012; Seyhan 2019, Gambardella et al. 2000).

Table 5.1 maps the translational roadblocks with the enabling factors that can ease the barriers to translational research.

Universities and trained manpower play an essential role in narrowing down the translational gap. The design of an effective education and training program in translational research remains a challenge because the program must offer each of its candidates and trainees the opportunity to master a combination of skills (Rubio et al. 2010). In the US, the National Institutes of Health (NIH) has made translational research a priority. Its institution of the NCATS and the CTSA are a great step forward for translational medicine. The NCATS Division of Preclinical Innovation (DPI) provides a variety of opportunities for undergraduate, graduate, and postdoctoral level trainees. DPI scientists participate in a team environment in which each project brings together expertise in the following areas (NCATS 2020):

- Biology (biological and disease assay development)
- Automation and engineering (high-throughput screening robotics)
- Informatics and data analysis
- Medicinal and analytical chemistry

Outside the US, the European Society for Translational Medicine (EUSTM) is a global non-profit interdisciplinary initiative based upon three main pillars: bench-side, bedside, and community. In the absence of the involvement of a public institution such as the NIH, market forces cannot be relied upon for effecting the translation from bench to bedside. The US experience suggests that such translation requires institutional and organizational arrangements that provide the essential infrastructure for building research teams and supporting collaborative projects.

Table 5.1 Enabling factors of biopharmaceutical innovation

Research Stages	*Enabling Factors*
Basic or early-stage research	• World Class Institutions (IFPMA 2021) • Highly trained labor force (retained or attracted back to the country) (IFPMA 2021) • Clusters of innovative companies providing support on core technologies (IFPMA 2021) • High-throughput screening, gene sequencing, etc. (IFPMA 2021) • Adequate public investment in basic science research
Translational Research ('bench to bedside' therapy)	• Well-trained cadre of "translational" investigators (Crowley 2003) • Substantive collaboration between scientists, doctors, and industry professionals (Crowley 2003; Fernandez-Moure 2016) • Development of multidisciplinary training institutions incorporating translational research into their curriculums (Fernandez-Moure 2016) • Paradigm shift in training and career development that lays the foundation for funding and commercialization of breakthroughs (Fernandez-Moure 2016) • Multisource open innovation models (Schuhmacher et al. 2016; Seyhan 2019) • Strong medical schools and clinicians for designing managing and reporting trials design (IFPMA 2021) • Strong investment in digital technologies (IQVIA 2019a, 2019b) • Training health scientists in the "next-generation biotherapeutics (NGB)" including cell, gene, and nucleotide therapies (IQVIA 2019a, 2019b) • Capability of using predictive analytics and artificial intelligence to obtain value and evidence from big real-world data (IQVIA 2019a, 2019b) • Effective funding mechanism (Seyhan 2019; Tassey 2014)

Tapping the potential of frontier technologies

The innovative applications of the advances in digital technologies characterizing the fourth industrial revolution (Industry 4.0) are expected to have positive effects on drug discovery and development. Several innovations are shaping the process of pharmaceutical R&D, from artificial intelligence to 3D printing for drug design and production (Pammolli et al. 2020). These emerging technologies are being used in all aspects of the pharmaceutical sector like patients' data analysis, disease diagnosis, manufacturing of medical goods, and packaging (Sharma et al. 2023).

The creative applications of the above-mentioned emerging technologies have resulted in many seminal advances in disease diagnosis and treatment in recent years. The following subsection presents a brief review of their flourishing role in revolutionizing healthcare. Table 5.2 presents a brief snapshot of

Table 5.2 Frontier technologies and the health sector

Industry 4.0 Technologies	*Brief Description*	*Applications in Health*
Machine learning and artificial intelligence (AI)	Machine intelligence—machines performing human-like cognitive functions	• AI and machine learning algorithms analyze big data sets generated by "omics" technologies faster and more accurately (human error-free) for rapid decision-making • Image analysis algorithms help to identify malignancies and other diseases faster • Drugs repurposing and cost efficiency • Diseases forecasting and predictive analysis
3D Printing	Additive manufacturing (or industrial 3D printing) refers to a group of technologies that build physical objects directly from 3D (computer-aided design—CAD) data; use of laser printers to produce objects by printing very thin layers of material onto one another	• Tissue and organ fabrication; creation of customized prosthetics, implants, and medical devices • Bioprinters can create models with living cells • Just-in-time inventories that economize hospital resources
The IoT (Internet of Things)	Increased programmability, memory storage capacity, and sensor-based capabilities that allow physical world objects to become intelligent and communicate independently, online	• Application in many medical instruments such as ECG monitors, glucose level sensing, and oxygen concentration detection • Remote control by patients, and remote health monitoring of patients • The wearable Internet of Things (WIoT) facilitate telehealth to achieve automated interventions
Nanotechnologies and advanced new materials (biomaterials, nanomaterials)	Nanotechnology is the understanding and control of materials on the atomic or molecular scale. Matter can exhibit unusual physical, chemical, and biological properties at the nanoscale (Richard Feynman, a Nobel prize physicist)	• Ability to manipulate individual atoms and molecules in health care beyond the ability of doctors and humans • Platform technology for rapid development of next-generation vaccines (new class of DNA- and RNA-based vaccines) (Shin et al 2020)

Source: Compiled from different sources

the upcoming frontier technologies and their broad applications to the health sector.

Artificial intelligence (AI) and machine learning

Artificial intelligence is not one technology, but rather a collection of them (Davenport and Kalakota 2019). Some important AI technologies of high importance to healthcare are machine learning, natural language processing (such as speech recognition, etc.), physical robots (surgical robots), and others (see details in Davenport and Kalakota 2019). These technologies are used in diagnosis and treatment applications.

Machine learning (neural networks and deep learning) is a computer science methodology that aims to identify complex patterns in data that can be used to make predictions or classifications on new unseen data or for advanced exploratory data analysis (MacEachern and Forkert 2021, Davenport and Kalakota 2019). The basic unit of a neural network is a neuron. A neuron takes inputs, does some statistical data processing, and produces an output. Deep learning is increasingly being applied to radiology images for the detection of clinically relevant features in imaging data (identifying cancerous lesion) beyond what can be perceived by the human eye (Davenport and Kalakota 2019).

Biological and chemical scientists are extensively incorporating AI algorithms in drug designing and discovery processes. The most important positive contribution from AI/ML is in clinical trial design, conduct, and analysis (Kolluri et al. 2022). With AI principles along with ML (machine learning) and DL (deep learning) algorithms, virtual screening of compounds from chemical libraries, which comprise more than 10^6 million compounds, has become easy and time-effective (Gupta et al. 2021, IQVIA 2022b). With the large and complex datasets generated using precision medicine diagnostic approaches, novel techniques to process and understand these complex data are needed (MacEachern and Forkert 2021, Davenport and Kalakota 2019).

AI is proving to be very valuable when it comes to detecting diseases early and for confirming an accurate diagnosis quicker. AI algorithms help reading digital scans more accurately than doctors. For example, in breast cancer care, the use of AI is enabling the review of mammograms to be 30 times faster with 99% accuracy, reducing the need for unnecessary biopsies (Burke 2022). Machine learning, with access to patient data, can compare and predict individual profiles and medicine effectiveness (GHP News 2023). By doing this, manufacturers can adapt their medicines to create improved predictions on the demand of medicines and their effectiveness (GHP News 2023).

The convergence of artificial intelligence (AI) and precision medicine promises to revolutionize health care (Johnson et al. 2021). Precision or "personalized medicine," as mentioned earlier, is an approach to tailoring disease prevention and treatment that takes into account differences in people's genes, environments, and lifestyles (FDA home page). A vast amount of data remains untapped as it exists outside medical systems. Our individual health is heavily influenced by our lifestyle, nutrition, environment, and access to care (Johnson et al. 2021).

AI technologies and drug repurposing

AI and machine learning (ML) techniques are being utilized in drug repurposing to align existing drugs with specific indications or combine drugs to address pressing medical needs. Drug repurposing strategy is gaining importance as, with the use of AI-powered methodologies, this approach can reduce failure rate while saving time and cost (IQVIA 2022b). AI technologies sift through massive amounts of data records stored in digital form to identify new therapeutic uses of existing drugs.

It is estimated that as much as 30% of repurposed drugs are approved compared to only about 10% of new drugs gaining market approval resulting from traditional drug discovery and development (IQVIA 2022b). Well-known examples include sildenafil citrate for erectile dysfunction, thalidomide for multiple myeloma (cancer of the plasma/white blood cells), and remdesivir for the treatment of COVID-19 (Zhou et al. 2020). The strategy of drug repurposing is seen as a powerful solution for emerging diseases about which there is a lack of knowledge of drug–target interaction. AI can quickly detect drugs that can fight against emerging diseases (Mohanty et al. 2020).

Big data analytics, "OMICS," and machine learning tools

The creation and analysis of large databases of genetic, phenotypic, prescribing, and health outcome information are essential for predictive analysis and for developing preventive medicine (OECD 2009). Advances in "omics" technologies, also called "systems biology," are enabling scientists and clinicians to generate a learning dataset consisting of molecular insights into the disease pathogenesis (Seyhan and Carini 2019). OMICS data set is a high dimensional data set that consists of thousands to millions of molecule measurements (e.g., genes, or genes products, such as RNA or proteins) (National Academies of Sciences, Engineering, and Medicine 2012). Genomics investigates thousands of DNA sequences, and proteomics examines large numbers of proteins (National Academies of Sciences, Engineering, and Medicine 2012).

Although "omics" datasets have provided remarkable insights, it is by analyzing, linking, and comparing different large datasets (genomic, clinical outcomes, bio-banks, imaging, etc.) that the greatest insights have been gained—so-called "big data" (EBE 2015). Advanced data analytics algorithms are required to identify, evaluate, and rank assumed drug targets from omics data (Paananen and Fortino 2020). With the availability of big data, including biological, clinical, and open data (scientific publications and data repositories), novel AI and machine learning algorithms are capable of leveraging these large sets of biomedical data which are in high demand (Seyhan and Carini 2019; Zhou et al. 2020).

Big data analytics has the potential of improving healthcare practices and research in the following key areas:

- Analyzing clinical trials and patient records, using predictive modeling to reduce attrition rates, better matching patients with treatment (Raghupathi and Raghupathi 2014)
- Analyzing public health and epidemiological data (structured and unstructured data)[7] for turning large amounts of data into actionable information (Raghupathi and Raghupathi 2014)
- Conducting genomic analytics: screening gene sequencing more efficiently and to capture gene-to-drug-response relationships that may lead to more personalized, effective treatments (Aronson and Rehm 2015; Chen and 2016; He et al. 2017; Seyhan and Carini 2019)
- Improving the speed and quality of medical decision-making (Popov et al. 2022)

Accurate analysis of medical data benefits early disease detection, patient care, and saving of national resources (Chen et al. 2017). Big-data analytics in demand forecasting can make GVCs more responsive to sudden surge in health needs (Bhaskar et al. 2020).

Role of nanotechnologies in health care

Nanotechnology is a multidisciplinary field, which covers a vast and diverse array of devices derived from engineering, biology, physics, and chemistry (Ferrari 2005). This area of science involves working with materials and devices on a nanoscale level. Nanoparticles of dimensions ranging between 1 and 100 nm are designed and used for diagnostics, therapeutics, and as biomedical tools for research.

Biological processes, including ones necessary for life, occur at the nanoscale (NIH 2017). Nanoscale devices are similar in size to large biological molecules ("biomolecules") such as enzymes and receptors. By gaining access to cells, blood vessels, and areas of the body, they have the potential to detect disease and deliver treatment in many ways. It is now possible to provide therapy at a molecular level with the help of these tools, thus treating the disease and assisting in the study of the pathogenesis of the disease (Surendiran et al. 2009). Designing drugs with a greater degree of cell specificity improves efficacy and minimizes adverse effects (Surendiran et al. 2009). In the fight against cancers, nanodevices such as nanovectors help in the targeted delivery of anticancer drugs and imaging contrast agents (Ferrari 2005). Nanoscience provides technology to design and develop newer cardiac instruments, which are not only smaller in size but also more effective (Shetty 2006).

Among the several uses and benefits, the following are some notable developments and applications of nanotechnology-based tools and techniques.

- Medical imaging and targeted drug delivery (Caruthers et al. 2007)
- Robotic surgery—the use of micro- and nanoscale robots to enable the extended reach of the surgeon's hand movements into smaller, precise movements of tiny instruments within the patient's body (Li et al. 2017; Mali 2013; Brodie and Vasdev 2018)
- Nanomaterials embedded in many novel medical devices (Pallotta et al. 2019)
- Early detection of cancer (Choi et al. 2010)
- Development of modern vaccines (mRNA vaccines) (Khurana et al. 2021)

Among the above listed uses of nanotechnologies, two remarkable applications—viz., early detection of cancer and use in modern vaccines—merit more details.

Nanotechnology and early detection of diseases

Current imaging devices (X-ray, magnetic resonance imaging (MRI), computed tomography (CT), endoscopy, and ultrasound) can only detect cancer when there is a visible change to the tissue (Zhang et al. 2019). By that time, thousands of cancer cells may have proliferated and even metastasized (Zhang et al. 2019). Diagnostic methods with a greater degree of sensitivity aid in the early detection of the disease and provide better prognosis (Surendiran et al. 2009; Eniola-Adefeso et al. 2012; NIH 2017). Molecular imaging can provide functional and molecular information at the cellular or subcellular level in vivo in a non-invasive manner (Ma and Xia 2021). Nano-biosensors have the capability to diagnose Alzheimer's disease in an early stage and thus treat it better. A nano-filter can selectively fish toxins out of the blood (Tiwari and Tiwari 2022).

Nanotechnologies and new vaccines

Viruses are nanoscale objects; nanoparticles and viruses operate at the same scale, meaning that nanoscale technology approaches in vaccine development can be a powerful approach (Shin et al. 2020). Traditional vaccines trigger immune responses by injecting the entire viruses, either as attenuated live viruses (weakened form of the germ that causes a disease), inactivated viruses (the killed version of the germ that causes a disease), or engineered viruses, into the body (National Institutes of Health 2020). The new class of DNA- and RNA-based vaccines deliver the genetic sequence of specific viral proteins to the host cells using nanotechnology platforms. mRNA-based therapies have several advantages: mRNA delivery is safer than the whole virus; mRNA has a short half-life, which can be regulated by molecular design; and mRNA vaccine is immunogenic (National Institutes of Health 2020). These nanotechnology-based vaccines are scalable, since mRNA can be engineered using standard laboratory techniques (National Institutes of Health 2020). mRNA vaccines combine desirable immunological properties with an outstanding safety profile and the unmet flexibility of genetic vaccines (Schlake et al. 2012). mRNA presents a promising vector that may well become the basis of a game-changing vaccine technology platform (Schlake et al. 2012). This vector virus is not a live virus, and therefore no risk of causing disease in the person getting vaccinated.

3D printing technology in medicines and medical devices

3D printing or additive manufacturing (AM) is a family of technologies that implement layer-by-layer processes in order to fabricate physical models, based on a computer-aided design (CAD) model. 3D printing permits the fabrication of high degrees of complexity with great reproducibility, in a fast and cost-effective fashion (Mathew et al. 2020). 3D technology makes it possible to construct devices with intricate structures, internal cavities, and unconventional geometries that are very difficult or impossible to construct using traditional manufacturing. Due to its versatility, 3D printing has medical applications in drugs, medical devices, and biologics (FDA 2020). 3D printing software can be used to extract digital data from patient images such as computed tomography, magnetic resonance imaging, or laser scanning to yield custom-made and personalized constructs for surgical planning and implantation (Jovic, Combellack, Jessop, Whitaker). Scientists have been able to create blood vessels, synthetic ovaries, and even a pancreas. These artificial organs then grow within the patient's body to replace the original faulty one (Burke 2022).

3D printing technology offers several long-term benefits:

- Technology is expected to play a significant role in personalized medicine (Awad et al. 2018)
- Development of tailored medical devices and vaccines (Awad et al. 2018)
- 3D bioprinting, which is a convergence of biology and engineering technologies, is projected to drastically reduce the wait time for organ/tissue transplantation (Jovic et al. 2020)

The following discussion elaborates on these projected benefits.

3D printing and personalized medicines

In 2015, the US FDA approved the first medicine called levetiracetam (medication to treat epilepsy) that was produced by 3D printing. The precision of the machine allowed manufacturers to create a pill with a high drug load. In one dose, patients were now able to receive 1,000 milligrams of levetiracetam. This quick-dissolving pill (CAPRA 2022) was a revolutionary treatment for sufferers of epileptic seizures (GHP 2023).

With 3D printing, the drugs can be manufactured and tailored to individual cases. The dosing and release characteristics of the drug delivery devices can be easily changed by altering the geometries of the 3D design using computer-aided design (CAD) (Mathew et al. 2020).

3D printing and tailored medical devices

Additive manufacturing enables manufacturers to create devices matched to a patient's anatomy (patient-specific devices) or devices with very complex internal structures (FDA 2020). Medical devices produced by 3D printing include orthopedic and cranial implants, surgical instruments, dental restorations such as crowns, and external prosthetics (FDA 2020). In medical devices, 3D printing applications are generally categorized into the following applications: anatomical models (e.g., for surgical preparation, planning, or to aid diagnosis), surgical guides, tools and instruments, implants and therapeutic devices, prosthetics, tissues and organs, and dental applications (CAPRA 2022).

3D technology and modern vaccines

3D technology is enabling the development of vaccine patches which enable much more precise delivery to immune cells in the dermis of the skin, compared to the shots in someone's arm muscle (Miller 2022). Researchers have found that there are 100 to 1,000 times more migratory immune cells in the dermis of the skin than in the muscle (Miller 2022). Moreover, the patches are also easy to self-administer, freeing up hundreds of thousands of health-care workers to do things other than give vaccines. During the COVID-19 pandemic, 3D printing played a role in the manufacturing of PPE, swabs, and other medical devices, enabling greater access across the globe (GHP 2023).

3D bioprinting and the future of artificial organ transplantation

Bioprinting is a type of 3D printing technique that combines living cells (e.g., stem cells) and supportive biomaterials (e.g., scaffolds on which cells can grow) into so-called bioinks, an evolving technology with various applications in making three-dimensional functional artificial tissue structures and organs to replace injured or diseased tissues or organs (CAPRA 2022). 3D computer models using socket designs can make bionic limbs such as hands, arms, feet, and legs. 3D bioprinting can print human organs on demand, no longer necessitating the need for living or deceased human donation or animal transplantation (Vermeulen et al. 2017).

IoT (Internet of Things) and the health industry

The Internet of Things (IoT) is a system of wireless, interrelated, and connected digital devices that can collect, send, and store data over a network without requiring human-to-human or human-to-computer interaction (Kelly et al. 2020). The IoT brings together physical objects with embedded electronics, software, sensors, and network connectivity which means they are able to collect and exchange data with each other. IoT allows the people seamless interactions among different types of devices such as medical sensors, monitoring cameras, home appliances, and so on (Gope and Hwang 2016). The IoT has important applications in health domain as this technology can result in significant advancements in patient care management (Riazul Islam et al. 2015). Various medical devices, sensors, and diagnostic and imaging devices can be viewed as smart devices or objects constituting a core part of the IoT (Riazul Islam et al. 2015; Gope and Hwang 2016). IoT is considered to have advantages for managing chronic disease, medical emergencies, better patient care, and fitness (Javaid and Khan 2021). Some prominent IoT-based healthcare applications include blood glucose (sugar) level sensing, monitoring of the electrocardiogram (ECG), BP monitoring, blood oxygen saturation monitoring, smart wheelchairs management, use of smartphones in health care, and numerous others (Riazul Islam et al. 2015).

A note of precaution about the use of some technologies

It is argued that the advances of new frontier technologies are not unmixed blessings for humanity. Concerns have been expressed that progress in biotechnologies might make it easier to manufacture extremely dangerous pathogens (whether deliberately or accidentally), potentially far worse than the SARS-CoV-2 virus that causes COVID-19. Uncontrolled applications of AI technologies could be existential—meaning they could cause human extinction or an equally permanent and severe disempowerment of humanity (Carlsmith 2022). Caution is required to prevent potentially existential risks. Some experts have warned about the toxic health hazards of NPs (nanoparticles) in vivo and in vitro because we know little about these effects given our current state of knowledge.

The realization of the potential new advances in basic sciences and emerging frontier technologies on human well-being will depend on well-designed innovation policies, the development environment that supports these efforts, international coordination of cybersecurity risk measures, as well as on efforts of supranational organizations to promote the equitable access of countries to any new technologies (WHO, WIPO, and WTO 2020).

Summary

The "productivity crisis" in pharmaceutical R&D and the existence of monopoly power (discussed in the earlier chapter) are documented as among the key factors of soaring drug prices. For improving productivity, the top priority for the industry is to increase R&D efficiency and R&D effectiveness, both of which matter for R&D productivity growth. Advances in medical sciences are widening the gap between "bench-side" research and bedside clinical benefits. Bridging this gap is one of the roadblocks to productivity growth. Based on the research literature, this chapter has highlighted the following proposals for augmenting productivity:

- Reducing late-stage (Phase II and III) attrition rates and cycle times during drug development through research collaboration strategies with public agencies and external partners
- Increasing public investment in biomedical research for laying down the strong foundations for applied research and product development
- Tapping the potential of frontier technologies for reversing the productivity slowdown trend
- Venturing into new forms of multisource open innovation alliances with a strategic intent of integrating external assets for strengthening the R&D capabilities
- The use of novel adaptive design of clinical trials
- Applying cost-effectiveness analysis in drugs pricing
- Sharing global databases relating to clinical, genomic, and proteomic data across a large population with diverse demographic character for aiding research in "precision" therapies

Notes

1 The phrase "me-too drug" refers to medication that offers minor improvement over the existing drugs.
2 Research and development (R&D) consortia are performed by manufacturing companies, often with the support of government, for the purpose of conducting shared research on new technologies for the benefit of the consortium's member companies.
3 "Generally speaking, pharmacogenetics and pharmacogenomics deal with the genetic basis underlying variable drug responses in individual patients. The traditional pharmacogenetic approach relies on studying sequence variations in candidate genes that are thought to affect drug response, whereas pharmacogenomic studies encompass the sum of all genes (i.e., the genome)" (Vogenberg et al. 2010 P 561).
4 Smaller EBP companies have been to be the most active in the fastest-growing areas: oncology and orphan drugs (IQVIA 2019a).
5 Interorganizational networks can be defined as formally established cooperation arrangements spanning different organizations (Perkmann and Walsh 2007).
6 Phenotype refers to an individual's observable traits, such as height, eye color, and blood type. A person's phenotype is determined by both their genomic makeup (genotype) and environmental factors.
7 Structured data (also known as relational data) is data that can be easily queried, recalled, analyzed, and manipulated through a relational database management system (RDBMS). These data include integers, decimals, dates, time, strings, and Booleans. Unstructured data refers to data in the form of images, videos, audio, webpages, free text, and even social media content. This type of data is too complex to be parsed and interpreted. This data can still be stored, retrieved, and edited by other advanced programming methods.

References

Aronson, Samuel J., and Heidi L. Rehm. 2015. "Building the Foundation for Genomics in Precision Medicine." *Nature* 526 (7573): 336–342. https://doi.org/10.1038/nature15816.

Askariazad, M., & Wanous, M. 2009. A proposed value model for prioritizing supply chain performance measures. *International Journal of Business Performance and Supply Chain Modelling* 1: 115–128.

Awad, Atheer, Sarah J. Trenfield, Alvaro Goyanes, Simon Gaisford, and Abdul W. Basit. 2018. "Reshaping Drug Development Using 3D Printing." *Drug Discovery Today* 23 (8): 1547–1555. https://doi.org/10.1016/j.drudis.2018.05.025.

Baldwin, C., and Hippel, . 2009. *Modeling a Paradigm Shift: From Producer Innovation to User and Open Collaborative Innovation, MIT Sloan School of Management.* Working Paper # 476409. INFORMS.

Bandali, R., and G. Scott. 2018. *How Translational Science Can Solve pharma's Productivity Puzzle, Sponsored Insight Syneos Health STAT.* News.com.

Berry, Scott R., William K. Evans, Elizabeth L. Strevel, and Chaim M. Bell. 2012. "Variation and Consternation: Access to Unfunded Cancer Drugs in Canada." *Journal of Oncology Practice* 8 (1): 35–39. https://doi.org/10.1200/JOP.2011.000278.

Bhaskar, Sonu, Jeremy Tan, Marcel L. A. M. Bogers, Timo Minssen, Hishamuddin Badaruddin, Simon Israeli-Korn, and Henry Chesbrough. 2020. "At the Epicenter of COVID-19-the Tragic Failure of the Global Supply Chain for Medical Supplies." *Frontiers in Public Health* 8: 562882. https://doi.org/10.3389/fpubh.2020.562882.

Bianchi, M., A. Cavaliere, D. Chiaroni, F. Frattini, and V. Chiesa. 2011. "Organisational Modes for Open Innovation in the Bio-pharmaceutical Industry: An Exploratory Analysis." *Technovation* 31 (1): 22–33. https://doi.org/10.1016/j.technovation.2010.03.002.

Brodie, Andrew, and Nikhil Vasdev. 2018. "The Future of Robotic Surgery." *Annals of the Royal College of Surgeons of England* 100(Suppl. 7): 4–13. https://doi.org/10.1308/rcsann.supp2.4.

Burke, H. 2022. "Top 10 New Medical Technologies 2022, Preclinical Post, 2022, April 14". https://www.proclinical.com/blogs/2022-4/top-10-new-medical-technologies-2022.

CAPRA. 2022. "3D Printing Our Way to Better" Health Care, June. *Canadian Association of Professionals in Regulatory Affairs* 27, author, Duggal, Pratibha. https://capra.ca/en/blog/3d-printing-our-way-to-better-health-care-2022-06-27.

Carlsmith, J. 2022. "Is Power-Seeking AI an Existential Risk?" *Arxiv, Admin.*/2206.13353. https://arxiv.org/pdf/2206.13353 DOI:10.48550/arXiv.2206.13353

Caruthers, Shelton D., Samuel A. Wickline, and Gregory M. Lanza. 2007. "Nanotechnological Applications in Medicine." *Current Opinion in Biotechnology* 18 (1): 26–30. https://doi.org/10.1016/j.copbio.2007.01.006.

Chen, B., and A. J. Butte. 2016. "Leveraging Big Data to Transform Target Selection and Drug Discovery." *Clinical Pharmacology & Therapeutics* 99 (3): 285–297. https://doi.org/10.1002/cpt.318.

Chen, M., Y. Hao, K. Hwang, L. Wang, and L. Wang. 2017. "Disease Prediction by Machine Learning over Big Data from Healthcare Communities." In *IEEE Access* 5: 8869–8879. https://doi.org/10.1109/ACCESS.2017.2694446.

Choi, Young-Eun, Ju-Won Kwak, and Joon Won Park. 2010. "Nanotechnology for Early Cancer Detection." *Sensors* 10 (1): 428–455. https://doi.org/10.3390/s100100428.

Cockburn, I. M., and R. M. Henderson. 2001. "Publicly Funded Science and the Productivity of the Pharmaceutical Industry, NBER Chapters." In *Innovation Policy & the Economy*. National Bureau of Economic Research, Inc 1: 1–34.

Cockburn, I M. 2007. "Is the Pharmaceutical Industry in a Productivity Crisis?," NBER Chapters, In *Innovation Policy and the Economy*, 7, 1–32, National Bureau of Economic Research, Inc.

Crowley, William F. Jr. 2003. "Translation of Basic Research into Useful Treatments: How Often Does It Occur?" *American Journal of Medicine* 114 (6): 503–505. https://doi.org/10.1016/s0002-9343(03)00119-0.

Danzon, Patricia M., and Erin Taylor. 2010. "Drug Pricing and Value in Oncology." *Oncologist* 15(Suppl. 1): 24–31. https://doi.org/10.1634/theoncologist.2010-S1-24.

Danzon, Patricia M., Sean Nicholson, and Nuno Sousa Pereira. 2005. "Productivity in Pharmaceutical-Biotechnology R&D: The Role of Experience and Alliances." *Journal of Health Economics* 24 (2): 317–339. https://doi.org/10.1016/j.jhealeco.2004.09.006.

Davenport, T., and R. Kalakota. 2019. "The potential for artificial intelligence in healthcare." *Future Healthcare Journal* 6 (2): 94–98. https://doi.org/10.7861/futurehosp.6-2-94

EBE. 2015. "White Paper on Personalized Medicine." *Eu/Media/413495/29-ebe-biopharma_whitepaperonpm_rgb.pdf.* https://www.efpia.

EFPIA. 2023. "Precision medicine: Giving the right medicine, to the right patient, at the right time." Retrieved from https://www.efpia.eu/about-medicines/development-of-medicines/precision-medicine/

Eniola-Adefeso, O., M.J. Heslinga, and T.M. Porter. 2012. Design of nano vectors for therapy and imaging of cardiovascular diseases. *Methodist Debakey Cardiovascular Journal* 8 (1):13–7.

FDA 2020. "What Is Digital Health?" Accessed September 22 https://www.fda.gov/medical-devices/digital-healthcenterexcellence/what-digital-health.

Fernandez-Moure, Joseph S. 2016. "Lost in Translation: The Gap in Scientific Advancements and Clinical Application." *Frontiers in Bioengineering & Biotechnology* 4: 43. https://doi.org/10.3389/fbioe.2016.00043.

Ferrari, Mauro. 2005. "Cancer Nanotechnology: Opportunities and Challenges." *Nature Reviews. Cancer* 5 (3): 161–171. https://doi.org/10.1038/nrc1566.

Fishburn, C. Simone. 2013. "Translational Research: The Changing Landscape of Drug Discovery." *Drug Discovery Today* 18 (9–10): 487–494. https://doi.org/10.1016/j.drudis.2012.12.002.

Gambardella, A., L. Orsenigo, and F. Pammolli,. 2000. "Global competitiveness in pharmaceuticals. A European perspective." Report prepared for the Enterprise Directorate-General of the European Commission.

Gassmann, O., and G. Reepmeyer. 2005. "Organizing Pharmaceutical Innovation: From Science-Based Knowledge Creators to Drug-Oriented Knowledge Brokers." *Creativity & Innovation Management* 14 (3): 233–245. https://doi.org/10.1111/j.1467-8691.2005.00344.x.

GHP (Global Health and Pharma). 2023. *The Transformation of Pharmaceutical Manufacturing by Technology*, Posted on April 17, 2023. GHP.

Ginsburg, Geoffrey S., and Kathryn A. Phillips. 2018. "Precision Medicine: From Science to Value." *Health Affairs (Project Hope)* 37 (5): 694–701. https://doi.org/10.1377/hlthaff.2017.1624.

Gope, P., and T. Hwang. 2016. "BSN-Care: A Secure IoT-Based Modern Healthcare System Using Body Sensor Network." In *IEEE Sensors Journal* 16 (5): 1368–1376. https://doi.org/10.1109/JSEN.2015.2502401.

Gregson, N., K. Sparrowhawk, J. Mauskopf, and J. Paul. 2005. "Pricing medicines: theory and practice, challenges and opportunities." *Nature Reviews Drug Discovery* 4: 121–130.

Gupta, Rohan, Devesh Srivastava, Mehar Sahu, Swati Tiwari, Rashmi K. Ambasta, and Pravir Kumar. 2021. "Artificial Intelligence to Deep Learning: Machine Intelligence Approach for Drug Discovery." *Molecular Diversity* 25 (3): 1315–1360. https://doi.org/10.1007/s11030-021-10217-3.

Haghani, Milad, and Michiel C. J. Bliemer. 2020. "Covid-19 Pandemic and the Unprecedented Mobilisation of Scholarly Efforts Prompted by a Health Crisis: Scientometric Comparisons Across SARS, MERS and 2019-nCoV Literture." *Scientometrics* 125 (3): 2695–2726. https://doi.org/10.1007/s11192-020-03706-z.

He, K. Y., D. Ge, and M.M. He. 2017. "Big Data Analytics for Genomic Medicine." *International Journal of Molecular Sciences* 18 (2): 412.

Henderson, R., and I. Cockburn. 1996. "Scale, scope, and spillovers: The determinants of research productivity in drug discovery." *The RAND Journal of Economics* 27 (1): 32–59.

Henderson, R., G. P. Pisano, and L. Orsenigo. 1999. "The Pharmaceutical Industry and the Revolution in Molecular Biology: Interactions Among Scientific, Institutional, and Organizational Change." In *Sources of Industrial Leadership: Studies of Seven Industries*, edited by David Mowery, and Richard Nelson. Cambridge University Press.

Hensher, M., K. Kish, J. Farley, S. Quilley, and K. Zywert. 2020. "Open Knowledge Commons Versus Privatized Gain in a Fractured Information Ecology: Lessons from COVID-19 for the Future of Sustainability." *Global Sustainability* 3: E26. https://doi.org/10.1017/sus.2020.21.

Hollis, A. 2004. *Me-Too Drugs: Is There a Problem* [WHO report]. Accessed December 13, 2004. https://www.who.int/intellectualproperty/topics/ip/Me-tooDrugs_Hollis1.pdf.

IFPMA. 2012. "The New Frontiers of Biopharmaceutical Innovation." Report 27 Jan International Federation of Pharmaceutical Manufacturers and Associations., IFPMA Geneva. https://www.ifpma.org/publications/the-new-frontiers-of-biopharmaceutical-innovation/

IFPMA. 2023. Biopharmaceutical Innovation and Global Public Health, Facts and Figures 2022. International Federation of Pharmaceutical Manufacturers and Associations., IFPMA Geneva, https://www.ifpma.org/wp-content/uploads/2023/01/i2023_IFPMA-Facts-And-Figures-2022.pdf

IQVIA. 2019a. *Digital Health Trends 2021, Innovation, Evidence, Regulation, and Adoption*. IQVIA.

IQVIA. 2019b. *Emerging Biopharma's Contribution to Innovation, Assessing the Impact*. IQVIA.

Riazul Islam, S. M. R., D. Kwak, M. H. Humaun Kabir, M. Hossain, and K. S. Kwak. 2015. "The Internet of Things for Health Care: A Comprehensive Survey." *IEEE Access* 3: 678–708. https://doi.org/10.1109/ACCESS.2015.2437951.

Javaid, Mohd, and Ibrahim Haleem Khan. 2021. "Internet of Things (IoT) Enabled Healthcare Helps to Take the Challenges of COVID-19 Pandemic." *Journal of Oral Biology & Craniofacial Research* 11 (2): 209–214. https://doi.org/10.1016/j.jobcr.2021.01.015.

Johnson, Kevin B., Wei-Qi Wei, Dilhan Weeraratne, Mark E. Frisse, Karl Misulis, Kyu Rhee, Juan Zhao, and Jane L. Snowdon. 2021. "Precision Medicine, AI, and the Future of Personalized Health Care." *Clinical & Translational Science* 14 (1): 86–93. https://doi.org/10.1111/cts.12884.

Jovic, Thomas H., Emman J. Combellack, Zita M. Jessop, and Iain S. Whitaker. 2020 November 27. "3D Bioprinting and the Future of Surgery." *Frontiers in Surgery* 7: 609836. https://doi.org/10.3389/fsurg.2020.609836.

Kelly, Jaimon T., Katrina L. Campbell, Enying Gong, and Paul Scuffham. 2020. "The Internet of Things: Impact and Implications for Health Care Delivery." *Journal of Medical Internet Research* 22 (11): e20135. https://doi.org/10.2196/20135.

Khanna, I. 2012. "Drug Discovery in the Pharmaceutical Industry: Productivity Challenges and Trends." *Drug Discovery Today* 17 (19–20): 1088–1102.

Khurana, Amit, Prince Allawadhi, Isha Khurana, Sachin Allwadhi, Ralf Weiskirchen, Anil Kumar Banothu, Deepak Chhabra, Kamaldeep Joshi, and Kala Kumar Bharani. 2021. "Role of Nanotechnology Behind the Success of mRNA Vaccines for COVID-19." *Nano Today* 38: 101142. https://doi.org/10.1016/j.nantod.2021.101142.

Kituyi, M. 2020. *COVID-19: Collaboration Is the Engine of Global Science – Especially for Developing Countries.* World Economic Forum.

Kola, Ismail, and John Landis. 2004. "Can the Pharmaceutical Industry Reduce Attrition Rates?" *Nature Reviews. Drug Discovery* 3 (8): 711–715. https://doi.org/10.1038/nrd1470.

Kolluri, Sheela, Jianchang Lin, Rachael Liu, Yanwei Zhang, and Wenwen Zhang. 2022. "Machine Learning and Artificial Intelligence in Pharmaceutical Research and Development: A Review." *AAPS Journal* 24 (1): 19. https://doi.org/10.1208/s12248-021-00644-3.

Landry, Latrice G., Nadya Ali, David R. Williams, Heidi L. Rehm, and Vence L. Bonham. 2018. "Lack of Diversity in Genomic Databases Is A Barrier to Translating Precision Medicine Research into Practice." *Health Affairs (Project Hope)* 37 (5): 780–785. https://doi.org/10.1377/hlthaff.2017.1595.

Lee, Jenny J., and John P. Haupt. 2021. "Scientific Globalism During a Global Crisis: Research Collaboration and Open Access Publications on COVID-19." *Higher Education* 81 (5): 949–966. https://doi.org/10.1007/s10734-020-00589-0.

Li, Jinxing, Berta Esteban-Fernández de Ávila, Wei Gao, Liangfang Zhang, and Joseph Wang. 2017. "Micro/Nanorobots for Biomedicine: Delivery, Surgery, Sensing, and Detoxification." *Science Robotics* 2 (4): eaam6431. https://doi.org/10.1126/scirobotics.aam6431.

Li, Yvonne Y., and Steven Jm Jones. 2012. "Drug Repositioning for Personalized Medicine." *Genome Medicine* 4 (3): 27. http://doi.org/10.1186/gm326.

Ma, Tiancong, and Tian Xia. 2021. "Nanoparticle-Based Activatable Probes for Bioimaging." *Advanced Biology* 5 (1): e2000193. https://doi.org/10.1002/adbi.202000193.

MacEachern, Sarah J., and Nils D. Forkert. 2021. "Machine Learning for Precision Medicine." *Genome* 64 (4): 416–425. https://doi.org/10.1139/gen-2020-0131.

Mali, Shrikant. 2013. "Nanotechnology for Surgeons." *Indian Journal of Surgery* 75 (6): 485–492. https://doi.org/10.1007/s12262-012-0726-y.

Mathew, Essyrose, Giulia Pitzanti, Eneko Larrañeta, and Dimitrios A. Lamprou. 2020. "3D Printing of Pharmaceuticals and Drug Delivery Devices." *Pharmaceutics* 12 (3): 266. https://doi.org/10.3390/pharmaceutics12030266.

Mazzucato, M. 2013. *The Entrepreneurial State: Debunking the Public vs. Private Myth in Risk and Innovation*. Anthem Press; OECD. OECD (2016a): science technology and innovation outlook: (2015a): Government al Glance.

Miller, K. 2022. *A New Approach to Vaccinations: 3D Printed Patches, May 12, 2022, SCOPE Blog*. Stanford Medicine.

Mohs, Richard C., and Nigel H. Greig. 2017. "Drug Discovery and Development: Role of Basic Biological Research." *Alzheimer's & Dementia* 3 (4): 651–657. https://doi.org/10.1016/j.trci.2017.10.005.

Mohanty, S., M. Harun Ai Rashid, M. Mridul, C. Mohanty, and S. Swayamsiddha. 2020. "Application of Artificial Intelligence in COVID-19 drug repurposing." *Diabetes & Metabolic Syndrome* 14 (5): 1027–1031.

National Academies of Sciences, Engineering, and Medicine. 2012. "Evolution of translational omics: Lessons learned and the path forward." In *Omics-based clinical discovery: Science, technology, and applications*, edited by C. M. Micheel, S. J. Nass, and G. S. Omenn. National Academies Press (US).

National Institutes of Health. 2020. "Nanomedicine and the COVID-19 vaccines." *Nature Nanotechnology* 15: 963. https://doi.org/10.1038/s41565-020-00820-0.

National Pharmaceutical Council. 2012. "The State of Comparative Effectiveness Research and the Environment for Health Care Decision Making". https://www.npcnow.org/resources/state-comparative-effectiveness-research-and-environment-health-care-decision-making-2012.

Narang, A. K., and L. H. Nicholas. 2017. "Out-of-pocket spending and financial burden among Medicare beneficiaries with cancer." *JAMA Oncology* 3 (6): 757–765.

NCATS. 2020. *Translational Science Training at NCATS, Translational Science Training at NCATS*. nih.gov. National Center for Advancing Translational Sciences.

NIH. 2017. *Benefits of Nanotechnology for Cancer*. National Cancer Institute. Accessed August 8, 2017. https://www.cancer.gov/nano/cancer-nanotechnology/benefits.

O'Connell, Damian, and David Roblin. 2006 September. "Translational Research in the Pharmaceutical Industry: From Bench to Bedside." *Drug Discovery Today* 11 (17–18): 833–838. https://doi.org/10.1016/j.drudis.2006.07.009.

OECD. 2009. *The Bioeconomy to 2030, Designing a Policy Agenda*. OECD International Future Project, Organization for Economic Co-operation and Development Publishing.

OECD. 2015. *Innovation Policies for Inclusive Development. Scaling up Inclusive Innovation*. OECD.

OECD. 2016a. *Increasing Productivity in Small Traditional Enterprises: Programs for Upgrading*. OECD.

OECD. 2016b. "G20 Innovation Report, Report prepared for the G20 Science." Technology and Innovation Ministers Meeting: (2015). OECD: The Innovation Imperative: Contributing to Productivity, Growth and Well-Being.

OECD. 2020. *Challenges in Access to Oncology Medicines: Policies and Practices Across the OECD and the EU, OECD Health Working Papers, No. 123 (November 2020).* OECD.

OECD. 2021. *Using Trade to Fight COVID-19: Manufacturing and Distributing Vaccines.* OECD.

Paananen, J., and V. Fortino. 2020. "An omics perspective on drug target discovery platforms." *Briefings in Bioinformatics*, 21 (6): 1937–1953.

Pallotta A, I. Clarot, J. Sobocinski, E. Fattal, and A. Boudier. 2019. "Nanotechnologies for Medical Devices: Potentialities and Risks." *ACS Applied Bio Materials* 2 (1): 1–13.

Pammolli, Fabio, Lorenzo Righetto, Sergio Abrignani, Luca Pani, Pier Giuseppe Pelicci, and Emanuele Rabosio. 2020. "The Endless Frontier? The Recent Increase of R&D Productivity in Pharmaceuticals." *Journal of Translational Medicine* 18 (1): 162. https://doi.org/10.1186/s12967-020-02313-z.

Paul, Steven M., Daniel S. Mytelka, Christopher T. Dunwiddie, Charles C. Persinger, Bernard H. Munos, Stacy R. Lindborg, and Aaron L. Schacht. 2010. "How to Improve R&D Productivity: The Pharmaceutical Industry's Grand Challenge." *Nature Reviews. Drug Discovery* 9 (3): 203–214. https://doi.org/10.1038/nrd3078.

Pénin, J., and D. Neicu. 2018. "Patents and Open Innovation: Bad Fences Do Not Make Good Neighbors." *Journal of Innovation Economics* 25 (1): 57–85. https://doi.org/10.3917/jie.025.0057.

Perkmann, M., and K. Walsh. 2007. "University-Industry Relationships and Open Innovation: Towards a Research Agenda." *International Journal of Management Reviews* 9 (4): 259–280. https://doi.org/10.1111/j.1468-2370.2007.00225.x.

Popov, Vladimir V., Elena V. Kudryavtseva, Nirmal Kumar Katiyar, Andrei Shishkin, Stepan I. Stepanov, and Saurav Goel. 2022 March 14. "Industry 4.0 and Digitalisation in Healthcare." *Materials* 15 (6): 2140. https://doi.org/10.3390/ma15062140.

Raghupathi, Wullianallur, and Viju Raghupathi. 2014. "Big Data Analytics in Healthcare: Promise and Potential." *Health Information Science & Systems* 2: 3. https://doi.org/10.1186/2047-2501-2-3.

Roland, A., and A. Baker. 2023. *A New Look at R&D Productivity, How Small Changes to Key Levers Can Dramatically Impact Cost per Output, WHITE PAPER IQVIA 2023 Feb 3.* IQVIA.

Rosenblatt, Michael (2012). Feb. 2013. "How Academia and the Pharmaceutical Industry Can Work Together: The President's Lecture, Annual Meeting of the American Thoracic Society, San Francisco, California" [Special article]. *Annals of the American Thoracic Society* 10 (1): 31–38. https://doi.org/10.1513/AnnalsATS.201209-075PS.

Rubio, Doris McGartland, Ellie E. Schoenbaum, Linda S. Lee, David E. Schteingart, Paul R. Marantz, Karl E. Anderson, Lauren Dewey Platt, Adriana Baez, and Karin Esposito. 2010. "Defining Translational Research: Implications for Training." *Academic Medicine* 85 (3): 470–475. https://doi.org/10.1097/ACM.0b013e3181ccd618.

Schlake, Thomas, Andreas Thess, Mariola Fotin-Mleczek, and Karl-Josef Kallen. 2012. "Developing mRNA-Vaccine Technologies." *RNA Biology* 9 (11): 1319–1330. https://doi.org/10.4161/rna.22269.

Schuhmacher A., P.G. Germann, H. Trill, and O. Gassmann O. 2013. Models for open innovation in the pharmaceutical industry. *Drug Discovery Today* 18 (23–24): 1133–7. doi: 10.1016/j.drudis.2013.07.013. Epub 2013 Jul 26. PMID: 23892183

Schuhmacher, A., O. Gassmann, and M. Hinder. 2016. Changing R&D models in research-based pharmaceutical companies. *Journal of Translational Medicine* 14 (105). https://doi.org/10.1186/s12967-016-0838-4

Schuhmacher, Alexander, Oliver Gassmann, Nigel McCracken, and Markus Hinder. 2018. "Open Innovation and External Sources of Innovation. An Opportunity to Fuel the R&D Pipeline and Enhance Decision Making?" *Journal of Translational Medicine* 16 (1): 119. https://doi.org/10.1186/s12967-018-1499-2.

Seyhan, Attila A., and Claudio Carini. 2019. "Are Innovation and New Technologies in Precision Medicine Paving a New Era in Patients Centric Care?" *Journal of Translational Medicine* 17 (1): 114. https://doi.org/10.1186/s12967-019-1864-9.

Seyhan, A. A. 2019. "Lost in Translation: The Valley of Death Across Preclinical and Clinical Divide – Identification of Problems and Overcoming Obstacles." *Translational Medicine Communications* 4 (1): 18. https://doi.org/10.1186/s41231-019-0050-7.

Sharma, D., P. Patel, and M. A. Shah. 2023. "A Comprehensive Study on Industry 4.0 in the Pharmaceutical Industry for Sustainable Development." *Environmental Science & Pollution Research* 30 (39): 90088–90098. https://doi.org/10.1007/s11356-023-26856-y.

Shaw, Daniel L. 2017. "Is Open Science the Future of Drug Development?" *Yale Journal of Biology & Medicine* 90 (1): 147–151.

Shetty, R. C. 2006. "Benefits of Nanotechnology in Cardiovascular Surgery—A Review of Potential Applications." *US Cardiology* 3 (1): 95–6.

Shin, Matthew D., Sourabh Shukla, Young Hun Chung, Veronique Beiss, Soo Khim Chan, Oscar A. Ortega-Rivera, David M. Wirth, Angela Chen, Markus Sack, Jonathan K. Pokorski, and Nicole F. Steinmetz. 2020. "COVID-19 Vaccine Development and a Potential Nanomaterial Path Forward." *Nature Nanotechnology* 15 (8): 646–655. https://doi.org/10.1038/s41565-020-0737-y.

Shiroiwa, Takeru. 2020. "Cost-Effectiveness Evaluation for Pricing Medicines and Devices: A New Value-Based Price Adjustment System in Japan." *International Journal of Technology Assessment in Health Care* 36 (3): 270–276. https://doi.org/10.1017/S0266462320000264.

Smith, R. D., H. Thorsteinsdóttir, A.S. Daar, E.R. Gold, and P.A. Singers. 2004. "Genomics knowledge and equity: A global public goods perspective of the patent system." *Bulletin of the World Health Organization*, 82 (5): 385–389.

Stiglitz J E., and Wallsten. 1999. "Public-Private Technology Partnerships: Promises and Pitfalls. *American Behavioral Scientist*, 43 (1): 52–73. https://doi.org/10.1177/00027649921955155

Surendiran, A., S. Sandhiya, S. C. Pradhan, and C. Adithan. 2009. "Novel Applications of Nanotechnology in Medicine." *Indian Journal of Medical Research* 130 (6): 689–701.

Talaga, Patrice. 2010. "The Future of Pharmaceutical R&D: Somewhere Between Open and Reverse Innovation." *Future Medicinal Chemistry* 2 (9): 1399–1403. https://doi.org/10.4155/fmc.10.213.

Tassey, G. 2014. "Competing in Advanced Manufacturing: The Need for Improved Growth Models and Policies." *Journal of Economic Perspectives* 28 (1): 27–48. https://doi.org/10.1257/jep.28.1.27.

Tiwari, S., and R. Tiwari. 2022. *Leveraging Biotechnology for Sustainable and Inclusive Growth: Prospects for India-German.* Collaboration for Affordable Health Care. Consulate General of India.

Toole, A. A. 2007. "Does Public Scientific Research Complement Private Investment in Research and Development in the Pharmaceutical Industry?" *Journal of Law & Economics* 50 (1): 81–104. https://doi.org/10.1086/508314.

Tran, George, and S. Yousuf Zafar. 2018. "Financial Toxicity and Implications for Cancer Care in the Era of Molecular and Immune Therapies." *Annals of Translational Medicine* 6 (9): 166. https://doi.org/10.21037/atm.2018.03.28.

Tucker, Joseph D., Suzanne Day, Weiming Tang, and Barry Bayus. 2019. "Crowdsourcing in Medical Research: Concepts and Applications." *PeerJ* 7: e6762. https://doi.org/10.7717/peerj.6762.

Ural, A. 2023. "As Patent Cliff Looms for Biopharma Giants, Smaller Biotechs Face Cash Crunch, June 21, GEN Edge". https://www.genengnews.com/news/industry-news/as-patent-cliff-looms-for-biopharma-giants-smaller-biotechs-face-cash-crunch/.

Vermeulen, Niki, Gill Haddow, Tirion Seymour, Alan Faulkner-Jones, and Wenmiao Shu. 2017. "3D Bioprint Me: A Socioethical View of Bioprinting Human Organs and Tissues." *Journal of Medical Ethics* 43 (9): 618–624. https://doi.org/10.1136/medethics-2015-103347.

Vogenberg, F. Randy, Carol Isaacson Barash, and Michael Pursel. 2010. "Personalized Medicine: Part 1: Evolution and Development into Theranostics." *P & T: A Peer-Reviewed Journal for Formulary Management* 35 (10): 560–576.

WHO. 2018a. "International Agency for Research on cancer, press release 12 September 2018." World Health Organization Geneva.

WHO. 2018b. "Pricing of cancer medicines and its impacts, Technical Report, licence: CC BY-NC-SA 3.0 IGO." World Health Organization, Geneva.

WHO, WIPO and WTO. 2020. "Promoting Access to Medical Technologies and Innovation: Intersections between public health, intellectual property, and trade, 2nd Edition." World Health Organization, Geneva.

WHO. 2021a. "External reference pricing: WHO guideline on country pharmaceutical pricing policies. A plain language summary."

WHO. 2021b. "Value based pricing: WHO guideline on country pharmaceutical pricing policies. A plain language summary."

Woolf, Steven H. 2008. "The Meaning of Translational Research and Why It Matters." *JAMA* 299 (2): 211–213. https://doi.org/10.1001/jama.2007.26.

Zerhouni, E. A. 2003. "The NIH Road Map." *Science* 302 (63–64): 72.

Zhang, Y., Maoyu Li, Xiaomei Gao, Yongheng Chen, and Ting Liu. 2019. "Nanotechnology in Cancer Diagnosis: Progress, Challenges and Opportunities." *Journal of Hematology & Oncology* 12 (1): 137. https://doi.org/10.1186/s13045-019-0833-3.

Zhou, Y., F. Wang, J. Tang, R. Nussinov, and F. Cheng. 2020. "Artificial intelligence in COVID-19 drug repurposing." *The Lancet. Digital Health* 2 (12): e667–e676.

6 Controlling neglected tropical diseases and containing the growing risks of pandemics

Introduction: Neglected tropical diseases (NTDs) and pandemics

Neglected tropical diseases (NTDs) are a group of bacterial, parasitic, viral, and fungal infections that affect more than a billion people (one-sixth of the world's population) in the tropical and sub-tropical developing countries, where they mostly affect impoverished communities and disproportionately affect women and children (WHO 2020). Neglected tropical diseases (NTDs) are closely related to poverty.[1] The present system for developing medicines has largely failed to produce much-needed products that address the health needs of millions of people worldwide (Smith et al. 2009; Wirtz et al. 2017). The unmet treatment of medical needs causes high mortality and disability in developing poor countries (Weng et al. 2018). Neglected diseases are classified as those for which the market for medical treatment is insufficient to attract investment from the drug industry (Yamey et al. 2002). Global R&D efforts focus on diseases prevalent in wealthy countries (such as coronary heart disease) rather than those that primarily affect poor-country populations (such as malaria and HIV/AIDS) (World Bank Organization 2022; WTO 2022). Developing and low-income countries, accounting for nearly 85% of the global disease burden (Acharya and Pathak 2019), face several challenges, including limited human development resources, inadequate investment in basic and applied scientific research, under-resourced healthcare sector, poor institutions, inadequate health infrastructure and limited buffer capacity, and weak enforcement of disease prevention programs.

Pandemics—large-scale outbreaks of infectious and contagious diseases—are occurring frequently over the past century because of increased global travel and integration, urbanization, changes in land use, and greater exploitation of the natural environment (Madhav et al. 2017). The global scale outbreaks—"Black Swan" events[2]—pose a serious risk of greatly increasing morbidity and mortality over a wide geographic area and cause significant economic, social, and political disruption.

The above challenges warrant the critical role of the various actors: industry, public bodies, not-for-profit organizations, and supranational institutions toward the discovery of new therapies for neglected diseases and to control the

DOI: 10.4324/9781003449331-6

risks of pandemics. Concerted efforts are required to build production capacity in developing countries; otherwise, people in the least developed economies would remain vulnerable to tropical diseases and contagion (WHO 2021b). NTDs are formally recognized as targets for global action in SDG target 3.3, which calls to "end the epidemic of ... neglected tropical diseases" by 2030, as part of Goal 3 (Ensure healthy lives and ensure well-being for all at all ages) (WHO 2020, p 4). Pandemic preparedness plans are also essential to counter the recurring global threat to human lives and economic stability.

Addressing the challenge of NTDs

Stimulation of R&D and production of drugs to treat tropical diseases require strategies and measures other than the conventional patent tool, since in developing countries consumers' ability to pay is insufficient to recoup R&D investments (Stigliz and Jayadev 2010; Danzon 2011; Wirtz et al. 2017; WHO, WIPO, and WTO 2020). For health interventions to achieve the desired health improvement outcome, a range of market "Push" and "Pull" mechanisms are proposed to tackle NTDs (Trouiller et al. 2002; Weng et al. 2018; WHO, WIPO, and WTO 2020). "Push" mechanism aims at cutting the cost of R&D for industry (such as open sources, public investment in R&D, grants, subsidized loans, and investment tax credits), and the "Pull" mechanism aims at increasing market attractiveness (through instituting innovation, "prizes," rewards, orphan drug status, advance purchase commitment) (Weng et al. 2018). Together, these mechanisms create more attractive markets, lower uncertainty, and raise profit margins, thereby stimulating increased investment in R&D. The following are among the most prominently suggested strategies aimed to deliver new health solutions with greater speed and less cost:

- Donations from the philanthropic organizations
- Open-source innovation network, including PDP model for tropical diseases
- Complementing the patent system with supplementary strategies (such as prizes and awards)
- Improving manufacturing capabilities in developing countries
- Preventive strategies for ending tropical diseases

Donations from philanthropic organizations

The member states of WHO, the pharmaceutical industry, charitable foundations, and non-governmental organizations have jointly engaged in initiatives in recent years to fund and develop new treatments for diseases affecting developing countries and to increase access to existing healthcare products (WHO 2008). Product development partnerships (PDPs) are typically funded by philanthropic organizations in collaboration with public agencies since such projects for NTDs lack commercial profitability. Funding from philanthropic organizations, however, has been found to be inadequate, and it rarely is effective at moving products through the pipeline to patients (Hecht et al. 2009; Moran 2011).[3] The strategy for improving access to medicines for NTDs through donation programs has achieved only partial success and lacks long-term sustainability. Several new financing mechanisms have been launched recently, such as the Global Health Innovative Technology Fund, the European and Developing Countries Clinical Trials Partnership, and the RIGHT Fund, to attract the necessary funding to maintain progress towards elimination of neglected diseases (WHO 2021b; WIPO 2022). Public-private partnerships that provide funding to bridge research gaps are considered to be an effective needs-driven approach to deal with NTDs. The search for medicines to combat NTDs has resulted in the booming collaboration of not-for-profit organizations with industry, global research networks, and international initiatives to boost the prevention, control, elimination, and eradication of NTDs toward 2020 (Engels and Zhou 2020).

Open-source drug discovery model for controlling tropical diseases

Research is an essential component of every tropical disease control program (Hotez et al. 2004). Open-source drug discovery and development builds on two principles (WHO, WIPO, and WTO 2020). First, open-source models are based on the idea of collaboration, that is, organizing and motivating groups of independent researchers to contribute to research projects. Second, it is based on an open approach to sharing of IP in the public domain or the use of customized licenses. The development of the COVID-19 vaccine in a record time is a remarkable example that can be credited to open science, industry partnerships, harmonization of clinical trials, sharing of collective research knowledge, and the altruism of study participants (Golob et al. 2021; Besançon et al. 2021). The urgency associated with the pandemic had created an imperative to accelerate the adoption of open science. Bringing the vaccine to market with billions of doses produced in record time was made possible by the vital role played by the governments and the collective and collaborative work of thousands of researchers and research institutions (Stiglitz 2022).

Open-source approaches can yield several benefits:

(a) Cost reduction through collaboration (Masum and Harris 2011; Besançon et al. 2021)
(b) The creation of commons (Masum and Harris 2011)
(c) Access to non-exclusive licenses to build production capacity where it is lacking (WHO 2021a)
(d) Sharing of large data sets in the public domain to foster "repurposing" of existing clinical drugs (Nwaka et al. 2009; Allarakhia 2013; Weng et al. 2018)[4]

International organizations, industry, and not-for-profit organizations including World Health are playing strategic roles in coordinating and promoting joint research and production activities to control NTDs. In the late 1990s, an innovative collaboration model for R&D for neglected diseases emerged in the form of public-private partnerships (PPPs) that came to be known as product development partnerships (PDPs). PDPs address the lack of commercial incentive to undertake R&D for vaccines, diagnostics, and drugs for neglected diseases of the developing world. To fast-track medicine development, one of the imperatives is the sharing of intellectual capital resources on the basis of royalty agreements (Edlin 2011; Lezaun and Montgomery 2015). WIPO Re: Search initiative emphasizes the role of IP sharing as a partnering mechanism (Lezaun and Montgomery 2015). WIPO Re: Search Consortium unites public and private market forces to address neglected tropical diseases (NTDs), malaria, and tuberculosis (TB) through the sharing of intellectual property across sectors and geographies. These open-science initiatives, discussed below, are used as catalyst strategies.

Product development partnerships (PDPs) and WIPO Re: Search initiative

PDPs are public-private partnerships established to address the lack of commercial incentive to undertake R&D for vaccines, diagnostics, and drugs for neglected diseases of the developing world. WHO works closely with PDPs to support them in their efforts to develop much-needed new health technologies to fight poverty-related and neglected diseases and to ensure that these technologies become quickly accessible to the most vulnerable populations (WHO 2021b). PDPs, such as "Open-Source," involve the collaboration of not-for-profit organizations and international agencies, such as DNDi (Drugs for Neglected Disease Initiative) and Tropical Disease Research (TDR) (Special Program for Research and Training), as a global vehicle of scientific collaboration.

DNDi is a not-for-profit drug R&D organization in NTDs based in Geneva, Switzerland, whose aim is to respond to the dire need for safe, affordable, easy to-use, and efficacious treatments for the neglected population. This initiative has delivered 12 affordable new treatments for six deadly diseases, as of 2022 (DNDi webpage). In 2021, WHO, together with the Drugs for Neglected Disease initiative (DNDi), established the Global Antibiotic Research and Development Partnership (GARDP) to develop new treatments for drug-resistant infections (WHO 2022a).

TDR was formed in 1974 with the two interdependent objectives of developing improved tools for the control of tropical diseases and strengthening the research capability of affected countries themselves. Thousands of scientists worldwide have benefited from training and research support facilitated by TDR (Reeder 2014). The open-access, web-accessible TDR Targets database is particularly important in tropical infectious disease research (Magariños et al. 2012).

WIPO Re: Search is a unique initiative of working on 19 neglected diseases, some of which had not yet been included in the prevailing list of NTDs. WIPO, in collaboration with public-sector and private-sector researchers and BIO Ventures for Global Health, has launched a new consortium called WIPO Re: Search in October 2011. This consortium is increasingly filling research gaps by bringing together knowledge, tangible assets, skills, and infrastructure from the private, non-profit, and academic sectors in the quest for new treatments for NTDs (Bombelles et al. 2015; Weng et al. 2018). Under this program, public-sector and private-sector organizations share IP (intellectual property) assets and expertise with the global health research community, using selected royalty-free licenses (Bombelles et al. 2015; WHO, WIPO and WTO 2020). Companies participating in WIPO Re: Search have agreed to grant royalty-free licenses for R&D and manufacture for the sole purpose of addressing public health needs for NTDs in least-developed countries (WHO, WIPO, and WTO 2020; WIPO 2022). Progress has been made in the direction of developing critical disease-specific technologies—drugs, vaccines, diagnostics, and vector control agents[5]—that are facilitating the control or elimination of many of the world's NTDs (Hotez et al. 2016).

Prizes and awards for incentivizing R&D for NTDs

Market mechanisms, such as intellectual property rights (IPRs), do not work for incentivizing medical R&D for NTDs (WHO, WIPO, and WTO 2020). A key factor of the above market failure is the limited purchasing power of both governments and patients in the countries where such diseases predominate.

There are suggestions to create a Global Fund for Public Goods (GFPG) to ensure sustainable financing for global public goods (Peacock 2022; Moon et al. 2017). Other measures for promoting medical R&D in lower and middle income countries (LIMCs) include the establishment of disease-specific partnerships, such as the International AIDS Vaccine Initiative, the Global Alliance for Tuberculosis Drug Development, and the Medicines for Malaria Venture, for example, which have resulted in over 70 such global health partnerships (Smith et al. 2004). Such global models of collaborations require all countries to make funding contributions for research, development, and manufacture of COVID-19 vaccines to help reduce barriers to making vaccination a global public good.

South-south cooperation: A network to strengthen developing countries capabilities

Most of the product development public-private partnerships (PD-PPP) referred to in the earlier section are funded by industrialized countries. However, there are concerns about sufficiency and sustainability of such partnerships in future, because of the sheer magnitude of the problem. (Morel et al. 2005). Developing countries with innovation capabilities can play a significant role of leading innovations in health products for NTDs by sharing experiences and conducting collaborative programs and public-private collaborations (Morel et al. 2005). South-south cooperation in the area of medicine offers real hopes for the achievement of several MDGs, and such cooperation may be the only viable way to improve the availability and affordability of essential medicines and vaccines (Nwaka et al. 2009).

Innovative developing countries (IDCs): Their potential role in south-south cooperation

Innovative developing countries (IDCs) are themselves advancing new health technologies, products, and services (Morel et al. 2005). Rapidly growing health innovation capabilities of some developing countries' IDCs are distinguished by the following capabilities (Morel et al. 2005, Vasconcellos et al. 2018):

- They have the capacity to develop, manufacture, ensure safety, and market new health products and to develop, test, and introduce new health policies or strategies.
- They are distinguished by their rapidly growing strength in health innovation as illustrated by increasing patenting and publishing activities and increasing investments in technology by both the public and private sectors.
- They have a rapidly growing number of health technology companies
- They are able to analyze, evaluate, and adopt new practices and technologies

Among the scientific publications in international journals, evidence shows that IDCs do prioritize NTDs as an area of research (Vasconcellos et al. 2018). Brazil, Thailand, Argentina, Indonesia, India, Mexico, Singapore, and Malaysia are found to be the counties with the larger proportion of publications in NTDs compared to the global average of publications addressing at least one NTD during the period 2005–2017 (Vasconcellos et al. 2018). In regard to the research publications addressing E-Bola (in West Africa) and Zika (in South America) epidemics during 2014–2016, Brazil ranked among the top five countries (just behind the US but ahead of France, UK, and Italy) in the co-authorship networks focusing on the epidemics (Vasconcellos et al. 2018).

Table 6.1 presents evidence on the research specialization of selected IDCs' three broad areas of NTDs (tropical communicable diseases, medicines, and vaccines for tuberculosis and HIV). This specialization is measured as the proportion of research publications by a given country on a given disease divided by the proportion of global publications on the disease (UNESCO 2021). For example, a country that devotes 2% of its output to a research topic that represents 1% of all research output worldwide on the same topic would score 2.00, as it produces twice as much output as expected, relative to the global average (UNESCO 2021). The Table 6.1 shows varying patterns of specialization of countries in basic research on communicable and contagious diseases.

Through intensive research collaboration in tropical diseases, these countries can generate innovative medical products at affordable prices. The success

Table 6.1 Research publications in tropical diseases: specialization of emerging nations

Specialization Index (2011–2019)			
Countries	*Tropical Communicable Diseases*	*Medicine and Vaccines for Tuberculosis*	*Human Immunodeficiency Virus (HIV)*
Brazil	4.16	1.46	1.3
China	0.34	0.53	0.3
India	1.86	NA	0.97
Russia	0.17	0.87	0.33
South Africa	2.41	9.13	10.23
Singapore	1.58	1.05	0.54

Source: UNESCO 2021

depends upon the effective strong public-private partnership in filling the knowledge gaps. Evidence is now emerging from the north-south and south-south drug discovery networks that human and institutional capacity can be built around drug discovery projects with clear product milestones and deliverables (Morel et al. 2005; Nwaka et al. 2009).

International initiatives to promote local manufacturing base in developing countries

To strengthen the global supply system and to increase timely access to essential medicines, numerous concerned stakeholders (government leaders, industry associations, technology experts and innovators, civil society, and the international community) have stressed the importance of local production. The World Local Production Forum (WLPF) is a new initiative of WHO with a focus on improving access to quality, safe, and effective tropical medicines (WHO 2021a). Encouraging local production is deemed a long-term sustainable solution ('t Hoen and Moon 2001; UNCTAD 2011; Stevens and Huys 2017).

Bringing biomedical inventions to populations in less-developed regions of the world has a great potential of narrowing down the large disparity emerging between the developed and developing world in accessing affordable medicines (WHO 2010). Since the 1970s, multilateral organizations and donor governments have played various facilitating roles in supporting the development of local pharmaceutical production capacity and relevant technology transfer. WHO's Special Program for Research and Training in Tropical Diseases (TDR) initiated in 1975 is a critical global program aimed at strengthening research capacity of poor affected countries to tackle NTDs (Minja et al. 2011).

TDR: A global program to develop research capabilities in developing countries

TDR is co-sponsored by the United Nations Children's Fund (UNICEF), the United Nations Development Program (UNDP), the World Bank, and the World Health Organization (WHO). TDR works with a vast network of researchers and public health practitioners in low- and middle-income countries to ensure that scientific evidence continues to be generated and translated into safe, effective, equitable, and accessible health solutions for populations (WHO 2023). Currently, TDR is engaged with 12 countries for implementation of a multisectoral approach (MSA) to control vector-borne diseases, of which six started implementing in 2022 (WHO 2023).

The engagement of stakeholders at the country level facilitates the design of more specific and comprehensive strategies based on local needs (Minja et al. 2011). TDR supports the career development of young scientists to pursue studies leading to acquisition of a postgraduate degree (MSc or PhD) at the institutions of their home countries (Minja et al. 2011). With the help of this program, it is estimated that in 2021, 25% fewer people required interventions against NTDs than in 2010, and more than one billion people were treated for NTDs each year between 2016 and 2019 through mass treatment interventions (WHO 2023). As of December 2022, 47 countries had eliminated at least one NTD (WHO 2023).

Preventive measures: The WHO roadmap of ending tropical diseases by 2030

Poverty, lack of sanitation, poor knowledge of tropical diseases among the inhabitants, and inadequate health resources are among the leading obstacles to the prevention of NTDs. A number of NTDs are zoonotic (an infectious disease that is transmitted between species from animals to humans, or from humans to animals) and most are vector borne, the control strategies based only on treating the infected human population are unlikely to be successful (Weng et al. 2018). To control the occurrence and spread of tropical diseases, the World Health Organization (WHO 2010) has recommended five public health strategies for the prevention: preventive chemotherapy; intensified case management; vector control[6]; the provision of safe water, sanitation, and hygiene; and veterinary public health (to control the illnesses that spread between animals and people). The least developed countries also have the poorest health and sanitation infrastructure. More than 950 million people still have inadequate sanitation, and 553 million lack access to clean drinking water (Reed and McKerrow 2018).

WHO (2021b), in its new release of a road map for ending tropical diseases by 2030, has suggested the use of new interventions (new advanced treatment approaches), tools (Novel vector control tools), and diagnostics. One key requirement for countries to achieve the targets is to develop a national health system that will ensure the delivery of interventions through existing infrastructures, improve the sustainability and efficiency of interventions, and ensure that patients have equitable access to all aspects of treatment, care, and support (WHO 2021b). WHO has urged developing countries to invest $1 per person per year until 2030 to tackle 17 neglected tropical diseases (NTDs) and improve the health and well-being of more than 1.5 billion people (Kelland 2015). The funding of basic research on NTDs needs to be increased to capitalize on new, innovative technology in order to discover new drug targets, biomarkers, and strategies for vector control (Reed and McKerrow 2018).

Combating pandemics: Preparedness and resilience for future threats

There is always a lingering danger of the onset of pandemics due to the growing interactions of humans with animals, mostly wildlife, to meet the daily needs of life such as food, fiber, livelihoods, travel, sport, companionship, etc. (Leach et al. 2021). Animals can sometimes carry harmful germs that can spread to people and cause illness—these are known as zoonotic diseases or zoonoses. Further, the unabated hazardous effects of climate change also pose a grave risk of bringing more extreme weather events and new outbreaks of infectious diseases (Javorcik 2020; WTO 2021). With increased globalization and migration of people, the likelihood of pandemics is projected to increase. The Threat of Impending Pandemics calls for a proactive approach.

Safeguarding against future pandemics

COVID-19 has challenged local, national, regional, and global capacities to prepare and respond. The pandemic has made it clear that we need anticipatory rather than reactive systems to protect humanity from pandemics. Future preparedness requires addressing the major vulnerabilities of the international production and trading system, as well as addressing the fragilities of the public health system and global inequity in the availability of essential medical products.

The key strategic options for future preparedness taken at country and international levels include the following (see Table 6.2):

- Strengthening the global supply chains
- Addressing inequity in access to vaccine-promoting technology transfer
- Building surge capacity and rejuvenating the national public health system
- Public health surveillance and information management
- Global governance to coordinate the global health response

Strengthening the global supply chain

Global pandemics have revealed the critical importance of the supply chain to deliver medicines and medical products across the globe without much loss of human life. Epidemic outbreaks are a special case of supply chain risks (Ivanov 2020). The global supply chain during the COVID-19 pandemic has been a center of controversy. A closer examination of the developments during COVID-19, however, reveals that it was not the failure of the global supply chain per se, there were several other factors that caused severe disruptions.

Table 6.2 Pandemic preparedness

Measures of Future Preparedness	*Goals*
Expanding international production sites for manufacturing intermediates and medical supplies (Gereffi 2020)	Strengthening the global supply chains resilience
Building surge capacity (contingency planning for extending the capacity of intensive care units and beds, augmenting front-line staff, rapid testing and detection facilities, and training arrangement for health workers in critical areas) (Hick et al. 2014)	To contain the infection chain and to handle sudden spurt in demand for health resources
Pathogen surveillance and sharing of information on viruses (IFPMA 2023)	Sharing of pathogen genome data is critical for preventing, detecting, and responding to epidemics and pandemics at national and international levels, and is in the interest of all member states (WHO 2022b).
Commitment to Global Equity and Solidarity (IFPMA 2023)	Prevent the spread of infectious diseases, reduce the global disease burden, achieve UN's Sustainable Goal 3 on health
Technology transfer to enhance developing countries' indigenous production of essential medical goods (IFPMA 2023)	Technology sharing helps develop absorptive capacity and narrow the technology gap in developing countries
Integrating the fast-emerging countries in the global supply chain (Nicita et al. 2013; WHO 2013; Gereffi 2020)	Strengthening the global supply chain, tapping the market potential of fast emerging countries, and promoting "frugal" innovations in medical products
Strengthening the healthcare system of countries (IFPMA 2023)	Universal Health Care System (IFPMA 2023)
Carbo vigilance: curtailing the global pharmaceutical carbon footprint (Belkhir and Elmeligi 2019; Ray et al. 2021)	Monitoring sustainable development goal 12 (SDG12: ensuring sustainable consumption and production patterns, which is key to sustaining the livelihoods of current and future generations)

One of them was heavy dependence of the world on China with regard to the critical imports of medical components and products. It has been reported that around 51,000 companies around the world have one or more direct suppliers in Wuhan and at least five million companies around the world have one or more tier-two suppliers in the Wuhan region, COVID-19's origin (Ivanov 2020). Chinese industrial disruption, due to the COVID-19 outbreak, hit other nations via "supply-chain contagion" (Baldwin and Tomiura 2020). Other major accountable factors include COVID-19-related restrictions (like quarantine measures) imposed by the countries (Miroudot 2020), sudden massive surge of demand for medical goods (Gereffi 2020), trade restrictions imposed by exporting countries to hoard medical supplies (World Bank Organization and WTO 2022), limited surge capacity of hospitals' resources, among others.

Despite the significant strains on supply chains at the national and international levels, the coordinating and monitoring efforts of the WTO and WHO, along with the emergence of new supply sources, kept the global chain moving and resilient. Given the integrated nature of global manufacturing, there is no alternative to international trade to meet the swift rise in pandemic-driven demand for essential medical goods (Baldwin and Tomiura 2020). Trade data derived from the international input-output tables[7] of OECD countries sheds evidence that a typical vaccine-manufacturing plant uses about 9,000 different materials sourced from some 300 suppliers across approximately 30 different countries (WTO 2021). Trade also plays a critical role in the distribution of vaccines, requiring optimal levels of temperature for storage (WTO 2021).

Supply chain resilience and responsiveness are important to cope with sudden variations. Resilience can be defined as the ability to return to normal operations over an acceptable post-disruption period. Miroudot (2020) makes a distinction between resilience and robustness. Miroudot (2020) defines robustness as the ability to maintain operations during a crisis. In his view, GVCs proved to be rather robust during the pandemic and addressed the shortages in the supply of essential medical goods. There are many noteworthy instances of speedy responses to meet sudden upsurge of medical needs. In a short span of time, the pharmaceutical companies built new supply chains, sourced mRNA[8] and other key ingredients from foreign suppliers, and scaled up production to deliver more than 11.5 billion doses in less than two years (WTO 2022). In Korea, a new industry emerged that started exporting COVID-19 test kits to more than 100 countries in a short span of time (Miroudot 2020). Within weeks of the pandemic's spread, garment-makers in India, Malaysia, and Sri Lanka had transformed themselves into personal protective equipment (PPE) manufacturers, taking advantage of surging global demand for face masks, rubber gloves, and protective gowns (WTO 2021). Several manufacturers have successfully developed COVID-19 vaccines in less than 12 months—an extraordinary achievement, given it typically takes a decade or longer to develop new vaccines (Wouters et al. 2021).

Expanding international production sites for manufacturing

Currently, a few countries dominate and control the production and trade of medical goods and devices because high R&D intensity and advanced manufacturing capabilities are needed to develop novel and innovative therapeutics. Internationally, more diversified supply sources and expanding networks generate benefits of reducing vulnerability in disruptive times (OECD 2020; IMF 2022; Malacrino et al. 2022).

Integration of emerging economies into the global supply chains with untapped potential can mitigate the vulnerability of the global supply of critical components and medical supplies to disruptions, as many have untapped potential. Many emerging nations, besides offering a cost advantage in such key areas as clinical research, are attracting foreign investment for reasons including the abundance of young talent in science and technology and their rapidly expanding healthcare markets (Grimes and Miozzo 2015). Countries in Eastern Europe and Eastern and Southern Mediterranean possess good production capabilities and export potential but have remained less popular destinations for foreign investment (Javorcik 2020). These markets are attractive for investment, because of the increasing income, availability of human capital, and low-cost wages. Greater participation of countries in global trade and manufacturing are more likely to encourage greater competition and ensure access to quality and affordable medical products. Governments can incentivize the production in medical supplies in critical areas that meet the global demand. Through FDI or compulsory licensing, firms in developing countries can integrate into the global value chains, and partake in technology transfer with the help of international suppliers (Brach and Kappel 2009; Rodrik 2018). Evidence indicates that global value chains (GVCs) are a vehicle for the transfer of technology to trading partners (Rodrik 2018; Rigo 2021).[9]

Addressing vaccine inequity challenge

There is a lack of equitable access to vaccines in the low- and middle income developing nations. Vaccines are manufactured and exported by fewer countries, since their production is more complex and R&D-intensive (OECD 2021; Bown and Bollyky 2021). It is estimated that 74% of the eight billion global population live in low- and middle-income countries. The limited supply of COVID-19 vaccine has posed a serious threat to the lives and well-being of billions of people in LIMCs and herd immunity (which states that only a proportion of a population needs to be immune). The world had a normal capacity of production of 3.5 billion doses of vaccines at the time of the outbreak, which fell short by 10 million required doses to enable more equitable global access ('t Hoen et al. 2021). Addressing vaccine inequity is of paramount need for future preparedness. Inequity affects us all, with ongoing risk of new variants emerging until global herd immunity is strengthened (Hunter et al. 2022; Pilkington et al. 2022). Prevention of diseases by vaccination has become a key to the cost-effective reduction of mortality, improvement of life expectancy, and economic growth (Kumraj et al. 2022). Inadequate global production capacity of vaccine represents an unprecedented and urgent need for scale-up to achieve global vaccine equity (Asundi et al. 2021; 't Hoen et al. 2021). It is growingly realized that without the push toward vaccine self-reliance and decentralized bottom-up manufacturing worldwide, vaccine equity cannot be achieved (Yamey et al. 2022).

Scaling up vaccine production capacity: Need for technology and technical-know transfer to LIMCs

The long-term solution to global inequity requires persistent efforts to strengthen the local production capacity in economically poor regions and countries through technology transfer and sharing of knowledge on how to make vaccines, including ingredients, methods, sourcing, and technologies (Kavanagh et al. 2021; Asundi et al. 2021; Kumraj et al. 2022). Countries may not have the technical know-how and capability to produce such technologies. Transfer of know-how will therefore be critical to enable scale-up ('t Hoen et al. 2021). Technology transfer acts as a two-edged weapon: it is the best way to stop pandemics as well as it is an effective way to achieve equity (WTO 2022; News Room). Technology transfer requires promoting collective and coordinated management of IP rights and know-how, that call for a proactive role of multilateral organizations.

Multilateral initiatives

The WHO and other multilateral organizations (such as the World Bank) have launched several global initiatives to help developing countries to get access to required technology through collaborative efforts. The following are among the prominent initiatives:

- The formation of Coalition for Epidemic Preparedness Innovations (CEPI) in 2017
- Creation of COVAX, an initiative that supports the development and manufacture, procurement, and equitable distribution of COVID-19 vaccines
- Establishment of the COVID-19 Technology Access Pool (C-TAP) on May 29, 2020
- Creation of vaccine technology transfer hubs in developing countries

CEPI and COVAX

CEPI (pronounced "seppy") is a global partnership between public, private, philanthropic, and civil society organizations that aim to accelerate the development of vaccines against emerging infectious diseases and enable access to these vaccines for people during outbreaks. CEPI was officially launched in January 2017 as a global mechanism to explore and develop new ways to stimulate, finance, and coordinate vaccine development against priority public health threats, in alignment with the WHO.

COVAX is a collaboration between CEPI, Gavi (the vaccine alliance founded by the Gates Foundation), and the World Health Organization (WHO) with UNICEF established in June 2020. Its goal is to ensure that all countries and territories participating in COVAX have equitable access to COVID-19 vaccines.

Technology access pool (C-TAP) and MPP (Medicine Patent Pool)

In May 2020, WHO, the Government of Costa Rica, and other partners launched the COVID-19 Technology Access Pool (C-TAP) to facilitate faster equitable and affordable access to COVID-19 health products for people in all countries. C-TAP is a single platform for the developers of COVID-19 health products—vaccines, tests, medical devices, and treatments—to share their know-how, intellectual property (IP), and data with quality-assured manufacturers. A "pool" is an effective and efficient tool to bring new technologies together to be used at a fair price and be subject to payment of "royalties" to the developers. The non-exclusive licensing agreements under C-TAP increase the global production capacity and reduce the dependency on just a few companies for the production.

The existing Medicines Patent Pool (MPP) shows that such a pool is a realistic and efficient option that is compatible with international human rights and trade law. The Medicines Patent Pool is a UN-based organization dedicated to increasing access to affordable medicines through voluntary patent licensing. It was created in 2010 with the initial mandate of expanding access to treatment to combat the HIV pandemic. Its mandate has since been expanded several times, and now includes all patented medicines on the WHO's Essential Medicines List, as well as new technologies to combat COVID-19. The MPP works by negotiating non-exclusive, transparent licenses to use patents on key medical technology in low- and middle-income countries.

The most important difference between C-TAP and the Medicines Patent Pool (MPP) is that the MPP develops licensing deals for a limited set of countries, whereas C-TAP seeks to conclude global licensing agreements. The success of C-TAP to mitigate the vaccine inequity hinges on the willingness of the pharmaceutical industry to engage and share the knowledge of modern vaccine technology.

Creation of vaccine technology transfer hub

The WHO has created vaccine hubs, such as the mRNA vaccine hubs in South Africa and five other African countries (Hunter et al. 2022). The hub is a partnership between Afrigen (a biotech company), Biovac (a vaccine manufacturer), universities, and Africa CDC. Since the project's start, *hubs* in Argentina, Bangladesh, Brazil, India, Indonesia, South Africa, and Vietnam have built laboratories to develop their own *vaccines.* This holds a great promise of locally developed and manufactured vaccines for COVID-19 and protection against future pandemics (Hunter et al. 2022). Under this initiative, WHO and its partners will provide training and financial support to build the necessary human capital for production know-how, quality control, and product regulation, and will assist where needed with the necessary licenses (WHO 2021c).

While the focus is currently on COVID-19, it is hoped that the hub can be used to develop and manufacture at-scale vaccines to tackle other killer diseases like HIV, tuberculosis, malaria, and leishmaniasis, putting countries in the driver's seat to produce the tools required to meet their health needs (Kagame et al. 2023).

Need for waiving IP rights for publicly funded vaccine

The success of the above-mentioned initiatives critically depends on the willingness of the pharmaceutical countries to let others use their technology through mechanisms that facilitate IP sharing ('t Hoen et al. 2021). But barriers exist in the form of multiple patent rights. The evidence shows that mRNA vaccine technologies are covered by more than 100 patents, with many different patent holders (Kavanagh et al. 2021). To address the legal barriers, the COVID-19 TRIPS waiver was proposed by India and South Africa jointly in October 2020.

Researchers have pleaded to consider COVID-19 vaccines as a universal public good[10] to be shared globally without IP protection claims (Yunus et al. 2020; WTO 2021; UNESCO 2021 press release Feb 2021; Brown and Susskind 2020; Sariola 2021; Peacock 2022; Padrós Selma 2022). International bodies such as UNESCO's International Bioethics Committee (IBC) and the World Commission on the Ethics of Scientific Knowledge and Technology (COMEST) have urged that vaccines be treated as a global public good to ensure they are made equitably available in all countries (UNESCO 2021).

Global public goods have two characteristics: (i) these goods are non-rivalrous—meaning that using them doesn't reduce the amount for anyone else, and (ii) they must also be non-excludable, meaning that it should be impossible to prevent anyone else from getting the benefits (Joi 2020). The rationale for treating COVID-19 vaccine as a public good is that much of the pioneering research work on mRNA vaccines was carried out using knowledge generated in the public domain by the collaborative work of thousands of researchers, and by using public research funds (Lalani et al. 2022; Stiglitz 2022; Peacock 2022). There is a consensus among experts that TRIPs-waiver proposal alone would not serve as a complete solution, insofar as it would not adequately address the critical issue of access to know-how and confidential data ('t Hoen et al. 2011; Perehudoff et al. 2021). Given that a successful scaling up of COVID-19 vaccine production is in everyone's interest, it is essential that governments and international agencies strongly support technology transfer and make available vaccines at affordable prices.

Building critical care capacity and rejuvenating the national health system

A sudden spurt of pandemics places extraordinary constraints on healthcare services due to increased demand, especially in intensive care units (ICU), combined with limited capacity. Healthcare organizations need to rapidly build surge capacity to expand their operations. Pandemic causes significant disruption in health service delivery particularly in resource-limited countries.

The evidence from COVID-19 shows that countries with an under-resourced health system and poor infrastructure suffered an avoidable heavy toll on human lives and the spread of the deadly virus. Patients waiting for life-saving surgery suffered physical and mental agony due to the cancellation or postponement. The following discussion sheds information on the measures to promote a resilient and sustainable healthcare system.

Building a resilient health system

A critical aspect of a country's response to an epidemic is the surge capacity of the health system; that is, the health system's capacity to absorb and accommodate the acute increase in the demand of healthcare services (Barasa et al. 2020). Surge capacity is considered to have four elements: (i) staff (medical personnel, doctors, nurses, pharmacists), (ii) stuff (critical care medicines equipment and supplies), (iii) structures (national laboratory networks, designated hospitals, senior homes and residential facilities, public health infrastructure[11]), and (iv) systems (successful intragovernmental coordination and management of various levels of the healthcare system, surveillance systems, adequate public funding, and support for the poor) (Ducharme 2020; Izmirlieva 2020; Legido-Quigley et al. 2020). As a part of the surge capacity, public health experts have stressed the need to create cohort ICUs for COVID-19 patients (areas separated from the rest of the ICU beds) to minimize the risk of in-hospital transmission (also called Nosocomial infections) (Aitken and Jeffires 2001; Grasselli et al. 2020).

China is a leading example of scaling up resources to improve the medical surge capacity to rapidly cope with public health emergencies, caused by the COVID-19 outbreak in Wuhan. To fight COVID-19, China adopted three methods of accommodating the health needs of patients for treatment in Wuhan: expanding hospitals' capacity and building newly temporary health centers and Fangcang shelter units. The Fangcang shelter hospitals in China are a novel concept of large-scale temporary hospitals, rapidly built (built overnight) by converting existing public venues, such as stadiums and exhibition centers, into healthcare facilities (Chen et al. 2020). These shelter hospitals had key three characteristics: rapid construction, massive scale, and low cost. China severely restricted movement across Hubei Province in 16 cities, affecting more than 50 million people. Authorities had closed public transit and canceled outbound transportation (air, train, and long-haul buses). Vehicular traffic in Wuhan was banned (Phelan et al. 2020). The Chinese government shored up its surge capacity in the nick of time by recalling and deploying 1,400 medical personnel from the military service.

Rejuvenating the national health systems with contingency plans

The pandemic, COVID-19, has exposed key deficiencies of emergency preparedness and contingency provisions in countries. These deficiencies include scanty strategic reserves of personal protective equipment, front-line resources for timely testing, intensive care unit (ICU) devices, consumables, and pharmaceuticals, among others (Arabi et al. 2021).

COVID-19 has also unmasked the crisis in quality of social care in long-term care homes, the epicenter of COVID-19 in most countries (Edwards and Curry 2020). It is estimated that up to half of those who have died from COVID-19 in Europe were residents in long-term care facilities.[12] According to the International Long-term Care Policy Network (Comas-Herrera et al. 2020), people living in these facilities are particularly vulnerable to severe COVID-19 infections and experience high rates of mortality as a result.

During the pandemic, the long-term care homes may need to implement staff contingency plans to complete the essential care and services required for residents. Contingency plans are policy instruments that outline protocols, guidelines, and rules to follow in the event of a pandemic (Mattei and Vigevano 2021). Healthcare sector needs to focus more at-risk older adults to ensure their inclusion, both in public health recommendations and considerations made by policymakers.

Global health surveillance and information management

Global public health surveillance is the ongoing systematic collection, analysis, and interpretation of data, closely integrated with the timely dissemination of these data to those responsible for preventing and controlling the diseases (Thacker and Berkelman 1988). The COVID-19 epidemic has underlined the critical role of surveillance in protecting individual nations and the global community. Real-time analyses of epidemiological data increase awareness about the problem and for prompt interventions. The development of molecular methods has provided new tools for enhanced surveillance and outbreak detection (Sabat et al. 2020). WHO (2022a) has suggested the member states to increase their capacity to detect new threats, including through laboratory techniques, such as genomic sequencing (WHO 2022b).[13] Genomic sequencing is a tool used in the investigation and acute management of diseases that could constitute public health emergencies (WHO 2022b). It is projected that by the next decade, medical researchers will supply and utilize vast genome-base data resources to gain insights into the molecular mechanisms of human disease and better understand the epidemiological landscape (Collins et al. 2003; IQVIA 2022a, b). Genomic surveillance can prevent future pandemics and help the world better prepare for future public health threats. If scientists can rapidly identify an unknown pathogen, they can understand better the epidemiology, and how it spreads. Genomics provides an opportunity for vaccine development in the case of pathogens for which the traditional approaches have failed (Bambini and Rappuoli 2009). Moreover, comparative genomics[14] can inform a deeper understanding of the pathogenesis of COVID-19 (Asrani et al. 2020; Bambini and Rappuoli 2009).

Genomic data currently collected by existing initiatives focus on populations in the United States and Europe and do not reflect the genomics of global populations well (IQVIA 2022a, b). Though Asia's population makes up 60% of the world's population, initiatives currently plan to sequence only six million Asian genomes by 2025—12% of the global target (IQVIA 2022a, b). Global disparities in genomic surveillance undermine the global pandemic preparedness. International technical cooperation is required to support low- and middle-income countries in improving their local sequencing capacity.

Predictive modeling

In pandemic, providing timely information to the public is paramount. Understanding of the process of emergence and spread has moved from anecdotal through analytical to potentially predictive with the advancements in data science modeling (Morse et al. 2012). AI models have been used in the past for estimating and predicting the spread rate of pandemics like Zika virus in 2015. In the wake of the Ebola outbreak in 2014, the Global Health Security Index (GHSI)[15] was developed with the aim of gauging countries' capacity to deal with infectious disease outbreaks (Aitken et al. 2020).

Predictive analytics is a specialized branch of data analytics for making better predictions using past data and using quantitative analytic and learning methods. Due to accurate and fast predictions, the spread rate can be minimized by taking necessary precautionary action before the time (Mahalle et al. 2020). Predictive models improve surveillance capabilities that help healthcare professionals to devise better resilience and decision-making for managing uncertainty and disruption in healthcare operations (Morse et al. 2012). Big data and AI have also augmented the research activities by simulating the viral morphology and its evolution, and providing quicker identification of potential drug candidates for treatment of COVID-19 patients (Mehta and Shukla 2021). Furthermore, these technologies have proven useful for hospitals in predicting the demand for healthcare resources and planning the allocation in advance. In these unprecedented times, big data and AI empower countries and the governing authorities with solutions that can reduce the impact of virus and be instrumental in effective planning to address immediate public health challenges (Mehta and Shukla 2021).

Global governance

Global governance is necessary to coordinate the global health response (Gostin et al. 2020). WHO is the leading organization to develop the global response to health threats. The most prominent role of the World Health Organization (WHO) in controlling COVID-19 has been to work closely with the medical community, governments, and partners to rapidly expand scientific knowledge on this new virus, to track the spread and virulence of the virus, and to provide advice to countries and individuals on measures to protect health and prevent the spread risk of this outbreak. Multilateral, rule-based governance is advocated as an effective way to provide international "common goods" (Brown and Rosier 2023). No country can overcome future pandemics in isolation.

To control future pandemics, researchers have highlighted the following key measures at the global scale with the support and under the governance of supranational organizations:

- Coordinated efforts among the government and private sector to find solutions to various constraints (WTO 2021)
- Increasing international cooperation around technology transfer and the sharing of essential manufacturing knowhow (Pilkington et al. 2022)
- A strong, shared, transparent information base to create models that can predict the future course of the pandemic (OECD 2020; Gereffi 2020)
- Dismantling of trade barriers by member countries on essential goods (OECD 2021; Gereffi 2020; Evenett 2020)
- A strong and well-connected logistic network (OECD 2021)
- Regulatory cooperation among countries (WTO 2021)
- Enhanced trade facilitation and smooth customs procedures (WTO 2021)
- Modernized port infrastructure on key global shipping routes to reduce global chokepoints (IMF 2022)
- Digitalization of customs procedures to boost efficiency in trade documentation and subsequently to reduce trade costs (WTO 2021)

Summary

The chapter has focused on addressing two formidable challenges facing the global health sector: neglected tropical diseases (NTDs) and looming risks of deadly pandemics.

The neglected tropical diseases (NTDs) constitute one of the major sources of the global "burden of disease" (the sum of mortality and morbidity). The emergence and spread of infectious diseases with pandemic potential is yet another formidable challenge.

About containing the global disease burden arising from NTDs, open-source collaborative arrangements involving multilateral institutions have shown success, though much remains to be done. To control the risks of pandemics, a resilient global chain of production and trade networks are considered an integral measure in delivering medicines, vaccines, and medical devices to countries across the world. Technology transfer has been fundamental to the global pharmaceutical industry's ability to rapidly scale up the production of COVID-19 vaccines and treatments.

Based on the research evidence obtained from published studies, the chapter has highlighted the following proposals to deal with NTDs and to control the pandemic risks.

- Implementing market push and pull measures to tackle the neglected tropical diseases
- Enforcing multi-sectoral collaboration and open-source research networks as vital strategies to control NTDs
- Promoting the potential of south-south cooperation in research and development for tropical diseases
- Accelerating the discovery and development of technologies for neglected tropical diseases through novel global initiatives such as product-partnership development collaboration and WIPO Re:Search
- Building a robust global supply chain of medical goods and vaccines to fight future pandemics
- Scaling up global production of vaccines to attain vaccine equity
- Critical role of the international community, led through the ACT-Accelerator and its COVAX facility, in administering the supply of vaccines to meet the needs of population in LIMCs
- Multilateral initiatives involving WHO and not-for-profit organizations effort to disseminate the mRNA technology in developing countries through establishing technology transfer hubs
- Controlling the risks of future pandemics through global health surveillance and information management

Notes

1 These diseases and conditions include Buruli ulcer, Chagas disease, taeniasis/cysticercosis, dengue, dracunculiasis, echinococcosis, endemic treponematoses, foodborne trematodes, human African trypanosomiasis, the leishmaniases, leprosy, lymphatic filariasis, onchocerciasis, rabies, schistosomiasis, trachoma, and soil-transmitted helminthiasis (WHO 2013).

2 The COVID-19 pandemic is being widely described as a Black Swan event, an event that has outsized impact, that is harder to predict and even harder to compute its probabilities (Mishra 2020, Antipova 2020).

3 These include U.S. National Institutes of Health, Bill & Melinda Gates Foundation, Aggregate Pharmaceutical and Biotechnology company respondents, The Welcome Trust, U.S. Department of Defense, European Commission, Brazilian Ministry of Health, Department of Science and Technology, Médecins Sans Frontières (MSF), State of Sao Paulo Research Foundation (FAPESP), Institute Pasteur, UK Medical Research Council (MRC), and UK Department for International Development (DFID).

4 Discovering new therapeutic uses for existing molecules, also called "repurposing" of existing clinical drugs, or previously shelved compounds, is undergoing a resurgence of interest in open-source model of collaborative research between academic scientists and pharmaceutical companies (Allarakhia 2013).

5 Vector control agents (such as insecticide-based interventions in case of malaria) are one of the most effective methods to curb vector-borne diseases.

6 Vectors are living organisms that can transmit infectious pathogens between humans, or from animals to humans. Vector-borne diseases include malaria, dengue, chikungunya, Zika virus, yellow fever, and others. Most of these are preventable (WHO 2010).

7 Detailed trade data derived from the international input-output tables confirm that there are strong international interdependencies in the supply chains of vaccines.

8 mRNA vaccines are a new type of vaccine. They don't use live virus to trigger an immune response. Instead, they teach your cells how to make a protein that will trigger an immune response. Once triggered, your body makes antibodies. Vaccines use mRNA created in a laboratory to teach our cells how to make a protein—or even just a piece of a protein—that triggers an immune response inside our bodies.
9 The research literature suggest that there are largely four channels through which technology may be transferred across international boundaries (Maskus 2004):
Trade in goods, especially capital goods, and technological inputs
Foreign direct investment (FDI) and technology licensing
Non-market channels of ITT, such as imitation through product inspection and reverse engineering
Temporary migration of students, scientists, conferences, and knowledge available in the public domain
10 Global public goods are non-rival and non-excludable: one country's enjoyment of the good does not affect (or reduce) its enjoyment by others and once the good becomes available, no country can be excluded from sharing its benefits. See more details in Stiglitz (1999).
11 Public health infrastructure refers to the capability of identifying, tracing, managing, and treating cases (Madhav et al. 2017).
12 Statement to the press by Dr Hans Henri P. Kluge, WHO Regional Director for Europe. Statement—Invest in the overlooked and unsung: build sustainable people-centered long-term care in the wake of COVID-19. April 23, 2020, Copenhagen, Denmark.
13 Genomics has also been widely applied to tracking infectious diseases by sequencing the genomes of bacteria, parasites, and viruses (Gardy and Loman 2018). Genomic surveillance is the process of constantly monitoring pathogens and analyzing their genetic similarities and differences.
14 Comparative genomics involves comparing the genomes of different organisms.
15 The 2021 GHS Index measures the capacities of 195 countries to prepare for epidemics and pandemics. GHS Index, launched in late 2019, has become a key reference tool. https://www.ghsindex.org/

References

Acharya, Krishna Prasad, and Santosh Pathak. 2019 November 14. "Applied Research in Low-Income Countries: Why and How?" *Frontiers in Research Metrics & Analytics* 4: 3. https://doi.org/10.3389/frma.2019.00003.

Aitken, C., and D. J. Jeffries. 2001. "Nosocomial Spread of Viral Disease." *Clinical Microbiology Reviews* 14 (3): 528–546. https://doi.org/10.1128/CMR.14.3.528-546.2001.

Aitken, Tess, Ken Lee Chin, Danny Liew, and Richard Ofori-Asenso. 2020. "Rethinking Pandemic Preparation: Global Health Security Index (GHSI) Is Predictive of COVID-19 Burden, but in the Opposite Direction." *Journal of Infection* 81 (2): 318 356. https://doi.org/10.1016/j.jinf.2020.05.001.

Allarakhia, Minna. 2013. "Open-Source Approaches for the Repurposing of Existing or Failed Candidate Drugs: Learning from and Applying the Lessons Across Diseases." *Drug Design, Development & Therapy* 7: 753–66. https://doi.org/10.2147/DDDT.S46289.

Antipova, T. 2020 May 5. "Coronavirus Pandemic as Black Swan Event." *Integrated Science in Digital Age* 136: 356–366.

Arabi, Yaseen M., Elie Azoulay, Hasan M. Al-Dorzi, Jason Phua, Jorge Salluh, Alexandra Binnie, Carol Hodgson, Derek C. Angus, Maurizio Cecconi, Bin Du, Rob Fowler, Charles D. Gomersall, Peter Horby, Nicole P. Juffermans, Jozef Kesecioglu, Ruth M. Kleinpell, Flavia R. Machado, Greg S. Martin, Geert Meyfroidt, Andrew Rhodes, Kathryn Rowan, Jean-François Timsit, Jean-Louis Vincent, and Giuseppe Citerio. 2021. "How the COVID-19 Pandemic Will Change the Future of Critical Care." *Intensive Care Medicine* 47 (3): 282–291. https://doi.org/10.1007/s00134-021-06352-y.

Asrani, Purva, Gulam Mustafa Hasan, Sukhwinder Singh Sohal, and Md Imtaiyaz Hassan. 2020 Nov. "Molecular Basis of Pathogenesis of Coronaviruses: A Comparative Genomics Approach to Planetary Health to Prevent Zoonotic Outbreaks in the 21st Century." *Omics* 24 (11): 634–644. https://doi.org/10.1089/omi.2020.0131.

Asundi, Archana, Colin O'Leary, and Nahid Bhadelia. 2021. "Global COVID-19 Vaccine Inequity: The Scope, the Impact, and the Challenges." *Cell Host & Microbe* 29 (7): 1036–1039. https://doi.org/10.1016/j.chom.2021.06.007.

Baldwin, R., and E. Tomiura. 2020 "Ch. 5. Thinking Ahead About the Trade Impact of COVID-19." In *Economics in the Time of COVID-19, A CEPR Press* eBook, CEPR, edited by Baldwin Rand, and B. W. di Mauro. VoxEU.org.

Bambini, Stefania, and Rino Rappuoli. 2009 March "The Use of Genomics in Microbial Vaccine Development." *Drug Discovery Today* 14 (5–6): 252–260. https://doi.org/10.1016/j.drudis.2008.12.007.

Barasa, Edwine W., Paul O. Ouma, and Emelda A. Okiro. 2020 July 20. "Assessing the Hospital Surge Capacity of the Kenyan Health System in the Face of the COVID-19 Pandemic." *PLoS One* 15 (7): e0236308. https://doi.org/10.1371/journal.pone.0236308.

Belkhir, L., and A. Elmeligi. 2019. "Carbon Footprint of the Global Pharmaceutical Industry and Relative Impact of Its Major Players." *Journal of Cleaner Production* 214: 185–194. https://doi.org/10.1016/j.jclepro.2018.11.204.

Besançon, Lonni, Nathan Peiffer-Smadja, Corentin Segalas, Haiting Jiang, Paola Masuzzo, Cooper Smout, Eric Billy, Maxime Deforet, and Clémence Leyrat. 2021. "Open Science Saves Lives: Lessons from the COVID-19 Pandemic." *BMC Medical Research Methodology* 21 (1): 117. https://doi.org/10.1186/s12874-021-01304-y.

Bombelles, T., J. Dent, M. Sharafudeen, P. Stevens, K. M. Graef, and A. Krattiger. 2015. *Re: World Intellectual Property Organization: Search: Sharing Innovation in the Fight Against Neglected Tropical Diseases.* Global Challenges Brief, WIPO.

Bown, Chad P., and Thomas J. Bollyky. 2021. "How COVID-19 Vaccine Supply Chains Emerged in the Midst of a Pandemic." *World Economy* 45 (2): 468–522. https://doi.org/10.1111/twec.13183.

Brach, Juliane, and R. T. Kappel. 2009. "Global Value Chains, Technology Transfer and Local Firm Upgrading in Non-OECD Countries", GIGA Working Papers 110. *SSRN Electronic Journal.* GIGA German Institute of Global and Area Studies. https://doi.org/10.2139/ssrn.1485508.

Brown, G., and D. Susskind. 2020. *International Cooperation During the COVID-19 Pandemic.* Oxford University Press.

Brown, S., and M. Rosier. 2023. "COVID-19 Vaccine Apartheid and the Failure of Global Cooperation." *British Journal of Politics & International Relations* 25 (3): 535–554. https://doi.org/10.1177/13691481231178248.

Chen, Simiao, Zongjiu Zhang, Juntao Yang, Jian Wang, Xiaohui Zhai, Till Bärnighausen, and Chen Wang. 2020. "Fangcang Shelter Hospitals: A Novel Concept for Responding to Public Health Emergencies." *Lancet* 395 (10232): 1305–1314. https://doi.org/10.1016/S0140-6736(20)30744-3.

Collins, F. S., E. D. Green, A. E. Guttmacher, and M. S. Guyer 2003. US National Human Genome Research Institute: "A vision for the future of genomics research." *Nature* 422 (6934): 835–47. https://doi.org/10.1038/nature01626

Curry, E. 2020. "Dataspaces: Fundamentals, Principles, and Techniques." In Real-time Linked Dataspaces. Springer, Cham. https://doi.org/10.1007/978-3-030-29665-0_3

Danzon, P. M., A. Towse, and A. W. Mulcahy. 2011. "Setting cost-effectiveness thresholds as a means to achieve appropriate drug prices in rich and poor countries." *Health Affairs* 30 (8): 1529–1538. https://doi.org/10.1377/hlthaff.2009.0702

Ducharme, J. 2020. *Even the Pandemic Hasn't Made Public Health Icon Paul Farmer to Lose Hope*. Time December 3 2021.

Edlin, Chris. 2011. "The Importance of Patent Sharing in Neglected Disease Drug Discovery." *Future Medicinal Chemistry* 3 (11): 1331–1334. https://doi.org/10.4155/fmc.11.101.

Engels, Dirk, and Xiao-Nong Zhou. 2020. "Neglected Tropical Diseases: An Effective Global Response to Local Poverty-Related Disease Priorities." *Infectious Diseases of Poverty* 9 (1): 10. https://doi.org/10.1186/s40249-020-0630-9.

Evenett, S. 2020. *Tackling COVID-19 Together, Global Trade Alert*. University of St. Gallen.

Gardy, Jennifer L., and Nicholas J. Loman. 2018. "Towards a Genomics-Informed, Real-Time, Global Pathogen Surveillance System." *Nature Reviews. Genetics* 19 (1): 9–20. https://doi.org/10.1038/nrg.2017.88.

Gereffi, G. 2020. "What Does the COVID-19 Pandemic Teach Us About Global Value Chains? The Case of Medical Supplies." *Journal of International Business Policy* 3 (3): 287–301. https://doi.org/10.1057/s42214-020-00062-w.

Golob, Jonathan L., Njira Lugogo, Adam S. Lauring, and Anna S. Lok. 2021. "SARS-CoV-2 Vaccines: A Triumph of Science and Collaboration." *JCI Insight* 6 (9): e149187. https://doi.org/10.1172/jci.insight.149187.

Gostin, Lawrence O., Suerie Moon, and Benjamin Mason Meier. 2020 November "Reimagining Global Health Governance in the Age of COVID-19." *American Journal of Public Health* 110 (11): 1615–1619. https://doi.org/10.2105/AJPH.2020.305933.

Grasselli, Giacomo, Antonio Pesenti, and Maurizio Cecconi. 2020. "Critical Care Utilization for the COVID-19 Outbreak inLombardy, Italy: Early Experience and Forecast During an Emergency Response." *JAMA*. Published online March 13 323 (16): 1545–1546. https://doi.org/10.1001/jama.2020.4031.

Grimes, S., and M. Miozzo. 2015. "Big Pharma's Internationalization of R&D to China." *European Planning Studies* 23 (9): 1873–194. https://doi.org/10.1080/09654313.2015.1029442.

Hecht, Robert, Paul Wilson, and Amrita Palriwala. 2009. "Improving Health R&D Financing for Developing Countries: A Menu of Innovative Policy Options." *Health Affairs (Project Hope)* 28 (4): 974–985. https://doi.org/10.1377/hlthaff.28.4.974.

Hick, John L., Sharon Einav, Dan Hanfling, Niranjan Kissoon, Jeffrey R. Dichter, Asha V. Devereaux, Michael D. Christian, Task Force for Mass Critical Care, and Task Force for Mass Critical Care. 2014. "Surge Capacity Principles: Care of the Critically Ill and Injured During Pandemics and Disasters: CHEST Consensus Statement." *Chest* 146 (4 Suppl) Suppl: e1S–e16S. https://doi.org/10.1378/chest.14-0733.

Hotez, Peter J., Jan H. F. Remme, Paulo Buss, George George, Carlos Morel, and Joel G. Breman. 2004. "Combating Tropical Infectious Diseases: Report of the Disease Control Priorities in Developing Countries Project." *Clinical Infectious Diseases* 38 (6): 871–878. https://doi.org/10.1086/382077.

Hotez, Peter J., Bernard Pecoul, Suman Rijal, Catharina Boehme, Serap Aksoy, Mwelecele Malecela, Roberto Tapia-Conyer, and John C. Reeder. 2016 March 2. "Eliminating the Neglected Tropical Diseases: Translational Science and New Technologies." *PLoS Neglected Tropical Diseases* 10 (3): e0003895. https://doi.org/10.1371/journal.pntd.0003895.

Hunter, David J., Salim S. Abdool Karim, Lindsey R. Baden, Jeremy J. Farrar, Mary Beth Hamel, Dan L. Longo, Stephen Morrissey, and Eric J. Rubin. 2022. "Addressing Vaccine Inequity – Covid-19 Vaccines as a Global Public Good." *New England Journal of Medicine* 386 (12): 1176–1179. https://doi.org/10.1056/NEJMe2202547.

IFPMA. 2023. "Preparing Society Against Future Pandemics, Policy Perspectives from the Innovative Biopharmaceutical Industry" International Federation of Pharmaceutical Manufacturers and Associations. https://www.ifpma.org/wp-content/uploads/2023/01/i2023_IFPMA_Preparing_society_against_future_pandemics_Full_Report.pdf 2023_IFPMA_Preparing_society_against_future_pandemics_Full_Report.pdf

IMF (International Monetary Fund) 2022. "World Economic Outlook: War Sets Back the Global Recovery". International Monetary Fund Washington, DC: April

IQVIA. 2022a. "Emerging Biopharma's Contribution to Innovation. June 2022." June 13, Institute Report, US.

IQVIA. 2022b. "Drug Repurposing Basics. Using AI-powered methodologies to reduce failure rate while saving time and cost. Blog by Nathan Sommerford, Global Lead, AI for Drug Discovery & Development May 12, 2022." US https://www.iqvia.com/blogs/2022/05/drug-repurposing-basics

Ivanov, Dmitry. 2020. "Predicting the Impacts of Epidemic Outbreaks on Global Supply Chains: A Simulation-Based Analysis on the Coronavirus Outbreak (COVID-19/SARS-CoV-2) Case." *Transportation Research. Part E, Logistics & Transportation Review* 136: 101922. https://doi.org/10.1016/j.tre.2020.101922.

Izmirlieva, M. 2020. "COVID-19 Pandemic: Health System Surge Capacity." *Pharmaceutical Technology, March* 19. https://ihsmarkit.com/research-analysis/covid19-pandemic-health-system-surge-capacity.html

Javorcik, B. 2020. "Global Supply Chains Will Not Be the Same in the Post-COVID-19 World." In *COVID-19 and Trade Policy: Why Turning Inward Won't Work*, edited by R. E. Baldwin, and S. J. Evenett: 111–116. CEPR Press.

Joi, P. 2020. *Are Vaccines a Public Good?* September 11, VaccinesWork, GAVI. https://www.gavi.org/vaccineswork/are-vaccines-global-public-good.

Kagame, P., E. Macron, C. Ramaphosa, Scholz O. Sall Macky, and T. A. Ghebreyesus. 2023. "Sharing Technology and Supporting Innovation Is Not Just About Equity. It's Also the Best Way to Stop Pandemics, WHO Newsroom." https://

www.who.int/news-room/commentaries/detail/sharing-technology-and-supporting-innovation-is-not-just-about-equity.-it-s-also-the-best-way-to-stop-pandemics.

Kavanagh, Matthew M., Lawrence O. Gostin, and Madhavi Sunder. 2021. "Sharing Technology and Vaccine Doses to Address Global Vaccine Inequity and End the COVID-19 Pandemic." *JAMA* 326 (3): 219–220. https://doi.org/10.1001/jama.2021.10823.

Kelland, K. 2015. *WHO Urges Developing Countries to Fund Tropical Diseases Fight, Healthcare and Pharma*. Reuters.

Kumraj, Ganesh, Sarang Pathak, Sanket Shah, Piyali Majumder, Jainendra Jain, Davender Bhati, Sarmad Hanif, Sushmita Mukherjee, and Syed Ahmed. 2022. "Capacity Building for Vaccine Manufacturing Across Developing Countries: The Way Forward." *Human Vaccines & Immunotherapeutics* 18 (1): 2020529. https://doi.org/10.1080/21645515.2021.2020529.

Lalani, Hussain S., Jerry Avorn, and Aaron S. Kesselheim. 2022 March "US Taxpayers Heavily Funded the Discovery of COVID-19 Vaccines." *Clinical Pharmacology & Therapeutics* 111 (3): 542–544. https://doi.org/10.1002/cpt.2344.

Leach, M., H. MacGregor, I. Scoones, and A. Wilkinson. 2021. "Post-pandemic Transformations: How and Why COVID-19 Requires Us to Rethink Development. Ledford, H." *Translational Research: The Journal of Laboratory & Clinical Medicine* (2011): 4 ways to fix the clinical trial, *Nature* 477: 526–528.

Legido-Quigley, Helena, Nima Asgari, Yik Ying Teo, Gabriel M. Leung, Hitoshi Oshitani, Keiji Fukuda, Alex R. Cook, Li Yang Hsu, Kenji Shibuya, and David Heymann. 2020 March 14. "Are High-Performing Health Systems Resilient Against the COVID-19 Epidemic?" *Lancet* 395 (10227): 848–850. https://doi.org/10.1016/S0140-6736(20)30551-1.

Lezaun, Javier, and Catherine M. Montgomery. 2015. "The Pharmaceutical Commons: Sharing and Exclusion in Global Health Drug Development." *Science, Technology & Human Values* 40 (1): 3–29. https://doi.org/10.1177/0162243914542349.

Madhav, N., B. Oppenheim, M. Gallivan, P. Mulembakani, E. Rubin, and N. Wolfe. 2017. "Chapter 17. Pandemics: Risks, Impacts, and Mitigation." In *Disease Control Priorities: Improving Health and Reducing Poverty*. 3rd ed., edited by D. T. Jamison, H. Gelband, S. Horton, et al. International Bank for Reconstruction and Development/The World Bank.

Magariños, María P., Santiago J. Carmona, Gregory J. Crowther, Stuart A. Ralph, David S. Roos, Dhanasekaran Shanmugam, Wesley C. Van Voorhis, and Fernán Agüero. 2012. "TDR Targets: A Chemogenomics Resource for Neglected Diseases." *Nucleic Acids Research* 40 (database issue): D1118–D1127. https://doi.org/10.1093/nar/gkr1053.

Mahalle, P. N., N. P. Sable, N. P. Mahalle, and G. R. Shinde. 2020. "Data Analytics: COVID-19 Prediction Using Multimodal Data." In *Intelligent Systems and Methods to Combat Covid-19. SpringerBriefs in Applied Sciences and Technology*, edited by A. Joshi, N. Dey, K. Santosh: 1–10. Springer. https://doi.org/10.1007/978-981-15-6572-4_1.

Malacrino, D., A. Mohommad, and A. Presbitero. 2022. *Diversify Supply Chains, Do Not Dismanle IMGF Blog*. April 12. Ch 4 from World Economic Outlook, International Monetary Fund, https://www.imf.org/en/Blogs/Articles/2022/04/12/blog041222-sm2022-weo-ch4

Maskus, K. E. 2004. *Encouraging International Technology Transfer, UNCTAD-ICTSD Project on IPRs and Sustainable Development.* https://doi.org/10.7215/IP_IP_20040501A.

Masum, H., and R. Harris. 2011. *Open Source for Neglected Diseases: Magic Bullet or Mirage?* Results for Development Institute.

Mattei, P., and L. Vigevano. 2021. "Contingency Planning and Early Crisis Management: Italy and the COVID-19 Pandemic." *Public Organization Review* 21 (4): 647–63.

Mehta, Nishita, and Sharvari Shukla. 2021. "Pandemic Analytics: How Countries Are Leveraging Big Data Analytics and Artificial Intelligence to Fight COVID-19?" *SN Computer Science* 3 (1): 54. https://doi.org/10.1007/s42979-021-00923-y.

Minja, Happiness, Christian Nsanzabana, Christine Maure, Axel Hoffmann, Susan Rumisha, Olumide Ogundahunsi, Fabio Zicker, Marcel Tanner, and Pascal Launois. 2011. "Impact of Health Research Capacity Strengthening in Low- and Middle-Income Countries: The Case of WHO/TDR Programmes." *PLoS Neglected Tropical Diseases* 5 (10): e1351. https://doi.org/10.1371/journal.pntd.0001351.

Miroudot, S. 2020, Ch. 9. "Resilience Versus Robustness in Global Value Chains: Some Policy Implications." In *COVID-19 and Trade Policy: Why Turning Inward Won't Work* eBook, edited by Richard Baldwin, J. Simon, A. Evenett, and C. E. P. R. Press. VoxEU.org.

Mishra, P. K. 2020. "COVID-19, Black Swan Events and the Future of Disaster Risk Management in India." *Progress in Disaster Science* 8: Article ID: 100137. https://doi.org/10.1016/j.pdisas.2020.100137.

Moon, Suerie, John-Arne Røttingen, and Julio Frenk. 2017 April "Global Public Goods for Health: Weaknesses and Opportunities in the Global Health System." *Health Economics, Policy, & Law* 12 (2): 195–205. https://doi.org/10.1017/S1744133116000451.

Moran, M. 2011. "Global Finding of New Products for Neglected Tropical Diseases." In *Forum on Microbial Threats. The Causes and Impacts of Neglected Tropical and Zoonotic Diseases: Opportunities for Integrated Intervention Strategies* vol. 2011: A16. Institute of Medicine, National Academies Press.

Morel, C. M., T. Acharya, D. Broun, A. Dangi, C. Elias, N. K. Ganguly, C. A. Gardner, R. K. Gupta, J. Haycock, A. D. Heher, P. J. Hotez, H. E. Kettler, G. T. Keusch, A. F. Krattiger, F. T. Kreutz, S. Lall, K. Lee, R. Mahoney, A. Martinez-Palomo, and M. Yun. 2005. Health Innovation Networks to Help Developing Countries Address S. G. Morgan, H. S. Bathula, and Suerie Moon. 2020. "Pricing of Pharmaceuticals Is Becoming a Major Challenge for Health Systems." *BMJ* 368: l4627. https://doi.org/10.1136/bmj.l4627.

Morse, Stephen S., Jonna A. K. Mazet, Mark Woolhouse, Colin R. Parrish, Dennis Carroll, William B. Karesh, Carlos Zambrana-Torrelio, W. Ian Lipkin, and Peter Daszak. 2012. "Prediction and Prevention of the Next Pandemic Zoonosis." *Lancet* 380 (9857): 1956–1965. https://doi.org/10.1016/S0140-6736(12)61684-5.

Nicita, A., V. Ognivtsev, and M. Shirotori. 2013. *Global Supply Chains: Trade and Economic Policies for Developing Countries*, UNCTAD Blue Series Papers 55, United Nations Conference on Trade and Development.

Nwaka, Solomon, Bernadette Ramirez, Reto Brun, Louis Maes, Frank Douglas, and Robert Ridley. 2009. "Advancing Drug Innovation for Neglected Diseases-Criteria for Lead Progression." *PLoS Neglected Tropical Diseases* 3 (8): e440. https://doi.org/10.1371/journal.pntd.0000440.

OECD. 2020. *Challenges in Access to Oncology Medicines: Policies and Practices Across the OECD and the EU, OECD Health Working Papers, No. 123 (November 2020).* OECD.

OECD. 2021. *Effective Policies to Foster High Risk/High-Reward Research OECD Scienvce, Technology and Industry Policy Papers* vol. 112. OECD.

Padrós Selma, Jaume. 2022. "Vaccines: A Universal Public Good." *Medicina Clinica* 158 (2): 93–94. https://doi.org/10.1016/j.medcle.2021.03.029.

Peacock, Stuart J. 2022 February 12. "Vaccine Nationalism Will Persist: Global Public Goods Need Effective Engagement of Global Citizens." *Globalization & Health* 18 (1): 14. https://doi.org/10.1186/s12992-022-00802-y.

Perehudoff, Katrina, Carmen Durán, Irina Demchenko, Veronica Mazzanti, Priya Parwani, Fatima Suleman, and Anke de Ruijter. 2021. "Impact of the European Union on access to medicines in low- and middle-income countries: A scoping review." *Lancet Regional Health - Europe* 9: 100219.

Phelan, Alexandra L., Rebecca Katz, and Lawrence O. Gostin. 2020. "The Novel Coronavirus Originating in Wuhan, China: Challenges for Global Health Governance." *JAMA* 323 (8): 709–710. https://doi.org/10.1001/jama.2020.1097.

Pilkington, Victoria, Sarai Mirjam Keestra, and Andrew Hill. 2022. "Global COVID-19 Vaccine Inequity: Failures in the First Year of Distribution and Potential Solutions for the Future." *Frontiers in Public Health* 10: 821117. https://doi.org/10.3389/fpubh.2022.821117.

Ray, Avik, Swati Sharma, and Balakrishnan Sadasivam. 2021. "Carbovigilance: Curtailing the Global Pharmaceutical Carbon Footprint." *Future Healthcare Journal* 8 (3): e683–e685. https://doi.org/10.7861/fhj.2021-0071.

Reed, S.L., J.H. McKerrow. 2018. Why Funding for Neglected Tropical Diseases Should Be a Global Priority. *Clinical Infectious Diseases* 67 (3): 323–326. doi: 10.1093/cid/ciy349. PMID: 29688342.

Reeder, John C. 2014. "TDR: (Back) Making a Difference." *PLoS Neglected Tropical Diseases* 8 (1): e2531. https://doi.org/10.1371/journal.pntd.0002531.

Rigo, D. 2021. "Global Value Chains and Technology Transfer: New Evidence from Developing Countries." *Review of World Economics (Weltwirtschaftliches Archiv), Springer;Institut für Weltwirtschaft* 157 (2): 271–294.

Rodrik, D. 2018. "New Technologies, Global Value Chains, and the Developing Economies." *SSRN Electronic Journal* 7307. https://doi.org/10.2139/ssrn.3338636.

Sabat, Isabella, Sabine Neuman-Böhme, Nils E. Varghese, Pedro Pita Barros, Werner Brouwer, Job van Exel, Jonas Schreyögg, and Thomas Stargardt. 2020. "United but divided: Policy responses and people's perceptions in the EU during the COVID-19 outbreak." *Health Policy* 124 (9): 909–918. doi:10.1016/j.healthpol.2020.06.009

Sariola, S. 2021 April 1. "Intellectual Property Rights Need to Be Subverted to Ensure Global Vaccine Access." *BMJ Global Health* 6 (4). https://doi.org/10.1136/bmjgh-2021-005656.

Smith, Richard D., Carlos Correa, and Cecilia Oh. 2009. "Trade, TRIPS, and Pharmaceuticals." *Lancet* 373 (9664): 684–691. https://doi.org/10.1016/S0140-6736(08)61779-1.

Smith, R. D., H. Thorsteinsdóttir, A.S. Daar, E.R. Gold, and P.A. Singers. 2004. "Genomics knowledge and equity: A global public goods perspective of the patent system." *Bulletin of the World Health Organization* 82 (5): 385–389.

Stevens, H., and I. Huys. 2017. "Innovative Approaches to Increase Access to Medicines in Developing Countries." *Frontiers in Medicine* 4. https://doi.org/10.3389/fmed.2017.00218.

Stiglitz, J. E. 1999. "Knowledge as a Public Good in International Cooperation in the 21st Century." In *Oxford Press*, edited by Inge Kaul, Isabelle Grunberg, Marc A. Stern. UNDP.

Stiglitz, J. E. 2022. "Vaccinating the World Against COVID-19 Is a No-Brainer." *PLOS Global Public Health* 2 (5): e0000427. https://doi.org/10.1371/journal.pgph.0000427.

Stiglitz, J. E., and A. Jayadev. 2010. "Medicine for Tomorrow: Some Alternative Proposals to Promote Socially Beneficial Research and Development in Pharmaceuticals." *Journal of Generic Medicines: The Business Journal for the Generic Medicines Sector* 7 (3): 217–226. https://doi.org/10.1057/jgm.2010.21.

't Hoen, E. and S. Moon. 2001. "Pills and Pocketbooks: Equity Pricing of Essential Medicines in Developing Countries (MSF Jul 11, 2001)". available online

't Hoen, E., J. Berger, A. Calmy, S. Moon. 2011. Driving a decade of change: HIV/AIDS, patents and access to medicines for all. *Journal of the International AIDS Society* 14: 15. doi: 10.1186/1758-2652-14-15. PMID: 21439089; PMCID: PMC3078828.

Thacker, S. B., and R. L. Berkelman. 1988. "Public Health Surveillance in the United States." *Epidemiologic Reviews* 10: 164–190. https://doi.org/10.1093/oxfordjournals.epirev.a036021.

Trouiller, P., P. L. Olliaro, E. Torreele, J. Orbinski, R. Laing, and N. P. Ford. 2002. "Drug Development for Neglected Diseases: A Deficient Market and a Public-Health Policy Failure." *Lancet* 359 (9324): 2188–2194. https://doi.org/10.1016/S0140-6736(02)09096-7.

UNCTAD, 2011 "World Investment Report" Non-Equity Modes of International Production and Development, UN Publication, World Investment Report 2011: Non-Equity Modes of International Production and Development (unctad.org).

UNESCO (2015). UNESCO science report: towards 2030. Paris: UNESCO Publishing,. https://uis.unesco.org/sites/default/files/documents/unesco-science-report-towards-2030-part1.pdf.

UNESCO (2021). "UNESCO Science Report: the Race Against Time for Smarter Development." Report written by S. Schneegans, T. Straza and J. Lewis (eds). UNESCO Publishing: Paris.

Vasconcellos, Alexandre Guimarães, B. P. Fonseca E. Fonseca, and Carlos Medicis Morel. 2018. "Revisiting the Concept of Innovative Developing Countries (IDCs) for Its Relevance to Health Innovation and Neglected Tropical Diseases and for the Prevention and Control of Epidemics." *PLoS Neglected Tropical Diseases* 12 (7): e0006469. https://doi.org/10.1371/journal.pntd.0006469.

Weng, Hong-Bo, Hai-Xia Chen, and Ming-Wei Wang. 2018. "Innovation in Neglected Tropical Disease Drug Discovery and Development." *Infectious Diseases of Poverty* 7 (1): 67. https://doi.org/10.1186/s40249-018-0444-1.

WHO. 2008. *Global Strategy and Plan of Action on Public Health, Innovation and Intellectual Property, SIXTY-FIRST World Health Assembly WHA61.21 Agenda Item 11.6 24 May 2008*. WHO.

WHO. 2010. *First WHO Report on Neglected Tropical Diseases: Working to Overcome the Global Impact of Neglected Tropical Diseases*. WHO.

WHO. 2013. *Sustaining the Drive to Overcome the Global Impact of Neglected Tropical Diseases: Second WHO Report on Neglected Tropical Diseases*. WHO.

WHO. 2020. *COVID-19 Pandemic: Countries Urged to Take Stronger Action to Stop Spread of Harmful Information, Joint News Release, Sep 23, 2020*. WHO.

WHO. 2021a. *External Reference Pricing: WHO Guideline on Country Pharmaceutical Pricing Policies. A Plain Language Summary*. WHO.

WHO. 2021b. *Ending the Neglect to Attain the Sustainable Development Goals A Road Map for Neglected Tropical Diseases 2021–2030 Overview, 28 January 2021 Executive Summary, WHO Reference Number: WHO/UCN/NTD/2020.01*. WHO.

WHO. 2021c. *World Local Production Forum: Enhancing Access to Medicines and Other Health Technologies, Report of the First WLPF*, 21-25 June 2021. WHO.

WHO. 2022a. *WHO Guiding Principles for Pathogen Genome Data Sharing*. WHO.

WHO. 2022b. *WHO Licensing Agreement Can Improve Access to COVID Health Technologies, May 16, Open Access News*. WHO.

WHO. 2023. "Home Newsroom." *Neglected Tropical Diseases, Q&A*. January 16. https://www.who.int/news-room/questions-and-answers/item/neglected-tropical-diseases.

WHO, WIPO, and WTO. 2020. *Promoting Access to Medical Technologies and Innovation Intersections Between Public Health, Intellectual Property and Trade*. 2nd ed. WHO, WIPO, and WTO.

WIPO. 2022. "How New Funding Models Tackle Challenges in the Development of Innovative Treatments for Neglected Tropical Diseases, News July 1." https://www.wipo.int/policy/en/news/global_health/2022/news_0118.html.

Wirtz, V. J., H.V. Hogerzeil, A.L. Gray, M. Bigdeli, C.P. de Joncheere, M.A. Ewen, M. Gyansa-Lutterodt, et al. 2017. "Essential medicines for universal health coverage." *The Lancet* 389 (10067): 403–476. doi:10.1016/S0140-6736(16)31599-9

World Bank. 2022. *Trade Therapy Cooperation to Strengthen Pandemic Defenses, A Joint World Bank Group, the WTO Report Launched on 3 June 2022*. World Bank.

Wouters, Olivier J., Kenneth C. Shadlen, Maximilian Salcher-Konrad, Andrew J. Pollard, Heidi J. Larson, Yot Teerawattananon, and Mark Jit. 2021. "Challenges in Ensuring Global Access to COVID-19 Vaccines: Production, Affordability, Allocation, and Deployment." *Lancet* 397 (10278): 1023–1034. https://doi.org/10.1016/S0140-6736(21)00306-8.

WTO. 2021. *World Trade Report 2021 Economic Resilience and Trade*. WTO.

WTO. 2022. *Trade Therapy Deepening Cooperation to Strengthen Pandemic Defenses, The World Bank and the World Trade Organization, A Joint World Bank Group, the WTO Report Launched on 3 June 2022*. WTO.

Yamey, G., and E. Torreele. 2022. "The world's most neglected diseases." BMJ. 325 (7357): 176–7. doi: 10.1136/bmj.325.7357.176. Erratum in: BMJ Aug 17; 325 (7360): 352.

Yamey, G., P. Garcia, F. Hassan, W. Mao, K. K. McDade, M. Pai, S. Saha, P. Schellekens, A. Taylor, and K. Udayakumar. 2022. "It is not too late to achieve global covid-19 vaccine equity." *BMJ (Clinical Research ed.)* 376: e070650.

Yunus, Muhammad, Cam Donaldson, and Jean-Luc Perron. 2020. "COVID-19 Vaccines a Global Common Good." *Lancet. Healthy Longevity* 1 (1): e6–e8. https://doi.org/10.1016/S2666-7568(20)30003-9.

7 The pharmaceutical industry—environmental footprint challenge

Environmental footprint challenge and Sustainable Development Goal 12

Environmental challenges, in general, refer to the industry's contribution to climate change, pollution, biodiversity, and the depletion of the world's natural resources. The pharmaceutical industry is particularly dependent on biodiverse tropical rainforests for new discoveries, with 25% of drugs used in modern medicine being derived from rainforest plants (WEF 2022 p. 18). The pharmaceutical industry is a major global polluter, generating 4.4% of global emissions, more per dollar of revenue than the automotive sector (Elder 2022; WEF 2022; IQVIA 2021). Its CO_2 footprint is forecast to triple by 2050 if left unchecked (WEF 2022).

Pharmaceutical companies rely on extensive energy, water, and raw material requirements—all of which make the industry one of the biggest contributors to global emissions (Booth et al. 2023). Besides production, the consumption and disposal activities are additional sources. Human and veterinary medicines in soils and water bodies affect human and environmental health (Boxall 2004). Some of the most common medicines, such as oral contraceptives, antibiotics, statins or cytotoxins used in cancer treatment, painkillers anthelmintics from veterinary medicine and antibacterial therapeutics, etc. eventually find their way into the environment, causing unintended effects on animals and microorganisms in the environment (Boxall 2004). Un-metabolized drugs and their metabolites (a substance made or used when the body breaks down food, drugs, or chemicals) are widely regarded as emerging trace pollutants which are problematic because conventional sewage treatment plants cannot destroy them (Yu et al. 2020). The presence of pharmaceutical residues in water bodies is well documented and the hazards this creates are beginning to be understood (OECD 2019a).

It is also now well recognized that "zoonotic" diseases have ecological sources, including anthropogenic factors (that is, resulting from the influence of human beings on nature). The emergence of zoonotic diseases and devastating global pandemics, including HIV/AIDS, Ebola, SARS, flu, yellow fever, and the COVID-19 outbreak, is arguably the result of our lack

DOI: 10.4324/9781003449331-7

of efforts to maintain a balanced ecosystem (Lawler et al. 2021). The WHO study (2005) has also endorsed the adverse environmental effect of intensified human encroachment on natural environments, including the long-distance trade in wild animal species (including as food).

It is observed that due to the lack of control over drug consumption and disposal regulation in some countries, there may be a significant negative global impact and harm to many ecosystems worldwide. The increased use of pharmaceuticals, primarily due to the aging population and growing demand from developing countries, is considered to have a more far-reaching impact on the environment in the coming years. Addressing global pharmaceutical pollution warrants a strong and integrated international strategy of helping countries to move toward the United Nations Sustainable Development Goal 12. Sustainable growth requires a substantial reduction in the natural resources and toxic materials used, and the waste and pollutants generated, throughout the entire production and consumption process by 2030. The UN has defined 11 *targets* and 13 *indicators* for SDG 12. Targets specify the goals and indicators represent the metrics by which the world aims to track whether these targets are achieved (Our World in Data Team 2023).

Meeting the SDG 12 goal requires understanding the sources of pollution and concerted global action to develop the value chain of medicines and devices with reduced impact on the environment during production and after use.

Sources of greenhouse gases and pollution

Research studies have suggested multiple sources of pollution that warrant attention with urgency:

- Global climate change
- Greenhouse gas emissions across the entire value chain of pharmaceutical goods
- Overprescription and self-medication
- Trade in counterfeit medicine

Global climate challenge and the health sector

At the global level, health and climate change are inextricably linked. The damaging effects of climate change can arise from increased allergens (a substance that can cause an allergic reaction) and changes in the ecology of disease vectors (Lafferty 2009; WEF 2022).

While climate change clearly impacts health and health systems, the pharmaceutical industry itself has been fueling the climate crisis (WEF 2022). Evidence from the UK and France suggest the contribution from medicines ranges between 25 and 33% of all healthcare emissions (WEF 2022). This calls for examining the entire production chain—both upstream and downstream processes connected with the industry. The pharma industry needs to target its entire value production if it wants to make a real dent in reducing carbon emissions.

One important area of concern is the high dependence on non-renewable sources of energy. If pharma and biotech companies are to meaningfully curb their carbon emissions over the next few years, a stronger reliance is required on the use of biological resources across all economic sectors (i.e., a bio-based transformation) for greening the supply chain.

Environmental issues across the entire value chain

Every stage of the pharmaceutical supply chain has a carbon footprint—right down to the very beginning, where the raw materials for active pharmaceutical ingredients (APIs) are sourced, and ending with the pharmacies, hospitals, and clinics that serve patients (Chatterjee 2023; Booth et al. 2023, MacNeill et al. 2020; Jimenez 2022). The manufacture of APIs for small-molecule drugs relies largely on chemicals derived from petroleum, a fossil fuel (Jimenez 2022). Manufacturing of the finished product is another carbon-intensive stage of a pharma company's supply chain.

In the global production chain, manufacturers of finished pharmaceutical products often rely on multiple partners to manufacture their API intermediates, excipients (substances other than the active pharmaceutical ingredients (APIs) used in the formulation of a drug product for long-term stabilization), and raw materials (IQVIA 2021). The presence of manufacturing activities in developing countries results in high carbon footprints and ecological risks due to the lack or inefficiency of treatment facilities or inappropriate disposable practices and industry residues (Kookana et al. 2014). It is observed that of the 500 companies that control 80% or more of the supply chain, 40% of them are headquartered estimated to be in India or China, 30% in Europe, and 20% in the US (IQVIA 2021). Developing countries haven't reached the same maturity in enforcing the same sets of standards or regulations used by the FDA. Evidence from 90 manufacturing units of bulk APIs in Hyderabad's industrial estate (India) indicates that the treatment plant on the sites mixed the effluent with domestic wastewater to enhance biodegradation. The water downstream of the treatment plants as well as lakes in the region were found to contain very high levels of API residues compared to the commonly reported levels in Europe and North America (Kookana et al. 2014).

Disposal of packaging materials, single-use medical devices, and plastics

Inactive ingredients such as packaging materials are potential threats to human and environmental health. Use and disposal of unused/unwanted drugs enter the environmental chain via excretion (mainly in urine and feces) both directly into the domestic sewage system and via burial in landfills (Daughton and Ternes 1999). Many medical devices require metals and minerals from controversial sources, and their extraction has been linked to incidents of child and forced labor and adverse environmental impacts. Single-use medical devices result in environmental and public health damage (MacNeill et al. 2020). Most of the plastic waste stems from medical waste generated by hospitals and online shopping package material (Peng et al. 2021). It is found that hospital waste represents the bulk of the global discharge (73%), and most of the global discharge is from Asia (72%), which calls for better management of medical waste in developing countries (Peng et al. 2021). Most plastic ends up in either landfills or the environment and very little is recycled or used for energy recovery. There have been allegations that pharmaceutical companies have produced medicines at pack sizes or dosages that would result in wastage (WHO 2018).

Overprescription and self-medication

The practices of overprescription, self-medication (over-the-counter pharmaceuticals), and misdiagnosis of symptoms can increase the amount of pharmaceuticals in the environment (OECD 2019b). According to the Infectious Diseases Society of America 2018, clinicians in the US prescribed antibiotics without an infection-related diagnosis nearly half of the time, and one in five prescriptions were provided without an in-person visit. Among other commonly overprescribed drugs such as statins, insulin, and proton pumps (for gastric disorders), there is also strong evidence of "opioids" being prominently overprescribed in the US (Jalali et al. 2020). A doctor's prescribing decisions may be influenced by other factors including vested interests (links to pharmacy, brand, or manufacturing units) and any incentives offered by the pharmaceutical industry (Kookana et al. 2014).

Self-medication is a global phenomenon (Bennadi 2013). The WHO defines "self-medication" as the selection and use of APIs by individuals to treat self-recognized illnesses or symptoms (Kookana et al. 2014). People have less knowledge regarding the risks associated with their self-medication. In many lower income countries, most APIs or almost any drug available in the market can be purchased without a prescription (so-called "self-medication").

Illicit trade in counterfeit pharmaceutical products

It is estimated that the trade in counterfeit and pirated goods amounted to up to 3.3% of world trade in 2016, up from 2.5% in 2013 (OECD/EUIPO 2020). Customs data shows that counterfeit antibiotics, lifestyle drugs, and painkillers were the most targeted by counterfeiters (OECD/EUIPO 2020). Counterfeiters also target diabetes treatments and central nervous systems medicines (OECD/EUIPO 2020). The materials used to build them are frequently toxic since these materials are cheaper to use, which puts end users at risk. Illicit trade is considered to have undesired consequences that compromise the attainment of the SDGs (Sustainable Development Goals). Within the pharmaceutical supply chain, from the initial raw materials to manufacturing and distribution, plenty of opportunities exist for providing fake or mislabeled materials and ingredients, leading to possibilities for creating counterfeit products.

Measures to mitigate pharma industry's carbon footprint

Several measures have been proposed in the literature to mitigate the environmental impact occurring at every stage of the supply chain—from raw material use stage to manufacturing, packaging, final consumption, and disposal of medical products (Larsson 2014; Caban and Stepnowski 2021; OECD 2019a). The following discussion considers selective strategies to address the environmental sustainability issues emerging from the pharmaceutical sector:

- Promoting bioeconomy and greening the supply chain
- International monitoring
- Greenhouse emission reporting
- Adopting ESG (Environmental, Social and Governance) Guidelines

Promoting bioeconomy and greening the supply chain

Bioeconomy is a bio-resources-based economy that supplies the renewable raw material, resources, and components along the value chain from natural resources and biological processes (Lokko et al. 2018, Dietz et al. 2018). Biotechnology and biomanufacturing are the pillars that are shaping the bioeconomy (see also, The White House 2022). Although the power of these technologies is well regarded at the moment in the context of human health, these pillars are unfolding new opportunities for effective innovative solutions in climate change, energy, and sustainability of the global commons.

Biotechnology and environment

Besides the health sector, modern biotechnology is expected to lead to important breakthroughs in many fields, such as food, energy, and the environment. Advances in biotechnology have enabled the scientists to replace non-renewable resources such as fossils fuels with renewable biomass[1]and have increased the reliance on environmentally friendly biomaterials (for example, bioplastics—plastics derived from renewable biomass sources, such as vegetable fats and oils, corn starch, and microbiota—to replace the current type of toxic plastic) (Gavrilescu and Chisti 2005; Bracco et al. 2018).

Development of bio-based materials has a great potential in reducing global dependence on petrochemicals. Bio-based polymers and composites are viable alternatives to conventional petroleum-based polymeric materials for a sustainable and green society. Accelerated use of modern bioenergy (in the forms of solid, liquid, and gas) for meeting the growing needs of heat and the transport sector, and the use of solar photovoltaic (PV) wind combined in the electricity sector, can have a significant future contribution to a sustainable energy system (IEA 2018). According to IEA (2018) estimates, half of all renewable energy consumed in 2017 came from modern bioenergy. The IEA (2018) anticipates that "bioenergy growth in the heat, transport and electricity sectors combined could be as considerable as that of other renewables in the electricity sector" (p. 16).

To realize the potential of biotechnologies for environmental benefits, a comprehensive approach and continued research are needed that involve a multidisciplinary team of plant breeders, agronomists, bioprocess engineers, biotechnologists, and microbiologists.

Bionanotechnologies

The two main supporting technologies for biotechnology are computing and nanotechnology (2009b). Advances in ICT have allowed an increasing integration of synthetic biology, systems biology, and functional genomics into biotechnology through the convergence of an ever-expanding range of "omics" technologies—genomics, proteomics (proteins) (UNCTAD 2018). Bionanotechnology (the convergence between biotechnology and nanotechnology) has many promising applications in environmental remediation (OECD 2009). Current developments in nanotechnology are anticipated to help generate electricity through solar cells at a competitive cost, remedy oil spills, remove plastic waste from oceans, remove contaminants from water (including oil spills, sewage, and air), and improve fuel cell-powered cars. They have also been used in environmental instruments such as sensors.[2]

Biomanufacturing and the environment

Biomanufacturing applies the principles of engineering and chemical design to engineer cell-based therapies (The White House Office of Science and Technology Policy 2022). At its core, biomanufacturing relies on using living systems (traditionally microorganisms) and, more recently, cell culture combined with advanced manufacturing approaches to produce biological molecules (StarFish medical team blog, Feb 3, 2022, The Future of Biomanufacturing). In the pharmaceutical sector, biomanufacturing is primarily associated with the production of biotherapeutic products. Biomanufacturing processes have many creative ways of reducing the adverse environment of pharmaceutical production and disposal of medicines. Some of the leading applications are listed below:

- Generating power from biomass materials (plants, wood, and waste)
- Bioremediation process—that is by using microorganisms to break toxic substances into those that are safe to dispose of
- Replacing energy-intensive processes with naturally occurring processes that often require only sunlight and a controlled environment

Biomanufacturing is poised to continue to expand, as it is already impacting a wide range of industries.

Government support and action to promote bioeconomy

Today's societal challenges call for mission-oriented initiatives and expanded public programs on projects where social returns to R&D are high. The available research evidence shows that policymakers can influence not only the rate but also the direction of innovation (Haščič et al. 2015). A critical task facing policymakers is to ensure investments in biotechnologies take place on an appropriate scale. Because of their large purchasing power, governments can pull demand for innovation, create a signaling effect as a lead user, and they can influence the diffusion of innovations more broadly (OECD 2011).

International monitoring

It has now been recognized that pharmaceuticals in the environment is a topic of global relevance, and not just an issue for industrialized countries, necessitating the collaborative attention of countries and international organizations (aus der Beek et al. 2016). To address environmental footprint problems, an international regime for chemicals and waste management was originally agreed upon in 2002 at the World Summit on Sustainable Development. In 2006, the United Nations Environment Programme (UNEP) facilitated negotiations toward a program that would lay out the work plan to achieve the 2020 goal. These negotiations led to the adoption of the Strategic Approach to International Chemicals Management (SAICM) (aus der Beek et al. 2016; Miettinen and Khan 2021).

Scientists, regulatory agencies, and the European Commission have developed a regulatory framework for environmental risk assessment (ERA) of pharmaceutical products (Küster and Adler 2014). ERAs play an important role in minimizing problems before pharmaceuticals enter the environment (Küster and Adler 2014). Reliably predicted or measured environmental concentrations (MECs) of chemicals are essential for the exposure assessment (Liebig et al. 2006). In 2014, worldwide environmental concentrations (MEC—Measured Environmental Concentrations) of human and veterinary pharmaceutical residues were compiled in a database within the framework of the research project. In respect of developing countries, research in this direction is at a nascent stage, as many of these countries lack equipped environmental laboratories as well as funds to monitor pharmaceuticals in environmental matrices (aus der Beek et al. 2016).

Greenhouse emissions reporting

An up-to-date assessment of environmental emissions in pharmaceutical firms is essential to help the management of pharma companies. By reporting greenhouse gas emissions, companies can demonstrate their commitment to reducing their environmental impact and mitigating the effects of climate change (Arias 2023). In addition to regulatory compliance, accounting for emissions can also provide benefits. For example, it can help companies identify opportunities for reducing waste, lowering energy costs, and improving their reputation and relationship with stakeholders (Arias 2023). Mandated emissions reporting would inform science-based interventions and facilitate the rapid adoption of sustainable practices.

Adopting ESG guidelines

Environmental Social and Governance (ESG) initiatives have become a strategic imperative for nearly all organizations. ESG guidelines for the pharmaceutical industry largely concern its way of manufacturing and marketing products to the public. Environmental guidelines include implementing standard policies that include investing in clean, renewable energy and lowering carbon footprint in the industry. Social guidelines include how well a company treats its clients and workers and maintaining concerns around diversity, inclusion, and rights. Governance involves how well-run a company is in terms of its corporate structure. In order to track the progress towards environmental sustainability goals (ESG), the pharma companies report their emissions in three scopes: Scope 1 are all direct emissions from activities under the company's control, Scope 2 are indirect emissions from purchased energy, and Scope 3 are all other indirect emissions from sources outside a company's control (Arias 2023). ESG is widely used by investors and other stakeholders to evaluate a company's impact beyond its balance sheet. ESG ratings and indices have gained consideration as investment assessment tools to contribute to low carbon transition (Boffo et al. 2020).

An innovative and sustainable use of bio-based resources in different sectors of the economy (i.e., a bio-based transformation or bioeconomy) provides opportunities for achieving a number of different Sustainable Development Goals (SDGs), which have been designed to improve social, economic, and ecological living conditions (Dietz et al. 2018).

Many drug companies have adopted an environmental, social, and corporate governance framework known as ESG. These frameworks are a way for corporations to evaluate how they are working on behalf of social goals that go beyond trying to maximize profits for shareholders. Companies with an ESG framework often release reports for investors that outline steps they've taken to increase their sustainability and social profiles.

Summary

The pharmaceutical industry is a major global polluter, generating more global emissions per dollar of revenue than the automotive sector. Every stage of the pharmaceutical supply chain has a carbon footprint—right down to the very beginning, where the raw materials for active pharmaceutical ingredients (APIs) are sourced. The following are some key measures needed to mitigate the adverse environmental impact:

- Developing a national strategy of integrating the advances in biotechnology and biomanufacturing into all sectors to create a sustainable bioeconomy
- Greening of the supply chain through applying the principles of green chemistry: reducing pollution at its source by minimizing or eliminating the hazards of chemical feedstocks, reagents, solvents, and products; and shifting to greener, renewable energy sources
- Limiting self-medication and overprescription practices
- Restricting trade in counterfeit pharmaceutical products
- Continuing dialogue between environmental experts and drug discovery and development experts in industry, academia, and authorities all over the world, to explore the feasibility of developing medicines with lower environmental impact
- Interventions of international organizations to enforce global environmental standards that target the key areas of the global value chain, and thereby limit the cross-border spillovers

Global interconnectedness requires us to address the health of the planet's entire population, irrespective of national borders. Engagement in global health is not simply a humanitarian concern but a priority for our collective well-being, efficient use of resources, and safeguarding our future (De Cock et al. 2013).

Notes

1 Biomass is an organic material that comes from plants and animals, and it is a renewable source of energy. Biomass is an "umbrella" term that includes renewable feedstocks such as wood, straw, sugar, maize, cassava, algae, or biowaste. Biomass generally consist of a very complex mixture of organic compounds, the separation of which is a rather challenging task.

2 Scientists have, however, raised concerns that the basic building blocks of nanotechnologies—particles smaller than one billionth of a meter—pose a potential new class of risk to health and the environment (OECD—Allianz-Aktiengesellschaft 2005). Adequate studies in the field of nano-ecotoxicology are required to assess the real risks of using nanoparticles, the safety and hazards related to them, etc. (Bundschuh et al. 2018, Taghavi et al. 2013).

References

Arias, A. 2023. *Is Pharma on Track to Reduce Its Carbon Emissions?* Blog January 12, 2023. IQVIA. https://www.iqvia.com/blogs/2023/01/is-pharma-on-track-to-reduce-carbon-emissions

Aus der Beek, Tim, Frank-Andreas Weber, Axel Bergmann, Silke Hickmann, Ina Ebert, Arne Hein, and Anette Küster. 2016. "Pharmaceuticals in the Environment—Global Occurrences and Perspectives." *Environmental Toxicology & Chemistry* 35 (4): 823–835. https://doi.org/10.1002/etc.3339.

Bennadi, Darshana. 2013. "Self-Medication: A Current Challenge." *Journal of Basic & Clinical Pharmacy* 5 (1): 19–23. https://doi.org/10.4103/0976-0105.128253.

Boffo, R., C. Marshall, and R. Patalano. 2020. *ESG Investing: Environmental Pillar Scoring and Reporting*. OECD.

Booth, Amy, Alexandra Jager, Stuart D. Faulkner, Christopher C. Winchester, and Sara E. Shaw. 2023. "Pharmaceutical Company Targets and Strategies to Address Climate Change: Content Analysis of Public Reports from 20 Pharmaceutical Companies." *International Journal of Environmental Research & Public Health* 20 (4): 3206. https://doi.org/10.3390/ijerph20043206.

Boxall, Alistair B. A. 2004. "The Environmental Side Effects of Medication." *EMBO Reports* 5 (12): 1110–1116. https://doi.org/10.1038/sj.embor.7400307.

Bracco, S., O. Calicioglu, M. G. Juan, and A. Flammini. 2018. "Assessing the Contribution of Bioeconomy to the Total 2 Economy: A Review of National Frameworks." *Sustainability* 3: 1–17.

Bundschuh, M., J. Filser, S. Lüderwald, M.S. McKee, G. Metreveli, G.E. Schaumann, R. Schulz, S. Wagner. 2018. "Nanoparticles in the Environment: Where do We Come from, Where Do We Go To?" *Environmental Sciences Europe* 30 (1): 6. doi: 10.1186/s12302-018-0132-6.

Caban, M., and P. Stepnowski. 2021. "How to Decrease Pharmaceuticals in the Environment? A Review." *Environmental Chemistry Letters* 19 (4): 3115–3118. https://doi.org/10.1007/s10311-021-01194-y.

Chatterjee, B. 2023. "Sustainability: Multiple Approaches Exist to Reduce Pharma's Environmental." *Footprint*, March 2, Tablets and capsules. https://www.tabletscapsules.com/3641-Technical-Articles/594885-Sustainability-Multiple-Approaches-Exist-to-Reduce-Pharma-s-Environmental-Footprint/.

Daughton, C. G., and T. A. Ternes. 1999. "Pharmaceuticals and Personal Care Products in the Environment: Agents of Subtle Change?" *Environmental Health Perspectives* 107 (Suppl. 6): 907–938. https://doi.org/10.1289/ehp.99107s6907.

De Cock, Kevin M., Patricia M. Simone, Veronica Davison, and Laurence Slutsker. 2013 August. "The New Global Health." *Emerging Infectious Diseases* 19 (8): 1192–1197. https://doi.org/10.3201/eid1908.130121.

Dietz, T., J. Börner, J. J. Förster, and J. von Braun. 2018. *Governance of the Bioeconomy: A Global Comparative Study of National Bioeconomy Strategies*. Discussion Papers 275071. University of Bonn, Center for Development Research (ZEF).

Elder, D. 2022. "22 February 2022, EPR (European Pharmaceutical Review)". *Green Chemistry*. WEF 3 ways healthcare systems can reduce their carbon footprint, blog by Aurelio Arias and Sarah Rickwood. http://www.europeanpharmaceuticalreview.com/article/168537/green-chemistry/.

Gavrilescu, Maria, and Yusuf Chisti. 2005. "Biotechnology-A Sustainable Alternative for Chemical Industry." *Biotechnology Advances* 23 (7–8): 471–499. https://doi.org/10.1016/j.biotechadv.2005.03.004.

IEA. 2018. "*Global Energy and CO2 Status Report 2018, The latest Trends in Energy and Emissions in 2018*." International Energy Agency Report, France.

IQVIA. 2021. *Environmental Sustainability in Pharma A View on Pharma's Progress Towards Positive Impact*. IQVIA.

Jalali, Mohammad S., Michael Botticelli, Rachael C. Hwang, Howard K. Koh, and R. Kathryn McHugh. 2020. "The Opioid Crisis: A Contextual, Social-Ecological Framework." *Health Research Policy & Systems* 18 (1): 87. https://doi.org/10.1186/s12961-020-00596-8.

Jimenez, D. 2022. *Cutting the Carbon Footprint of pharma's Supply Chain.* Pharma TechnologyFocus. https://pharma.nridigital.com/pharma_mar22/cutting-carbon-footprint-pharma-supply-chain.

Kookana, Rai S., Mike Williams, Alistair B. A. Boxall, D. G. Joakim Larsson, Sally Gaw, Kyungho Choi, Hiroshi Yamamoto, Shashidhar Thatikonda, Yong-Guan Zhu, and Pedro Carriquiriborde. 2014. "Potential Ecological Footprints of Active Pharmaceutical Ingredients: An Examination of Risk Factors in Low-, Middle- and High-Income Countries." *Philosophical Transactions of the Royal Society of London. Series B, Biological Sciences* 369 (1656): 20130586. https://doi.org/10.1098/rstb.2013.0586.

Küster, Anette, and Nicole Adler. 2014. "Pharmaceuticals in the Environment: Scientific Evidence of Risks and Its Regulation." *Philosophical Transactions of the Royal Society of London. Series B, Biological Sciences* 369 (1656): 20130587. https://doi.org/10.1098/rstb.2013.0587.

Lafferty, Kevin D. 2009. "The Ecology of Climate Change and Infectious Diseases." *Ecology* 90 (4): 888–900. https://doi.org/10.1890/08-0079.1.

Larsson, D. G. Joakim. 2014. "Pollution from Drug Manufacturing: Review and Perspectives." *Philosophical Transactions of the Royal Society of London. Series B, Biological Sciences* 369 (1656): 20130571. https://doi.org/10.1098/rstb.2013.0571.

Lawler, Odette K., Hannah L. Allan, Peter W. J. Baxter, Romi Castagnino, Marina Corella Tor, Leah E. Dann, Joshua Hungerford, Dibesh Karmacharya, Thomas J. Lloyd, María José López-Jara, Gloeta N. Massie, Junior Novera, Andrew M. Rogers, and Salit Kark. 2021. "The COVID-19 Pandemic Is Intricately Linked to Biodiversity Loss and Ecosystem Health." *Lancet. Planetary Health* 5 (11): e840–e850. https://doi.org/10.1016/S2542-5196(21)00258-8.

Liebig, Markus, Johann F. Moltmann, and Thomas Knacker. 2006. "Evaluation of Measured and Predicted Environmental Concentrations of Selected Human Pharmaceuticals and Personal Care Products." *Environmental Science & Pollution Research International* 13 (2): 110–119. https://doi.org/10.1065/espr2005.08.276.

Lokko, Yvonne, Marc Heijde, Karl Schebesta, Philippe Scholtès, Marc Van Montagu, and Mauro Giacca. 2018. "Biotechnology and the Bioeconomy-Towards Inclusive and Sustainable Industrial Development." *New Biotechnology* 40 (A): 5–10. https://doi.org/10.1016/j.nbt.2017.06.005.

MacNeill, Andrea J., Harriet Hopf, Aman Khanuja, Saed Alizamir, Melissa Bilec, Matthew J. Eckelman, Lyndon Hernandez, Forbes McGain, Kari Simonsen, Cassandra Thiel, Steven Young, Robert Lagasse, and Jodi D. Sherman. 2020. "Transforming the Medical Device Industry: Road Map to A Circular Economy." *Health Affairs (Project Hope)* 39 (12): 2088–2097. https://doi.org/10.1377/hlthaff.2020.01118.

Miettinen, M., and S. A. Khan. 2021. "SA (2021) Pharmaceutical Pollution: A Weakly Regulated Global Environmental Risk." *Review of European Comparative & International Environmental Law* 31 (1): 75–88.

OECD. 2011. "OECD Factbook 2011–2012: Economic, Environmental and Social Statistics", OECD Publishing, Paris, https://doi.org/10.1787/factbook-2011-en.

OECD. 2009. *The Bioeconomy to 2030, Designing a Policy Agenda.* OECD International Future Project, Organization for Economic Co-operation and Development Publishing.

OECD. 2019a. *Pharmaceutical Residues in Freshwater: Hazards and Policy Responses, OECD Studies on Water.* OECD Publishing.

OECD. 2019b. *Excessive Prices in Pharmaceutical Markets.* OECD Publishing.

OECD. 2020, Chapter 3. "Industry Review." In *Trade in Counterfeit Pharmaceutical Products.* OECD Publishing.

Our World in Data team. 2023. "SDG Tracker: Measuring progress towards the Sustainable Development Goals" Published online at OurWorldInData.org. Retrieved from: https://ourworldindata.org/sdgs

Peng, Yiming, Peipei Wu, Amina T. Schartup, and Yanxu Zhang. 2021. "Plastic Waste Release Caused by COVID-19 and Its Fate in the Global Ocean." *Proceedings of the National Academy of Sciences of the United States of America* 118 (47): e2111530118. https://doi.org/10.1073/pnas.2111530118.

StarFish Medical.2022. "Top Medical Device Blogs." Blogarithmic Thinking, Star Fish Product Engineering Inc. https://starfishmedical.com/blog/medical-device-blogs/

Taghavi, S.M., M. Momenpour, M. Azarian, M. Ahmadian, F. Souri, S.A. Taghavi, M. Sadeghain, and M. Karchani. 2013. "Effects of Nanoparticles on the Environment and Outdoor Workplaces". *Electronic Physician* 5 (4): 706–712. https://doi.org/10.14661/2013.706-712

The White House. 2022. *Executive Order 14081: Advancing Biotechnology and Biomanufacturing Innovation for a Sustainable, Safe, and Secure American Bioeconomy.* The White House.

The White House Office of Science and Technology Policy. 2022. *Bold Goals for U.S. Biotechnology and Biomanufacturing Harnessing Research and Development to Further Societal Goals.* The White House.

UNCTAD. 2018. "World Investment Report, Investment and New Industrial Policies." UNCTAD 2018, United Nations Publication.

WEF. 2022. *6 Ways the Pharmaceutical Industry Can Reduce Its Climate Impact Blog by Jayasree K. Iyer.* WEF.

WHO. 2018. International Agency for Research on Cancer, Press Release 12 September, 2018. WHO.

Yu, Derrick Ethelbhert C., Luis F. Razon, and Raymond R. Tan. 2020. "Can Global Pharmaceutical Supply Chains Scale up Sustainably for the COVID-19 Crisis?" *Resources, Conservation, & Recycling* 159: 104868. https://doi.org/10.1016/j.resconrec.2020.104868.

8 Role of China and India in the emerging global supply chain

Prospects and challenges

Introduction

According to UNESCO (2021), the emerging markets of China, India, and Brazil are important partners in the global value chain. These countries possess the required infrastructure and the capacity to produce generics of many drugs for both their domestic markets and many low- and medium-income countries (Correa 2011; UNCTAD 2021). Both China and India have large talent pool and are offering the breadth of preclinical and clinical services at significant savings of 30–80% versus the cost in the USA (Khanna 2012). Advanced countries are maturing rapidly in competitive skills needed in various facets of pharmaceutical R&D. With signing of patent treaty, these markets are escalating with new partnering and business deals in R&D, manufacturing, clinical trials, and marketing (Khanna 2012).

Both China and India have a large and expanding middle class. They are undergoing demographic and epidemiological transition. With steady economic growth and health reforms in progress, they are contributing to the growth of the global medical goods industry, and their contribution is projected to grow and over time. This chapter deals with assessing the potential, opportunities, and challenges facing these countries.

China and India: Emerging players in healthcare products and services

China and India are at the forefront of globalization in the 21st century, and both are projected to have a tremendous impact on the world as economic powerhouses (Dummer and Cook 2008). This section provides a brief review of the strengths of China and India in the global healthcare industry. Table 8.1 presents comparative data on key indicators of innovation capabilities of BRICS nations. These indicators include research and development (R&D) expenditures, research publications in biotechnology and artificial intelligence, patents cited in health sciences, as well as annual expenditure on medicines (a rough proxy of market size). As observed from the table, China excels among BRICS countries in every indicator of innovative potential. China also has the

DOI: 10.4324/9781003449331-8

Table 8.1 Key indicators: R&D publications, researchers, patenting, and pharmaceutical spendings, BRICS

	Share in Global GERD (%)		*Share of Global Researchers*		*Share of Global Publications in AI and Robotics*		*Share of Global Publications in Biotechnology*		*Share in Global Health Sciences' Patents*	*Percentage of the US Invoice Spending*	
	2014	*2018*	*2015*	*2018*	*2015*	*2018*	*2015*	*2018*	*2015*	*2023*	*2028(P)*
Brazil	2.4	1.88	2.31		1.99	1.79	4.09	5.51	0.14	5.0	5.3
China	21.18	24.84	19.5	21.12	19.25	20.14	23.29	9.97	1.8	23.0	20
India	2.94	3.06		3.87	9.06	18.12	10.59	10.25	0.74	4.4	4.6
Russia (Fed)	1.62	1.8	5.71	4.59	1.94	3.86	1.52	1.46	0.11	2.6	2.6
South Africa	0.31	0.29	0.3	0.33	0.5	0.47	0.51	0.77	0.08		

Sources: UNESCO (2021) and IQVIA (2024)

largest market size (defined as the percentage of the US invoice spending) (IQVIA 2024). India ranks next to China and is making steady progress in innovative capability.

India and China are major producers of generic pharmaceuticals, vaccines, biosimilars, and active pharmaceutical ingredients (APIs) among the developing countries. Their role has been critical to meeting public health needs in many low-income developing countries, especially in Africa (WHO 2011). They have been on a high growth trajectory in the last few decades. China and India (and including Brazil) hold a great potential in meeting the medical needs of the poor and underserved population (Hafner and Popp 2011).

Advances in big data analytics and IoT (Internet of Things) have created opportunities for India, China, and other emerging economies to apply bio-scientific knowledge by designing new services that would improve health outcomes, offer more flexible care models, as well as realize cost savings in healthcare delivery (Shaw et al. 2018). In both India and China, the use of digital health technologies is growing. In 2020, both countries increased their capability to develop affordable medical technologies by serving their internal markets. The Indian medical device industry is dominated by small-scale domestic players, who focus primarily on consumables and disposables, which include high-volume low-end products such as syringes, needles, and catheters (EOS Intelligence 2019). Indian players are also looking at entering the high-end product segment by offering more affordable and locally customized solutions (EOS Intelligence 2019). As in India, most local players in the Chinese medical device sector focus on the high-volume low-technology segments (EOS Intelligence 2019; ITA 2023, 2024). At the same time, leading Chinese medical device companies are investing heavily in R&D to move up the value chain (EOS Intelligence 2019). In January 2020, the country took policy action in this direction with the release of the National Digital Health Blueprint (NDHB).

The growth of digital health technologies has been spurred by fast expanding frontier technologies, such as IoT (Internet of Things), AI (artificial intelligence), Big Data, 5G, and others (UNCTAD 2021a, b). Only a few countries have innovative capability and absorption capacity in these technologies. According to UNCTAD's Frontier Technology Readiness Index, India, China, and some other developing countries rank highly in their capacity to use, adopt, and adapt frontier technologies (Readiness for Frontier Technologies Index) (UNCTAD 2021b). The countries most ready for frontier technologies are also expected to be those most likely to use them (UNCTAD 2021b). This index comprises five building blocks: ICT deployment, skills, R&D activity, industrial activity, and access to finance. India has been found to be the greatest overperformer as determined by the difference between the actual index rankings and the index rankings predicted by per capita income (UNCTAD 2021b). India's estimated ranking based on per capita income was 108, which meant that India overperformed other countries by 65 ranking positions. In terms of R&D activity, China ranked at number one position, while India ranked at fourth position among 158 countries (UNCTAD 2021b).

The high performance of India and China in R&D activity is reflected in their abundant supplies of highly skilled human resources. They also have large local markets, which attract investment by multinational enterprises (UNCTAD 2021b, WHO 2017a, b).

Rezaie et al. (2012), in their survey of 165 innovative products of 41 indigenous firms in China, India, and Brazil, found evidence of India's considerable expertise in chemical-based pharmaceuticals and China's focus on biotech innovations (55% of its innovative products).

China's strength: Investor in R&D and supplier of medical goods

China has emerged as the second-largest largest country in R&D intensity, after the United States (Ni et al. 2017). China is also making rapid progress in cross-cutting strategic technologies such as artificial intelligence, robotics, biotechnology, or nanotechnology (UNESCO 2021). With these technologies, China increased its share of global research publications from 28.08% in 2015 to 32.03% in 2019, representing the highest national share in the world (UNESCO 2021). Similarly, the share of researchers from China out of total researchers worldwide stood at 21.2% in 2018, the highest in the world (UNESCO 2021). China has greatly outperformed India and other emerging countries in developing its innovative capabilities (R&D funding, scientific publications, and patents) and industrial structure.

China has progressed from producing low-value-added devices to medium- to high-value-added devices (Torsekar 2018). China is ranked among the leading manufacturers and suppliers of active pharmaceutical ingredients (APIs). As of August 2019, the US sourced 13% of its domestic market needs for APIs from China. Of the total of 1,079 API facilities worldwide that make the 370 drugs that the WHO lists as marketed in the US, China was home to 166 (15%) in 2019. The number of registered facilities making APIs in China for the US market more than doubled between 2010 and 2019 (Congressional Testimony 2019). China's strengths in gene therapy technology (DNA Sequencing), stem cell research, gene chips, and gene research of some major diseases is getting acknowledged internationally.

Chinese multinational firms, Sino bio-pharmaceuticals, Shanghai Pharmaceuticals and Jiangsu Hengrui Medicine were ranked among the top 50 global MNEs in the pharmaceutical industry in 2022, in terms of revenue from the sale of prescription medicines (See Appendix A).

China's performance in R&D is likely to improve since the number of university students and researchers is on the rise. China's policy of recruiting Chinese scientists living abroad is likely to bolster Chinese innovative capability in the coming years (Ni et al. 2017; UNESCO 2021). China is attracting a growing number of returnees who are staffing universities, research institutes, and enterprises (UNESCO 2021).

India: Emerging global partner

The Indian pharmaceutical industry owes its emergence as a global player, beginning in the 1980s, with the adoption of *Waxman-Hatch Act 1984* in the United States, which intended to accelerate entry of generic products. Indian companies seized the opportunity to enter the US and European markets by implementing strict product quality standards (set by FDA and the European Medicines Agency), by introducing TRIPS (WTO's agreement mandating the members to enforce the patent protection laws in the pharmaceutical products by 2005), and by capitalizing on the cost advantages conferred by integrated nature of its industry. The integrated companies were able to achieve cost economies by sourcing low-cost APIs locally for their efficient production of finished pharmaceutical products (FPPs) (WHO 2017a).

India's medical device manufacturing sector has been developing several frugal technologies (see details in UNESCO 2021). For example, India has achieved global success in manufacturing low-cost ventilators and selling them at 20% of the standard international price, Cat 29 scanner, and COVID-19 test (UNESCO 2015, 2021).

India has been steadily increasing its contribution to the global R&D in the health sector. In cross-cutting strategic technologies, India improved its share of global research publications from 6.47% in 2015 to 10.2% in 2019 (UNESCO 2021). India has been mobilizing resources to produce low-cost solutions for public health systems around the world in three areas: vaccine research and manufacturing; the manufacture of generic versions of "game-changer" drugs; and frugal engineering of medical devices (UNESCO 2021). Indian companies have successfully introduced generic products into the US market in the last few years (Kedron and Bagchi-Sen 2011; Correa 2011) and have overtaken the lead from US generic firms in the number of first-time ANDA approvals.[1] India's share of first-time ANDA approvals increased from 29% in 2016 to 33% in 2019 (FICCI 2021). Fifty Indian firms together have abbreviated new drug application (ANDA) market authorization for over 5000 medical products (Guerin et al. 2020).

India has focused its development of APIs in the areas of oncology, cardiology, diabetes, and tropical diseases. Its API industry is ranked as the third largest in the world, and it produces approximately 57% of the APIs on the WHO's prequalified list (KPMG 2020). Indian manufacturers produce 67% (379) of the 563 WHO prequalified pharmaceutical products for conditions such as diarrhea (1), hepatitis (13), HIV/AIDS (197), influenza (10), malaria (41), neglected tropical diseases (3), reproductive health (21), and tuberculosis (93) (Guerin et al. 2020; WHO 2020a). Patent data indicates that Indian pharma companies are home-grown, meaning that "almost all of the USPTO patents secured by Indian inventors do indeed belong to domestic pharmaceutical companies" (2015, p. 604).

India is the leading supplier of the inexpensive antiretroviral medicines that have revolutionized HIV/AIDS treatment in Sub-Saharan Africa (Hafner and Popp 2011). Indian companies meet 62% of the global demand for vaccines (FICCI 2021) and export vaccines to more than 150 countries. Indian companies contribute 40–70% of the WHO's demand for Diphtheria, Pertussis, and Tetanus (DPT), and Bacillus Calmette–Guérin (BCG) vaccines and 90% of WHO demand for the measles vaccine (FICCI 2021). More than half the world's children are immunized with vaccines produced in India (WHO 2011).

Indian pharmaceutical companies are increasing their global presence. As of 2023, Sun Pharma ranked at 33th position among worlds' top 50 pharmaceutical enterprises in terms of the revenue from the sale of prescription drugs (see Appendix A). Aurobindo pharma occupied 46th position among the top 50 global pharmaceutical firms in 2021. In terms of market capitalization, Sun Pharma, Devi's laboratories, Dr. Reddy's laboratory and Cipla were ranked among the top 50 multinationals as of 2019 (Wikipedia).[2]

Besides numerous achievements at the global level, there is, however, a long standing concern about the low level of R&D expenditure (as a ratio of revenue) by Indian pharmaceutical companies, which falls below half of the equivalent percentage of OECD originator companies (8% India versus 16–20% foreign multinational companies) (WHO 2017a). Research evidence shows that low R&D intensity at the firm level restricts the absorptive capability of the firm (Mowery 1989). Absorptive capability is the ability of a firm to exploit external sources of knowledge or technology.

A comparative view of India and China in serving the US manufacturing facilities for drugs

China and India are emerging as important and cost-efficient locations for serving the US pharmaceutical market in APIs, generics, and all drugs (FDF-finished dosage forms). Indian generics companies are leading suppliers of US FDA-approved generic drugs. It is estimated that API manufacturing in India can reduce costs for US and European companies by 30–40% (The White House 2021).

The table 8.2 shows that only 27% of the facilities manufacturing APIs for the US market were located in the United States. The remaining 73% were in the EU (25%), India (19%), China (13%), Canada (2%), and other countries (14%). For finished generics manufacturing for the US market, 37% of sites were located in the United States, 26% in India, 16% in EU, and 8% in China.

China specializes in the first step: transformation of raw materials into intermediates of active pharmaceutical ingredients (APIs), while India specializes in the second step of final API manufacturing stage (Chapman et al. 2022).

As global partners, both the countries have the potential to upgrade their status in the global supply chain.

Upgrading opportunities for India and China: Moving beyond low valued generics

The pharmaceutical GVC consists of three interrelated strands: innovative and branded products, quality generics for high-end markets, and low-value generics (Haakonsson 2009). Both China and India focus largely on low-value generics (see Mossialos et al. 2016); Atkinson 2019; FICCI 2021; WHO

Table 8.2 Distribution of sites involved in the manufacture of medicines for the US market, according to location (% of total sites by category), March 2021

Country/Region	*Sites Involved in the Manufacture of Finished Products (FDF—Tablets, Liquid) (Country's/ Region's Percentage Share of Total Sites Serving the US Market)*	*Sites of API Manufacturing Facilities for All Drugs (Country's/ Region's Percentage Share of Total Sites Serving the US Market)*	*Sites of FDF (Tablets and Liquids) Manufacturing Facilities for Generic Drugs (Approved under ANDAs) (Country's/ Region's Percentage Share of Total Sites Serving the US Market)*	*Sites of API Manufacturing Facilities for Generic Drugs (Approved under ANDAs) (Country's/ Region's Percentage Share of Total Sites Serving the US Market)*
USA	48	27	37	13
EU	18	25	16	27
India	9	19	26	29
China	6	13	8	16
Canada	4	2	4	2
Latin America	2	2	1	3
Rest of the world	13	12	8	10

Source: The White House (2021). Note: Abbreviated New Drug Application (ANDA) should prove that your generic drug is just as safe, does the work, and is of the same quality as the original brand drug.

2017a, b). While India ranks as the third-largest manufacturer of generic drugs worldwide in terms of production volume, accounting for 10% of the total, in terms of value India accounts for only 1.5% of the total value of drugs produced worldwide, making it 14th ranked among manufacturing nations (FICCI 2021). India and China have the potential to move beyond low-value generics toward higher value opportunities in complex generics, biosimilars, new chemical entities (NCEs), incremental vaccine innovations, new biological entities (NBEs), and drugs repurposing (repositioning) innovations. India is already accelerating its efforts to improve its research and institutional infrastructure to that end (FICCI 2021; Kale 2019).

Undertaking incremental innovations and low-cost medical solutions

IFPMA (2013) has classified pharmaceutical innovations into three categories: revolutionary, radical, and incremental. Revolutionary innovation is marked by conceptual advances, such as new scientific theories or principles, which form the basis for subsequent research. A new biological or metabolic pathway, for example, can be considered revolutionary (IFPMA 2013). Putting these conceptual advances into practice can produce radical innovations that set the standard for applying a scientific principle. A "first-in-class" medicine (the first medicine of its type) is normally considered a radical product (IFPMA 2013). An incremental innovation (or adaptive innovation) is an improvement to a radical product (IFPMA 2013).

IFPMA suggests that incremental innovations in medicines refers to the following advances: expanding therapeutic classes of existing medicine, increasing the number of available dosing options, discovering new physiological interactions of known medicines, and improving other properties of existing medicines. Consider a few examples of incremental innovations. Rituximab was originally approved for the treatment of cancer but was later found effective at treating rheumatoid arthritis (Lybecker 2014). Insulin, initially administered through injection, was shown to have more rapid onset action when administered through an inhaler. For Type-2 diabetes, two treatments, metformin and saxagliptin, were combined into a simpler, single-dose treatment (IFPMA 2013). In treating malaria, a new formulation of two anti-malarial drugs, artesunate and amodiaquine, simplified dosing regimens by reducing the required number of tablets a day from eight to two (IFPMA 2013).

Some Indian companies have been introducing incremental innovations in vaccines for some common diseases. Examples include Bharat Biotech's typhoid conjugate vaccine and "eco-friendly" recombinant hepatitis B vaccine (free of cesium chloride and thiomersal) and Serum Institute's liquid rotavirus vaccine (FICCI 2021).

China and India can deploy increasing R&D to improve the properties of medicines already approved by regulatory bodies. Such improvements expand the number of treatment and dosing options available, thereby allowing healthcare providers to better treat diverse patient groups (IFPMA 2013). They are valuable to both patients and payers, for both health and cost-saving reasons. (Lybecker 2014).

Frugal innovations: Tapping the "bottom of the pyramid" (BOP)

The real health challenge facing the world's developing countries is the lack of (access to) cost-effective medicines and devices. Medical products designed by firms for developed economies are not affordable for most people in low-income emerging markets. Although 95% of essential medicines, as defined by the WHO, are off-patent, one-third of the world's population does not have reliable access to them (IFPMA 2012). While many essential medicines cost as little as USD 0.02–1.50, these prices can still be prohibitively expensive for individuals earning less than USD 1 a day. Lower-income countries also often suffer from limited availability of low-cost medicines (IFPMA 2012).

Frugal and reverse innovations create new markets, both in emerging economies and developed countries, for previously underserved customer groups (Simula et al. 2015). "Reverse innovation" (RI) refers to the case where innovation is adopted first in poor (emerging) economies before "trickling up" to rich countries (Govindarajan and Euchner 2012). Frugal innovation, on the other hand, means doing more with less, and it means being creative,

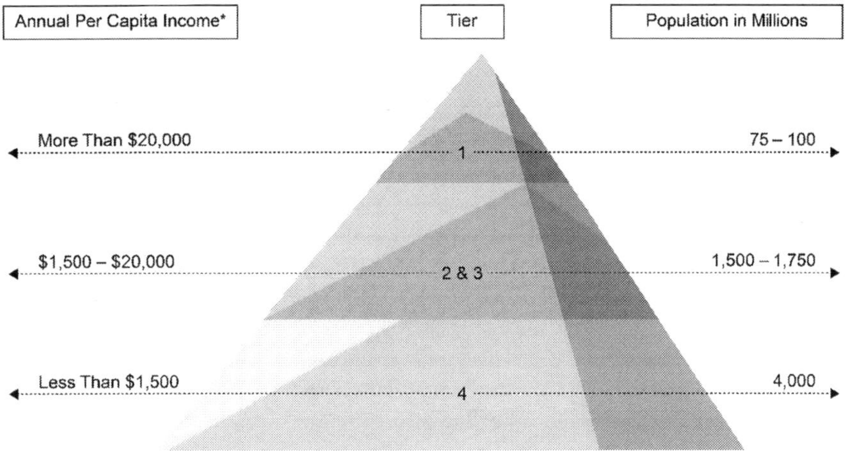

Figure 8.1 The economic development pyramids

innovative, and resourceful in the face of institutional voids (the absence of specialized intermediaries, regulatory systems, and contract-enforcement mechanisms) and resource constraints (Bhatti et al. 2018). A frugal innovation is a "good enough" product for resource-constrained consumers. Zeschky et al. (2011) have used the term "pro-inclusive innovations" instead of "frugal innovation" as these innovations often modify existing technologies, products, or services to supply a more inclusive customer base—including lower and middle income groups—while retaining the most critical functionalities.

There are global opportunities to serve the middle of the economic development pyramid as well as the bottom of the pyramid (Govindarajan and Euchner 2012). Figure 8.1 presents the concept of the economic development pyramid, comprising the four Tiers of the global market. The bottom of the pyramid (Tier 4) is the largest, but poorest, socio-economic group. According to Prahalad and Hart (2002), there exist tremendous innovation possibilities for markets at the bottom of the pyramid. But serving BOP markets requires a completely different approach from serving tiers higher in the pyramid. Serving the Tier 4 markets requires reinventing cost structures (in order to reduce cost levels relative to those in Tier 1) (Ostraszewska and Tylec 2014).

GE's Research Centre in India has developed several low-cost types of biomedical equipment, from scanners to portable electrocardiograms, while Bristol-Myers Squibb has developed many promising novel drugs at its partnered research center in Bangalore. Biocon, meanwhile, has not only developed insulins in India through proprietary technology in the early 2000s but also developed and delivered two affordable novel biologics for the benefit of cancer and psoriasis patients in India (Mazumdar-Shaw 2018).

The John F. Welch Technical Center (JFWTC), GE's research laboratory in India, introduced the MAC400 in India, an $800 portable ECG, into the market. Existing products had a digital signal processor (DSP), keyboard, and printer, which were all high-quality components that needed to be specially ordered (Motohashi 2012). In contrast, the MAC400 used standard, very low-cost components. Moreover, the product was lightweight, and battery-operated, thus making it popular in India. GE continued to improve the product, and it is now sold in 60 countries, including the United States, as an entirely new product category. This is an example of an R&D center spurring frugal innovation both globally and in the home country.

Several frugal innovations have turned into reverse innovations by seeping up into developed countries from developing countries (Hossain 2018). Zeschky et al. (2011) mention that very often reverse innovations have to be "re-engineered" to ensure that they are adapted to the norms and characteristics of their new markets. As a consequence, RI requires strong technological and managerial competencies (Le Bas 2016).

Exploring and entering markets of biosimilars, complex vaccines, and complex generics

Forecasts projecting from recent growth trends indicate that the markets for complex generics, biosimilars, and complex vaccines would offer significant opportunities to China and India in the coming years.

The market of biosimilars

At the global level, the market share of biosimilars (out of all biologics) has exhibited double-digit growth over 2015–2019 and is expected to continue to grow in the coming years (Kauser 2021).[3] The growth is being driven by the rising incidence of chronic diseases and the cost-effectiveness of biosimilars. With clinical testing not including large Phase III–type efficacy and safety studies, biosimilars require less investment and time for their development, thus providing cheaper alternatives and more competition for reference products previously lacking generic competition (Kale 2019; Rader and Langer 2019). Patent expirations (and the associated loss of market exclusivity) and ongoing regulatory improvements allowing for easier and more rapid market access are likely to aid the growth in biosimilars' market share (Kauser 2021).

More specifically, most recent blockbuster drugs (drugs generating revenue of > USD 1billion) are novel biologics which have lost their patents by 2020. A number of additional patent expirations of high-selling biological medicines are expected by 2030. This offers a great opportunity for other biopharmaceutical companies to develop similar biologics (Meher et al. 2019). Biosimilars have the potential to drastically reduce the overall cost of treatment, especially when the patient pool is large. This is evident from a study carried out in the United States where it was estimated over 10 years a biosimilar can save $54 billion (Meher et al. 2019).

Emerging markets have several advantages in developing biosimilars since potential entrants face lower entry barriers, a less stringent intellectual property regime (with less market exclusivity), and lower development and manufacturing costs (Blackstone and Joseph 2013). Dr. Reddy's (an Indian company) has been launching products in emerging markets four to five years ahead of the United States, allowing it to gather data in India before entering the US market. India's top pharmaceutical manufacturers (Cipla, Lupin, Aurobindo, Biocon, Reliance Life Sciences, Zydus Cadila, Enzene, and Intas) have entered the biosimilars market. Indian biosimilars have largely been sold to domestic and emerging markets. India leads globally at launching biosimilars in a domestic market. According to a WHO survey, India had approved 93 biosimilars for its domestic market (with at least 50 already on the market) by August 2019 compared to the US's 26 and the European Union's 61 (FICCI 2021).

India's Biocon is a major player in the biosimilar market. In 2016, Biocon's Insulin Glargine became the first biosimilar from India to be commercialized in Japan. In December 2017, Biocon got the US FDA's nod to market its novel biologic. Herceptin (or trastuzumab), which is used in certain breast and stomach cancer, was the first biologic to be approved by the FDA (Meher et al. 2019). Biocon developed the biosimilar in collaboration with US drug maker Mylan. The company has a rich pipeline of biosimilars and novel biologics at various stages of development including Insulin Tregopil. Biocon has rapidly developed a robust drug pipeline led by monoclonal antibodies and several other molecules at exciting stages in the biopharmaceutical value chain. Biocon's biosimilar products are sold in both bulk and formulation forms in several emerging markets. Biosimilars approved and used in India mainly consist of vaccines, monoclonal antibodies,[4] insulin, and recombinant proteins (Meher et al. 2019).[5]

India has other notable players. Low-cost/high-volume pharmaceutical and vaccine manufacturers in India, including the Serum Institute of India Private Ltd., Gennova Biopharmaceuticals, and Sun Pharma, are also investing in both biosimilar and novel monoclonal antibody development (IAVI 2019). The Department of Biotechnology (DBT) and Biotechnology Industry Research Assistance Council (BIRAC) are collaborating closely with industry and academia on multiple initiatives to promote research and manufacturing in biotechnology-based drugs (Birac 2019).

While India is a significant global player in the manufacturing and use of biosimilars, Indian biopharmaceutical companies need to upgrade their technology and improve the skills of their workforce. This will require the government and its regulatory agencies to enable such activities.

The biosimilar market in China is projected to quadruple from USD 2 billion in 2018 to USD 8.1 billion in 2025 (Xi 2020). Several biosimilars are in late-stage development by Chinese biopharmaceutical companies. China's policies support the upward trend. Its Food and Drug Administration (CFDA) has issued a number of legislative and regulatory policies (for example, in 2015) to promote research and development in, and production of, biosimilars (Zhang 2018). China's NMPA has standardized regulations governing the development and evaluation of biosimilars, clarified the definition of biosimilars, and set standards for preclinical R&D, clinical trials, and manufacturing. And the State Council,

China's cabinet, unveiled a new policy whereby some generics manufacturers could qualify for a "high-tech enterprise" designation that comes with a 15% corporate tax rate, compared to the 25% rate for other companies (GaBI 2019).

China's push to grow its biosimilar market is expected to significantly intensify competition faced by manufacturers of originators. For example, Roche, the maker of trastuzumab, bevacizumab, Rituxan, and rituximab, faces competition in China from locally made biosimilars (WHO 2017b). Meanwhile, Amgen has established a strategic collaboration with Simcere to develop and commercialize biosimilars in China. The partnership will focus on medicines in the areas of inflammation and oncology (Pategou 2019).

The biotech sector in both countries is, however, at a nascent stage (WHO 2017a, b). In India, a part of the challenge is its comparatively small biologicals manufacturing sector (WHO 2017a, b).

The market for vaccines

The market for vaccines is projected to grow in future, since vaccines are the most effective way to prevent infectious diseases. Vaccines "teach" our immune system how to create antibodies that protect us from diseases (NIPH 2020). Among other benefits, the vaccines are proving to be a potent weapon against the global fight against AMR (Utt and Wells 2016). AMR is an acronym for antimicrobial resistance (AMR), which has emerged as a significant threat to global health security. It is projected that if current trends in AMR continue unchecked, upward of ten million lives per year and trillions of dollars of losses to the global economy could occur annually by 2050 (Utt and Wells 2016). Vaccines can prevent infections and therefore lower the demand for therapeutic treatment with antimicrobials and, in turn, reduce disease with antimicrobial strains and also attenuate further increases in drug resistance (Utt and Wells 2016; Orenstein and Ahmed 2017). As per WHO's immunization records, current immunization programs have contributed to the marked reduction in mortality of children less than five years of age globally from 93 deaths per 1,000 live births in 1990 to 39 deaths per 1,000 live births in 2016 (Pollard and Bijker 2021).

MI4A (Market Information for Access to Vaccines, WHO) estimates the global market value for vaccines in 2019 to have been approximately $33 billion, or about 2% of the overall pharmaceutical market (WHO 2020b). Pneumococcal conjugate (PCV), diphtheria- and tetanus-containing, and human papillomavirus vaccines (HPV) are the highest-value vaccines, and it is projected that the PCV and HPV markets in particular will grow substantially by 2030 (WHO 2020b).

Though vaccine manufacturing remains concentrated among a few manufacturers in developed countries, with four (GSK, Pfizer, Merck, and Sanofi) controlling 90% of global vaccine value and five producing 60% of global volume (SII, GSK, Sanofi, BBIL and Haffkine), mid-size manufacturers from China, India, and other Asian countries are expanding their portfolios to compete in regional and new vaccine markets, such as HPV and PCV, offering additional and often more affordable choices (WHO 2020b).

India's pharmaceutical industry ranks among the largest in the world, currently producing 60% of the world's vaccines. Some of the top global companies have partnered with Indian companies to manufacture vaccines. India currently produces two vaccines—Covaxin and Covishield. Covaxin was developed by Bharat Biotech International. The other, Covishield (or AZD1222), is the product of a partnership between the Serum Institute (the world's largest vaccine manufacturer), the British-Swedish multinational pharmaceutical company AstraZeneca, and the University of Oxford.[6] The Serum Institute produces 2.5 million doses of Covishield daily (Blablová 2021) and has an agreement to manufacture one billion doses total. It serves customers worldwide, and its vaccines are accredited by the World Health Organization and used in 140 countries in their national immunization programs, saving millions of lives. In addition to the Serum Institute's partnership, India can expect more collaborations in the near future.

Serum Institute, the world's largest vaccine maker, has also reached an agreement with Novavax for the production of Novavax's NVX-CoV2373 (Covovax) vaccine for India and other low and middle-income countries. Novavax is an American biotechnology company that develops vaccines to combat serious infectious diseases. In December 2021, the World Health Organization (WHO) granted Emergency Use Listing (EUL) for Covovax for active immunization of individuals 18 years or older for the prevention of COVID-19. The EUL was based on the totality of preclinical, manufacturing, and clinical trial data submitted for review. The vaccine is also currently under review by multiple regulatory agencies worldwide. Novavax will also produce Codagenix's nasally administered COVID-19 vaccine CDX-005.

China, meanwhile, has developed four vaccines (produced by Sinovac, Sinopharm, CanSino and Anhui Zhifei Longcom) (Blablová 2021). Both China and India joined the COVAX initiative[7] aiming to ensure access to vaccines for developing countries.

The market of complex generics

As the market for simple generics has become saturated, biopharma companies are turning their focus to complex generic drugs, which deliver more value to patients by addressing additional unmet needs and which enable them to achieve market differentiation and opportunities for higher margins (IQVIA 2016). According to the US FDA, a complex generic is a generic with a complex active ingredient, complex formulation, complex route of delivery, or complex drug-device combinations, whereas a simple generic is a copy of a small-molecule reference drug and is chemically identical to its branded counterpart (IQVIA 2016; Lionberger 2021). Examples of complex products include inhalers, topical products, and extended release injectables (Lionberger 2021). The term "specialty generics" is often used interchangeably with "complex generics."

Generics of complex brand name drugs can be more difficult to develop than simple generics. Accordingly, a complex drug is less likely to come in generic form. According to IQVIA (2016), "Complex generic drug development is the current wave, and companies that can adapt to a more complicated development process are positioned to profit greatly in the years to come" (p. 10). In most cases with complex generics, the study design and plan will require more extensive clinical studies than are typical for simple generics (IQVIA 2016). It is challenging, time-consuming, and expensive to develop complex generics and demonstrate their safety, efficacy, and equivalence to their branded counterparts (IQVIA 2016).

China and India are the most attractive locations for manufacturing complex generics because of their strong R&D infrastructure and biologics capability. India, with its advantage of low-cost, high-quality generic manufacturing capability, is optimally suited to penetrate the complex generic market (Yes Global Institute 2017). Indian pharma players are following a differentiated market approach by manufacturing and distributing a broad range of products (Yes Global Institute 2017). Some of the top Indian companies, such as Dr. Reddy's, Zydus, Glenmark, Aurobindo, Torrent, Strides, Lupin, Cipla, and the globally acclaimed Sun Pharmaceutical Industries, have already started building their specialty generics pipelines (FICCI 2021; Sun Pharma, Annual Report 2019–2020).

Meanwhile, China's drug development expertise, understanding of the epidemiology of disease and medical practice in China, simplified regulatory system for drug registration, growing partnerships between major multinational pharmaceutical companies and domestic firms or research institutes, increasing number of foreign-trained graduates returning home with science backgrounds, and innovation-friendly policy environment are among the critical factors favoring the development of complex generics, in China (Su 2013; WHO 2016; Ding et al. 2011).

Harnessing the potential of drug repurposing (repositioning) market

Drug repurposing is becoming an effective approach to drug discovery, as it offers a new way to explore drugs. Drug repurposing, often referred to as drug repositioning, identifies new indications for approved or clinically failed/investigational drugs that have not been approved. Approved or failed compounds are then developed for alternative uses (IQVIA 2022). Drug repurposing is a strategy to accelerate drug development and skip the early phases of roadblocks (Seyhan 2019). Given that the repurposed drugs have been proven to be safe in humans in the early phases of clinical trials, drug repurposing can bring medications to patients much faster and with a much lower cost than developing new drugs (IQVIA 2022). Drug repositioning opens new opportunities for orphan diseases (diseases with a rare occurrence, affecting only a small population, typically less than 200,000), pandemic outbreaks (requiring faster, cheaper, less risky treatment), and highly resistant diseases (Low et al. 2020). To date, there are more than 7000 orphan diseases (affecting 20% of world population) for which there is insufficient research because of lack of profitability, and the number is continuously expanding (Low et al. 2020). With the advance of novel techniques based on machine learning, artificial intelligence, or in silico screens (performed on computer or via computer simulation), plus new data sources such as large-scale

Table 8.3 Research publications in artificial intelligence and robotics cross-cutting technology 2011–2019

Country	*Global Percentage Share of Research Publications in AI and Robotics Technologies*
Australia	2.3
Canada	2.6
United States of America	12.7
Brazil	1.9
France	4.3
Germany	5.7
Italy	3.7
The Netherlands	1.5
Spain	3.3
Sweden	0.8
United Kingdom	5.1
Switzerland	1.0
Russian Federation	2.2
South Africa	0.4
China	23.0
Singapore	1.0
India	9.3

UNESCO (2021)

electronic health records, repurposing may play an increasingly important role in the future (Greenblatt et al. 2023).

Bibliometric evidence indicates that the United States leads in this area of research, followed by China, the United Kingdom, and India (Sun et al. 2022). China and India, with their strength in AI technologies, have a great potential benefit in this area. On the basis of the global data on research publications in AI technologies, it is observed that China, USA, and India rank in the first three positions respectively in the recent available data from 2011 to 2019 form UNESCO (2021). US scientific publications in AI are more frequently cited than those from Europe and China, suggesting that US research has relatively more impact (de Kleijn et al. 2019).

Table 8.3 shows that compared to Europe, China and India are preparing to improve their scientific ability to adopt artificial intelligence and its tools. India lags behind China and USA by a great margin. China's progress with AI is largely the result of strong and direct government support for the technology, leadership from Chinese tech industry giants, and a robust venture capital community (Mou 2019). The most vibrant AI hubs worldwide are California's Silicon Valley, New York City, Beijing, Boston, London, and Shenzhen (Mou 2019).

Key challenge facing India and China: The weak innovation system

Moving up the value chain to develop and commercialize world-class innovative drugs and vaccines not only takes a significant investment in building

R&D capacity but also requires a public research institute and a well-functioning institutional environment that enables sustained innovation capability building (Intarakumnerd and Goto 2018; Chadee and Roxas 2013). China and India are facing common challenges in this regard.

Innovation policy in developing countries is more challenging and complex than in advanced countries because market failures and missing complementarities are likely to be more acute in them (Cirera and Maloney 2017). According to the National Innovation System (NIS) literature, raising R&D intensity alone would do little to improve innovation capability in the absence of critical complementary factors across many markets and, in particular, firm capabilities (Cirera and Maloney 2017). The literature emphasizes the critical role of interactions between organizations, institutions, and stakeholders. Organizations include firms, universities, financial institutions, and government agencies. Institutions are formal rules, informal norms, and the enforcement characteristics of both, which together determine innovation levels and economic performance (North 1992). Although institutions are formed to reduce uncertainty in exchange, weak institutions can significantly increase uncertainty in the business environment (Silvestre 2015).

One commonly identified impediment to innovation in developing countries is the difficulty of translating promising product concepts into affordable and accessible products (Morel et al. 2005). These countries need to develop capabilities to address this knowledge-application gap. In the medical sector, which relies on a technology base with high science content (such as biotechnology and biopharmaceutical technology), the public institutions that help transmit advances in basic research from academia to the private sector (Martin and Scott 2000)[8] are weaker and more failure-prone than in other sectors.

Institutional barriers and the absence of specialized intermediaries

Edquist (2001) have identified three categories of system failures in developing and emerging economies: organizations in the NIS might be inappropriate or missing, NIS institutions may be inappropriate or missing, or interactions or links between these elements might be inappropriate or missing.

As for the second category, one weakness in the innovation systems of most developing countries is institutional barriers to the timely enforcement of the codified rules and laws that facilitate transactions (Motohashi 2005). The inertia of informal rules, societal norms, and customs, poor government administration, red tape and bureaucratic corruption, a poorly functioning arbitration mechanism, lack of long-term commitment to development goals, and an inefficient legal system are examples of institutional barriers (or weaknesses). They hamper the enforcement of intellectual property laws, antimonopoly laws, rules governing the growth of businesses, and foreign investment. Missing actors and failures of rules[9] can cause systemic failure (Klein Woolthuis et al. 2005), depressing innovation.

Not only institutional weaknesses hold back developing nations such as China and India, but also institutional voids—the absence of specialized

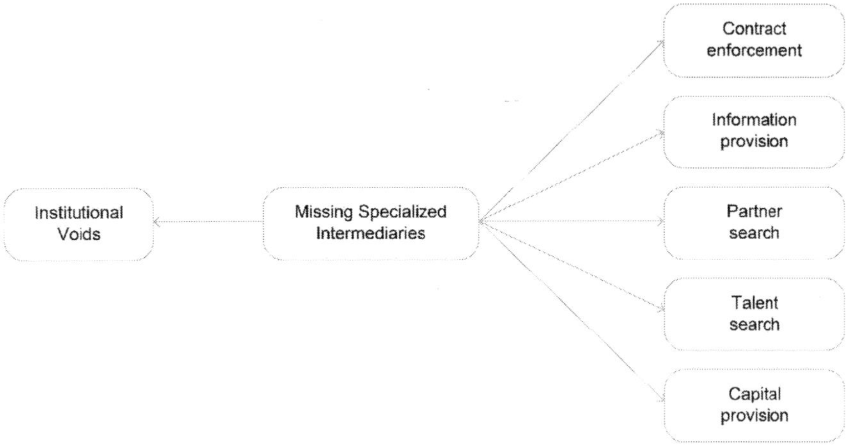

Figure 8.2 Khanna's concept on institutional voids based on missing intermediaries

Source: Schrammel (2013)

intermediaries, regulatory systems, and contract-enforcement mechanisms in emerging markets (see Figure 8.2)—hamper the goal of advancing global competitiveness. Institutional voids also disturb the functioning of markets by enhancing the likelihood of opportunism (including corruption), excessive rents to a few actors (reducing entrepreneurship), and market power (discouraging competition) (Doh et al. 2017). According to Khanna and Palepu (2015), "Institutional voids cannot be mandated away through deregulation and trade liberalization policies; it takes both significant time and substantial expertise to eliminate these voids" (p. 24). Institutional voids also depress investment in basic research and hinder the transfer of knowledge from academia to industry. And they entail a failure to counter market failures. Table 8.4 presents information on institutional factors, such as the freedom of the press, the incidence of corruption, and proactive features in labor market policies.[10]

Institutional development indicators in Table 8.4 reveal that BRICS nations fare poorly compared to developed countries in their freedom of the press, incidence of corruption, Intellectual Property Rights (IPRs) and efficiency of legal institutions—all of which form part of the "soft" infrastructure (Khanna et al. 2015) of the market economy. Other aspects of the soft infrastructure, including advertising agencies, media outlets, market research companies, logistic consultants, credit rating agencies, and regulators, are underdeveloped in emerging economies (Khanna et al. 2015).

Developing nations, including China and India, are slow to codify various rules regarding economic transactions (in the form of corporate law, contract law, property law including intellectual property law, and more) (Motohashi 2015). Even when they codify rules as laws, the laws' enforcement has often

Table 8.4 Selected institutional development indicators: Ordinal scale (1–7), (0-10) and (0–100) 2018

	Judicial Independence 1-7(best)	*Efficiency of Legal Framework in Challenging Regulations 1-7(best)*	*Freedom of Press (0–100 Worst)*	*Efficiency of Legal Framework in Settling Disputes 1-7(best)*	*Incidence of Corruption 0-100 (best)*	*Intellectual Property Rights Protection 1-7(best)*	*Active Labor Market Policies 1-7(best)*	*Venture Capital Availability 1-7(best)*	*Conflict of Interest Regulations 0-10(best)*
Belgium	6.7	4.2	3.1	4.2	75	6	4.6	3.8	7
Brazil	3.1	2.7	1.7	2.7	38	3.8	2.6	3.1	5.7
Canada	5.6	4.4	3.9	4.7	81	5.6	4.8	4	8.7
China	4.5	4.1	4.4	4.1	39	4.5	4.5	4.4	5.3
France	4.9	4.4	3.6	4.6	72	5.7	4.5	4.2	5.7
Germany	5	4.8	4.4	4.8	80	5.3	4.9	4.8	5
India	4.3	4	4.1	4.1	41	4.4	3.5	4.2	4.5
Russia	3.2	3.1	3.2	3.5	28	3.8	3.6	2.8	3.7
Singapore	5.6	4.6	5.5	6.2	85	6.4	5.5	4.8	6.3
SAF	5	4	3	4.6	43	4.7	2.5	3.1	3.3
Sweden	5.6	4.4	3.8	5.1	85	5.6	4.6	4.4	4.8
UK	5	4.5	4.3	5.1	80	5.5	4.3	4.5	4.6
USA	5.2	5	4.5	5.3	71	5.7	4.9	5.2	5.3

Source: Global Competitiveness Report 2019 WEF

been insufficient because the informal rules (country-specific societal norms, customs, and taboos) governing transactions and social behaviors stay in force (Motohashi 2015). In many cases, informal rules or codes of conduct exist even though they are not codified or are vague, so companies base their decisions on them. Thus, corporations, entrepreneurs, and individuals do not necessarily abide by formal institutions but are often influenced by informal institutions (Motohashi 2015).

Governments' shortcomings in developing nations affect innovation in other ways too. Such governments lack the resources and organizational efficiency to design and implement policies to redress market and system failures and hence foment innovation (Cirera and Maloney 2017). Their judicial systems lack resources and independence to enforce legal rules, including intellectual property right law. Lower institutional quality pertaining to rule of law, regulatory quality, and property rights and patent protection lowers the return to innovation for a large sample of firms in such countries (Nguyen and Jaramillo 2014). Innovation may also be stifled by the lack of coherence of policy across the NIS, by lack of policy coordination and consistency across ministries and agencies, and by lack of policy predictability (Cirera et al. 2017). As economic activities become more knowledge-intensive, a large and growing number of organizations with specialized expertise of very different kinds become involved in the production and diffusion of knowledge (OECD 1997).

Deficient basic research and non-existent translational research network

Moving up the value chain requires emerging countries to invest heavily in basic research and to invigorate their respective innovation systems to enable them to develop and commercialize new drugs and vaccines. The critical role of the public funded basic research in promoting innovation capability of firms was underlined in Chapter 4. Basic research consists of describing properties, structures, and relationships to formulate and test hypotheses, theories, or laws (Machado 2021). It is experimental or theoretical work undertaken primarily to acquire new foundational knowledge of scientific phenomena and observable facts, without any particular application or use in view (OECD 2015). Basic science leads to new practical applications. It is the prerequisite for any scientific breakthrough (UNESCO 2021).

The importance of basic research as the engine of an innovation ecosystem has long been recognized by the scientific community (Galkina Cleary et al. 2018). Indeed, Dirk and Susanne (2012), using Flemish R&D survey data covering a period from 2002 to 2007, found that basic research exhibited a productivity premium when compared to applied research and development in high-tech sectors. And according to Gambardella (1992), the more basic research a pharmaceutical firm performs, the more patents it produces. Among the sectors analyzed by Jaffe (1989), drugs and medical technology showed the strongest influence of basic academic research on corporate patenting.

Max Planck's or Albert Einstein's contributions to quantum mechanics in 1900 and 1905, respectively, are examples of expansions of fundamental theoretical knowledge of nature. It took several decades, and large investments in applied and experimental follow-up research, to bridge the gap between basic and practical knowledge, but eventually direct applications of economic value that rely on quantum mechanics, such as the transistor (used for personal computers) or lasers (used for CT scans), emerged (Machado 2021; Kakalios 2010).

In developing economies, several organizational and institutional barriers to innovations exist, including a lack of a "culture of translation" within institutions and inadequate infrastructure, such as the lack of facilities to conduct clinical research and an inadequately trained workforce (Fudge et al. 2016). Successful bridging of the gap requires significant publicly funded research and close coordination and knowledge exchange among multidisciplinary groups, including not only basic scientists and clinicians, but also bioinformaticians, statisticians, engineers, and industry experts (Butler 2008).

Despite China's considerable attainments in research publications and patenting activities, translational science remains one of the weakest links in the innovation system China has begun to develop national TROs (translational research organizations). The first TRO, National Centre for Translational Medicine in Shanghai, became operational in 2020. This is the first of five institutions to engage in bridging the translational gap between basic research and clinical. One formidable challenge is to attract Chinese biomedical researchers who are working abroad. Zhou et al. (2013) found that most Chinese TROs were launched by groups of research institutions without government participation in their organizing, funding, and coordinating. Ni et al. (2017) report that in China, considerable pharmaceutical R&D input, scientific publications, and patents have not yet translated into innovative globally acclaimed pharmaceutical products.

While inventive activity appears to have heightened tremendously among Indians within and outside India, less developed translational ability remains a matter of concern. India has yet to make concerted and systematic efforts to improve its translational science. Judging from trends in the number of patents issued to Indian inventors by the India Patent Office and those issued to Indian inventors by the US Patent and Trademark Office, a closer look at the data, however, shows that about 85% of the assignees of these patents are foreign inventors, commonly represented by multinational corporations (UNESCO 2021). In India, the Department of Biotechnology (DBT), Ministry of Science and Technology (MoST), and GoI (Govt of India), established an autonomous institution named the Translational Health Science and Technology Institute in 2010. Still, institutional support for translational research is lacking, and no multidisciplinary groups are working together to conduct basic science studies or studies in clinical medicine or public health (Kelkar et al. 2012).

Skill gaps

India and China need to address the skill gaps in order to move up the innovation ladder. In a study of the innovation capacity of China and India in the biosciences sector, Fan (2008) observes that one major challenge they face is the deficiency of human resources in R&D. The reason is that university education is not meeting the standards of the sector (Fan 2008). In India, in particular, there is a dearth of workers with the requisite training, expertise, and skill to meet the demands of the pharmaceutical and biotechnology industries across the R&D life cycle (FICCI 2021). Less than 0.5% of Indian students pursue a PhD or equivalent level of education. As of 2018–2019, only 35% of Indian higher education institutions offered postgraduate programs and just 2.5% offered PhD programs (FICCI 2021). Put differently, there is a mismatch between industry needs and university curricula (FICCI 2021).

Gathering intelligence on current and future skills needs can support better matching of training and jobs, which is of paramount importance everywhere. But most developing countries do not have databases (such as O*NET online databases in the USA) for projecting future demand for skills and for planning the education of their youth. The resulting poor matching between skills supply and demand has many negative consequences for individuals, companies, the economy, and society more generally (Bakhshi et al. 2017).

China and India need to develop educational and skill development programs to catch up with the advances in biomedical sciences and to strengthen academia-industry collaboration and government-industry research collaboration.

Lack of risk capital

Venture finance plays a catalyst role in traversing the path from scientific ideas to the commercialization of novel products, as access to adequate capital markets is a major determinant of whether companies will have enough resources to invest in innovation (IFPMA 2012). Venture capital takes the form of equity investment in the pre-start-up, start up, and early growth stages of business development (UN 2018). But the venture capital market is not well-developed in developing economies.

China faces challenges from an underdeveloped venture capital system, poor links between research and industry (Zhang et al. 2011). For new drug developers, venture capital (VC) contributions were limited. SMEs considerably relied on government investment to support their innovation (Ni et al. 2017). White et al. (2002) observed that venture capital firms in China did not have the expertise or operational mechanism to adequately select and manage new technology ventures, nor have they been able to add much beyond financing.

India and China both suffer from a lack of venture finance for start-ups (Fan 2008; UNESCO 2021; FICCI 2021). Salter (2009) in his analysis of venture capital flows to the health biotechnology sector in China found that the majority of domestic and foreign venture capital investment did not go to the early stage and high-risk firms of health biotech but to the established industries with predictable markets such as IT. Many PE (private equity) and VC firms focus on short-term and less innovative projects. One reason for the bias against start-ups is the absence of a well-functioning exit mechanism (Qiu et al. 2014). A well-functioning exit mechanism, particularly in the form of initial public offerings (IPOs) on second-tier stock exchanges, is an important indicator of venture funds' performance in a country. Second-tier stock exchangers play an important role in making seed capital available.

Challenges for small and medium enterprises

SMEs and start-ups in developing countries face major constraints in seeking to become competitive players as innovators in local markets and the global marketplace. The most prominent hurdles include insufficient access to adequate technologies, limited resources for market research, an unfavorable institutional environment (unsupportive legislation, ineffective incentives), poor access to risk capital, and underdeveloped national innovation systems as reflected in a deficient amount of complementary assets (inadequate skilled manpower, underdeveloped financial system, poor-quality basic research, underdeveloped technology transfer system). Opacity and corruption in the public sector pose particular problems for SMEs. New and small businesses face barriers to market entry and growth when state-owned enterprises (SOEs) are privileged in domestic and cross-border activities (OECD 2018).

Asian economies have bank-dominated financial markets with inefficient capital markets. SMEs there have difficulty accessing cheap finance. Almost 70% of the Indian, 80% of the Chinese, and 90% of Malaysian financial systems are based on bank loans (Yoshino and Taghizadeh-Hesary 2017). Venture capital in particular is not a well-developed industry. Start-up companies are finding it increasingly difficult to borrow money from banks because of strict Basel capital requirements. Riskier SMEs also face difficulty in borrowing money from banks (Yoshino and Taghizadeh-Hesary 2017). Most SMEs have no connection with capital markets. Rampant inefficiency in the banking system constrains timely access to finance. In developed economies, start-ups, young entrepreneurs, university spin-offs, and small, highly innovative firms, more often than not, produce major technological breakthroughs and innovations (Dahlstrand and Stevenson 2010). In biotechnology, much research has been taking place in start-ups rather than in large pharmaceutical firms (Casper and Matraves 2003; Powell 1996). Estimates show that SMEs account for about 20% of patents in biotechnology-related fields in Europe (OECD 2017). A sound business environment and a well-functioning entrepreneurial "eco-system" for business are essential for countries and regions in a globalized and digital economy (OECD 2018).

Public policies to strengthen the innovation systems

State can play a central role as a coordinator agent in fostering the NIS (National Innovation system) (Soete et al. 2010). In an evolving economy, governments have to devise innovation policies and develop innovation infrastructure for emerging economies to transition to higher-value-added activities. An innovation policy is "a public action that influences technical change and other kinds of innovations" (Edquist 2001, p. 18).

Government support for basic science and translational science

In the pharmaceutical industry, basic research has been the critical source of drug discovery (Toole 2012). Since basic research has a public good character, so market forces may generate a suboptimal amount (Stiglitz 1999, and brief discussion in Chapter 4 in the text). Indeed, investment in basic research has been insufficient in China and India. In China, only 5.5% of R&D investment (GERD in current PPP-adjusted $) was spent on basic research in 2017, while developed countries spent much higher percentages—e.g., 17% in the US and 26% in France (UNESCO 2021; Ni et al. 2017; WHO 2017a). In India, high-quality basic research is especially lacking in academia. Basic research accounted for a paltry 1.4% of India's GERD in 2017.

At the company level, R&D expenditure as a ratio of revenue fall below half of the equivalent percentage of OECD originator companies (8% India versus 16–20% foreign multinational companies) (WHO 2017a). Research evidence shows that low R&D intensity at the firm level restricts the absorptive capability of the firm (Mowery 1989). Absorptive capability is the ability of a firm to exploit external sources of knowledge or technology. Both countries require strong industry-university connections and a vibrant venture capital market to improve in this regard and in turn to move up in the global value chain. And public policies are needed to support open innovation models that improve scientific collaboration by encouraging the establishment of joint ventures or strategic alliances and the sharing of internal and external R&D (Seyhan 2019).

Instituting sound regulatory standards

Regulatory agencies ensure that a medicine is high quality by checking the efficacy, quality, and safety of the drug. Pharmaceutical companies and organizations must abide by CGMP (Current Good Manufacturing Practices) regulations. The research-based pharmaceutical industry is highly regulated throughout its innovation, manufacturing, and distribution pipelines (IFPMA 2012). During the R&D phase, governments require companies to regularly submit scientific data to demonstrate safety and efficacy. National authorities then determine whether the medicine may enter the national market (IFPMA 2012).

Effective regulation should not stunt innovation but should provide guidelines to aid companies in their R&D. If these guidelines are not clear, innovation and manufacturing processes may be hampered because researchers might not know whether their efforts will yield a market-ready medicine. Coping with such uncertainty is expensive (IFPMA 2012). One way for governments to attract industry investment is to adopt stringent international regulatory standards designed to create certainty and promote efficient R&D (IFPMA 2012).

To determine safety, quality, and efficacy, regulatory authorities rely on data submissions from innovators. Data submissions often parallel the R&D process; research data showing the safety and efficacy of new molecules, formulations, and indications are submitted throughout all phases of R&D. The submitted R&D data and supporting material represent intellectual property. Without adequate IP protections, other parties could gain a competitive advantage by using the data and materials. Data exclusivity relieves innovative companies of some of this risk (IFPMA 2012).

India has established a strong regulatory framework, with its latest revision, "New Drugs and Clinical Trial Rules, 2019," (Singh et al. 2020) (FICCI 2021). However, it has shortcomings (FICCI 2021). Regulatory supervision is split between the national and state levels but not adequately coordinated. The Central Drugs Standard Control Organization (CDSCO), the national regulatory authority, splits regulatory duties with state drug regulatory authorities (SDRAs), and regulatory standards are not harmonized across the country (FICCI 2021).

Another shortcoming is the lack of guidance on the most appropriate methodology for developing complex generics and biosimilars (which the world generics market is moving toward) and for presenting evidence in support of drug approval. The regulatory system needs to provide such guidance (FICCI 2021). Unlike with small-molecule drugs, the challenge of producing biosimilars is not only getting R&D right but also abiding by regulatory requirements (Kale 2019).

Meanwhile, China has begun to strengthen and streamline its regulatory approval process since 2020 when the State Administration for Market Regulation (SAMR) enacted the Amended Drug Registration Regulation (DRR). While, in the past, it took two to three years for approval of clinical trial applications, now the default is a 60-working day "silent approval," meaning if no response is received in 60 working days the application is approved.

Finally, moving up the value chain in drugs and vaccines requires public policy and institutions that enable sustained investment. National innovation policy needs to be complemented with policies that address market failures and institutional barriers. The role of the state is to correct the imperfections in the functioning of the innovation system (Edquist 2001).

Summary

This chapter has assessed the strengths and weaknesses of the innovation systems of India and China. The following are the key strengths and weaknesses analyzed in relation to their innovation capabilities.

- First, both countries enjoy the benefits of a large market for medical goods which attracts FDI in these countries
- Second, India is a leading supplier of generic medicine with developed countries as destinations, while China is a leading supplier of intermediate chemicals such as APIs. China is also among the top suppliers of critical medical supplies for hospital use
- Third, these countries have shown impressive innovative capabilities in developing products needed to serve the "bottom of the market pyramid." Their success in developing frugal innovations carries immense value to serve the medical needs of poor patients in both advanced and poor nations. India supplies vaccines against diphtheria, tetanus, pertussis, hepatitis B, measles, mumps, and rubella at affordable prices to developing and poor countries
- Fourth, evidence indicates that these countries are expanding into more technology-intensive products, such as biosimilars, complex vaccines, and complex generics product areas successfully and steadily. Indian pharmaceutical companies supply more than 50% of the global demand for different vaccines needed for global immunization problems
- Fifth, these countries are important global partners in R&D and suppliers of clinical trials services
- Sixth, these countries suffer from institutional voids, which constrain their innovation capabilities
- Seventh, these countries have yet to develop venture capital to attract seed funding for new medical ventures
- Finally, they have to go a long way to overcome their translational research gap. Their innovation system is in the early stages of development.

Notes

1 Each year, FDA's Center for Drug Evaluation and Research (CDER) approves a wide range of new drug products. FDA provides the scientific and regulatory advice needed to bring safe, effective, high-quality generic alternatives to market, which in turn creates more affordable treatment options for patients.

2 Since the COVID-19 pandemic began, six Indian firms have been actively engaging in vaccine development. These include Zydus Cadila, The Serum Institute of India, Bharat Biotech, Indian Immunological, and Mynvax (see details in UNESCO 2021).

3 At the therapeutic level, the biosimilar industry is segmented into insulin, monoclonal antibodies, recombinant human growth hormone, granulocyte colony-stimulating factor, interferon, erythropoietin, etanercept, follitropin, glucagon, calcitonin, teriparatide, and enoxaparin sodium. Of these segments, monoclonal antibodies tend to capture the biggest market share owing to the rising incidence of cancer and the increase in the number of product launches and approvals.

4 Monoclonal antibody (mAbs) drugs are treatments that enlist your body's germ-fighting immune system against diseases, including cancer.

5 Recombinant protein is a manipulated form of protein which is generated in various ways to produce large quantities of proteins, modify gene sequences, and manufac-

ture useful commercial products. Recombinant proteins are formed by transfecting foreign genes into a host cell.

6 AstraZeneca plc is a British-Swedish multinational pharmaceutical and biotechnology company with its headquarters at the Cambridge Biomedical Campus in Cambridge, England. The company has innovation hubs in developed countries (US and Canada) and in emerging markets (Russia, India, Brazil, China, Argentina, Singapore, and Gulf Cooperation Council (GCC) countries).

7 COVAX is a partnership between the World Health Organization (WHO) and two international groups—the Gavi vaccine alliance and the Coalition for Epidemic Preparedness Innovations (CEPI)—which aims to send vaccines to developing countries.

8 Public bridging institutions investing in infrastructure technology would fill an essential gap in such cases. In the United States, the National Institute of Standards and Technology provides such investments that generate the foundation for commercialization (Martin and Scott 2000; Mowery, 1989).

9 Players act as policymakers. Firms, universities, and others realize policy objectives. Rules (or institutions), meanwhile, can be translated into the outcomes of their actions. For example, legal offices write law (hard/formal institutions), companies together form a cooperative culture (soft institutions), and universities and firms form R&D alliances (Klein Woolthuis et al. 2005).

10 In this table, proactive labor market policies consist of active labor market measures or other interventions that are implemented preemptively, with the aim of protecting people against a wide range of labor market problems and economic shocks (Malo 2018).

References

Atkinson, R. D. 2019. *China's Biopharmaceutical Strategy: Challenge or Complement to US Industry Competitiveness?* Information Technology and Innovation, August.

Bakhshi, H., J. Downing, M. Osborne, and P. Schneider. 2017. *The Future of Skills: Employment in 2030.* Pearson and Nesta.

Bhatti, Y., R. Basu, D. Barron, and M. Ventresca. 2018. *Frugal Innovation: Models, Means Methods.* Cambridge University Press.

Birac. 2019. *India: The Emerging Hub for Biologics and Biosimilar*, Special Report Biotechnology Industry Research Assistance Council, Department of Biotechnology Government of India, November 21-23, 2019

Blablová, V. 2021. *How China and India Are Competing in Vaccine Diplomacy, China Observer.* EU.

Blackstone, Erwin A., and P. Fuhr Joseph. 2013. "The Economics of Biosimilars." *American Health & Drug Benefits* 6 (8): 469–478.

Butler, Declan. 2008. "Translational Research: Crossing the Valley of Death." *Nature* 453 (197): 840–842. https://doi.org/10.1038/453840a.

Casper, S., and C. Matraves. 2003. "Institutional Frameworks and Innovation in the German and UK Pharmaceutical Industry." *Research Policy* 32 (10): 1865–1879. https://doi.org/10.1016/S0048-7333(03)00082-9.

Chadee, D., and B. Roxas. 2013. "Institutional Environment, Innovation Capacity and Firm Performance in Russia." *Critical Perspectives on International Business* 9 (1/2): 19–39. https://doi.org/10.1108/17422041311299923.

Chapman, S., G. Dedet, and R. Lopert. 2022. "Shortages of medicines in OECD countries." OECD Health Working Papers, No. 137. OECD Publishing.

Cirera, X., and W. F. Maloney. 2017, e-Book. *Paradox-Developing Country Capabilities and the Unrealised Promise of Technological Catch-Up*. World Bank Publications. ISBN: 9781464811609.

Galkina Cleary, E., J. M. Beierlein, N. S. Khanuja, L. M. McNamee, and F. D. Ledley. 2018. "Contribution of NIH Funding to New Drug Approvals 2010–2016." *Proceedings of the National Academy of Sciences* 115 (10): 2329–2334. https://doi.org/10.1073/pnas.1715368115.

Congressional Testimony. 2019 *Safeguarding Pharmaceutical Supply Chains in a Global Economy*. October 30. https://energycommerce.house.gov/.

Correa, C. M. 2011. *Pharmaceutical Innovation*. Incremental Patenting and Compulsory Licensing, South Centre.

Dahlstrand, A. L., and L. Stevenson. 2010. "Innovative Entrepreneurship Policy: Linking Innovation and Entrepreneurship in a European Context." *Annals of Innovation & Entrepreneurship* 1 (1): 5602. https://doi.org/10.3402/aie.v1i1.5845.

de Kleijn, M., M. Siebert, and Huggett. 2019. "Artificial Intelligence: How Knowledge is Created, Transferred, and Used." Knowledge Management with Digital Humanities/Digital Scholarship Date: 22 August 2019.

Ding, J., Y. Xue, H. Liang, R. Shao, and Y. Chen. 2011. "From Imitation to Innovation: A Study of China's Drug R&D and Relevant National Policies." *Journal of Technology Management & Innovation* 6 (2): 1–13. https://doi.org/10.4067/S0718-27242011000200001.

Dirk, C., and T. Susanne. 2012. *Productivity Effects of Basic Research in Low-Tech and High-Tech Industries, ZEW*. Discussion Papers, No. 12-027. Zentrum für Europäische Wirtschaftsforschung.

Doh, J., S. Rodrigues, A. Saka-Helmhout, and M. Makhija. 2017. "International Business Responses to Institutional Voids." *Journal of International Business Studies* 48 (3): 293–307. https://doi.org/10.1057/s41267-017-0074-z.

Dummer, Trevor J. B., and Ian G. Cook. 2008. "Health in China and India: A Cross-Country Comparison in a Context of Rapid Globalisation." *Social Science & Medicine* 67 (4): 590–605. https://doi.org/10.1016/j.socscimed.2008.04.019.

Edquist, C. 2001. *Systems of Innovation for Development (SID)*. Background Paper for Chapter" I: "Competitiveness, Innovation and Learning: Analytical Framework" for the UNIDO World Industrial Development Report (WIDR).

EOS Intelligence. 2019. *India and China Make Space for Domestic*. Medical Devices, February 12.

Fan, P. 2008. *Innovation Capacity and Economic Development: China and India, UNIWider*. Research Papers, no. 2008/31. United Nations University.

FICCI. 2021. *Indian Pharmaceutical Industry 2021: Future Is*. Now Publishers, February 2021.

Fudge, Nina, Euan Sadler, Helen R. Fisher, John Maher, Charles D A D. A. Wolfe, and Christopher McKevitt. 2016. "Optimising Translational Research Opportunities: A Systematic Review and Narrative Synthesis of Basic and Clinician Scientists' Perspectives of Factors Which Enable or Hinder Translational Research." *PLoS One* 11 (8): e0160475. https://doi.org/10.1371/journal.pone.0160475.

GaBI. 2018. "Patent expiry dates for biologicals: 2018 update Generics and Biosimilars." *Initiative Journal (GaBI Journal)* 8(1): 24–31. DOI: 10.5639/gabij.2019.0801.003

Gambardella, A. 1992. Competitive advantages from in-house basic research: The U.S. pharmaceutical industry in the 1980s. *Research Policy* 21: 391–407.

Govindarajan, V., and J. Euchner. 2012. "Reverse Innovation." *Research-Technology Management* 55 (6): 13–17. https://doi.org/10.5437/08956308X5506003.

Greenblatt, W., C. Gupta, and J. Kao. 2023. "Drug Repurposing During The COVID-19 Pandemic: Lessons For Expediting Drug Development And Access." *Health affairs (Project Hope)* 42 (3): 424–432.

Guerin, Philippe J., Sauman Singh-Phulgenda, and Nathalie Strub-Wourgaft. 2020. "The Consequence of COVID-19 on the Global Supply of Medical Products: Why Indian Generics Matter for the World?" *F1000Research* 9: 225. https://doi.org/10.12688/f1000research.23057.1.

Haakonsson, S. J. 2009. "The Changing Governance Structures of the Global Pharmaceutical Value Chain." *Competition & Change* 13 (1): 75–95.

Hafner, T., and D. Popp. 2011. *China and India as Suppliers of Affordable Medicines to Developing Countries*, NBER Working Papers 17249. National Bureau of Economic Research, Inc.

Hossain, M. 2018. "Frugal Innovation: A Review and Research Agenda." *Journal of Cleaner Production* 182: 926–936. https://doi.org/10.1016/j.jclepro.2018.02.091.

IAVI. 2019. *India's Biopharmaceutical Business: An Evolving Success Story, Supplement to the Report, Expanding Access to Monoclonal Antibody-Based Products: A Global Call to Action.* IAVI.

IFPMA. 2012. *The Changing Landscape on Access to Medicines.* Adapting to Patient Needs, International Federation of Pharmaceutical Manufacturers & Associations.

IFPMA. 2013. *Incremental Innovation.* Adapting to Patient Needs, International Federation of Pharmaceutical Manufacturers & Associations.

Intarakumnerd, P., and A. Goto. 2018. "Role of Public Research Institutes in National Innovation Systems in Industrialized Countries: The Cases of Fraunhofer, NIST, CSIRO, AIST, and ITRI." *Research Policy* 47 (7): 1309–1320. https://doi.org/10.1016/j.respol.2018.04.011.

IQVIA. 2016. *Complex Generics: Charting a New Path, White Paper Quintiles IMS.* IQVIA.

IQVIA. 2022. *Emerging Biopharma's Contribution to Innovation, Assessing the Impact.*

IQVIA. 2024. "Global Use of Medicines 2024. Outlook to 2028" Institute for Human Data Science, Jan 2024. US Available from www.iqviainstitute.org

ITA (International Trade Administration. 2016. Top Markets Report, Pharmaceuticals A Market Assessment Tool for U.S. Exporters, U.S. Department of Commerce, International Trade Administration, Industry & Analysis (I&A) May 2016

Jaffe, A. B. 1989. "Real Effects of Academic Research." *American Economic Review* 79 (5): 957–970.

Kakalios, J. 2010. *The Amazing Story of Quantum Mechanics: A Math-Free Exploration of the Science That Made Our World.* Gotham Books.

Kale, D. 2019. "From Small Molecule Generics to Biosimilars: Technological Upgrading and Patterns of Distinctive Learning Processes in the Indian Pharmaceutical Industry." *Technological Forecasting & Social Change* 145: 370–383. https://doi.org/10.1016/j.techfore.2018.09.020.

Kauser, S. and Naik, V. 2021. *Enhancing Biosimilar Analysis with IQVIA Analogue Planner Off-Patent* [Blog]. IQVIA, March 4, https://www.iqvia.com/blogs/2021/03/enhancing-biosimilar-analysis

Kedron, P., and S. Bagchi-Sen. 2011. "US Market Entry Processes of Emerging Multinationals: A Case of Indian Pharmaceuticals." *Applied Geography* 31 (2): 721–730. https://doi.org/10.1016/j.apgeog.2010.11.004.

Kelkar, Dhanashree, Sheela Galwankar, and Shrikant Kelkar. 2012. "Need for Encouraging Translational Research in India." *Journal of Emergencies, Trauma, & Shock* 5 (1): 107. https://doi.org/10.4103/0974-2700.93105.

Khanna, Ish. 2012. "Drug Discovery in Pharmaceutical Industry: Productivity Challenges and Trends." *Drug Discovery Today* 17 (19–20): 1088–1102. https://doi.org/10.1016/j.drudis.2012.05.007.

Khanna, T., and K.G. Palepu. 2010. "The Nature of Institutional Voids in Emerging Markets: Why Markets Fail and How to Make Them Work." Harvard Business Press.

Khanna, T., and K. G. Palepu. 2015. *The Nature of Institutional Voids in Emerging Markets. Why Markets Fail and How to Make Them Work.* Harvard Business Press.

KPMG. 2020. *Indian API Industry – Reaching the Full Potential.* KPMG in India And [CII report], 7 July 2020.

Le Bas, C. 2016. "Frugal Innovation, Sustainable Innovation, Reverse Innovation: Why Do They Look Alike? Why Are They Different?" *Journal of Innovation Economics & Management* 21 (3): 9–26. https://doi.org/10.3917/jie.021.0009.

Lionberger, R. 2021. *Generic Drugs in the 21st Century: FDA's Actions Create Transparency and Value for Complex Generic Product Development.* FDA. May.

Low, Z. Y., I. A. Farouk, and S. K. Lal. 2020. "Drug Repositioning: New Approaches and Future Prospects for Life-Debilitating Diseases and the COVID-19 Pandemic Outbreak." *Viruses* 12 (9): 1058.

Lybecker, K. M. 2014. *Incremental Innovation in the Pharmaceutical Industry in Steven Globerman and Kristina M. Lybecker Edited: The Benefits of Incremental Innovation, Focus on the Pharmaceutical Industry.* Fraser Institute.

Machado, D. 2021. *Quantitative Indicators for High-Risk/High-Reward Research, OECD Science, Technology and Industry Working Papers, No. 2021/07.* OECD Publishing.

Malo, M. A. 2018. "Finding Proactive Features in Labour Market Policies: A Reflection Based on the Evidence, Research Paper Series." *Research Papers* 8. ILO Future of Work.

Martin, S., and J. T. Scott. 2000. "The Nature of Innovation Market Failure and the Design of Public Support for Private Innovation." *Research Policy* 29 (4–5): 437–447. https://doi.org/10.1016/S0048-7333(99)00084-0.

Mazumdar-Shaw, K. 2018. "Leveraging Affordable Innovation to Tackle India's Healthcare Challenge." *IIMB Management Review* 30 (1): 37–50. https://doi.org/10.1016/j.iimb.2017.11.003.

Meher, Bikash R., Sakthi Balan, Rashmi R. Mohanty, Monalisa Jena, and Smita Das. 2019. "Biosimilars in India; Current Status and Future Perspectives." *Journal of Pharmacy & Bioallied Sciences* 11 (1): 12–15. https://doi.org/10.4103/jpbs.JPBS_167_18.

Morel, Carlos, Broun, Denis, Dangi, Ajit, Elias, Christopher, Gardner, Charles, Gupta, RK, Haycock, Jane, Heher, Tony Heher, Hotez, Peter Hotez, Juma, Calestous, Kettler, Hannah, Krattiger, Anatole, Kreutz, Fernando, Lee, Keun and et al. 2005. Health Innovation Networks to Help Developing Countries Address Neglected Diseases. *Science*. 309: 401–403.

Mossialos, E., Y. Ge, J. Hu, and L. Wang. 2016. *Pharmaceutical Policy in China: Challenges and and Opportunities for Reform*. WHO.

Motohashi, K., 2005. "University-industry collaborations in Japan: The role of new technology-based firms in transforming the National Innovation System." *Research Policy* 34 (5): 583–594.

Motohashi, K., 2012. "*Managing Competency Creating R&D Subsidiaries: Evidence from Japanese Multinationals*" (June 2012). Tokyo Center for Economic Research (TCER). Paper No. E-48.

Motohashi, K. 2015. *Global Business Strategy Multinational Corporations Venturing into Emerging Markets*. Springer.

Mou, X. 2019. "Artificial Intelligence: Investment Trends and Selected Industry Uses." International Finance Corporations and World Bank, Note 71, September 2019 EM Compass Emerging Markets.

Mowery, D. 1989. "Collaborative Research and High-Temperature Superconductivity." In *Institutions and Firms' Return to Innovation: Evidence from the World Bank Enterprise Survey* Policy Research Working Paper 6918, edited by A. Link, H. Nguyen, and P. A. Jaramillo. World Bank.

Nguyen, H., and P. A. Jaramillo. 2014. "Institutions and Firms' Return to Innovation: Evidence from the World Bank Enterprise Survey." Policy Research Working Paper 6918, World Bank, Washington, DC.

Ni, Jingyun, Junrui Zhao, Carolina Oi Lam O. L. Ung, Yuanjia Hu, Hao Hu, and Yitao Wang. 2017. "Obstacles and Opportunities in Chinese Pharmaceutical Innovation." *Globalization & Health* 13 (1): 21. https://doi.org/10.1186/s12992-017-0244-6.

NIPH. 2020. "Why Is Vaccination so Important?" https://www.fhi.no/en/id/vaccines/childhoodimmunisation-programme/why-isvaccination-soimportant.

North, D. C. 1992. "Institutions and Economic Theory." *American Economist* 36 (1): 3–6. https://doi.org/10.1177/056943459203600101.

OECD. 1997. *National Innovation Systems OECD*. OECD.

OECD. 2015. *Innovation Policies for Inclusive Development. Scaling up Inclusive Innovation*. OECD.

OECD. 2017. *Going Digital: Making the Transformation Work for Growth and Well Being, Meeting of the Counci*. OECD.

OECD. 2018. *Strengthening SMEs and Entrepreneurship for Productivity and Inclusive Growth, Key Issue Paper, SME Ministerial Conference, 22–23 February 2018 Mexico City*. OECD.

Orenstein, Walter A., and Rafi Ahmed. 2017. "Simply Put: Vaccination Saves Lives." *Proceedings of the National Academy of Sciences of the United States of America* 114 (16): 4031–4033. https://doi.org/10.1073/pnas.1704507114.

Ostraszewska, Z., and A. Tylec. 2014. "Reverse Innovation – How It Works." *International Journal of Business & Management* III (1): 57–74. https://doi.org/10.20472/BM.2015.3.1.004.

Pategou, J. 2019. *The China Biosimilars Market: Rise of a Potential Powerhouse, Guest Column, May 14, 2019*. Biosimilar Development.

Pollard, Andrew J., and Else M. Bijker. 2021. "A Guide to Vaccinology: From Basic Principles to New Developments." *Nature Reviews. Immunology* 21 (2): 83–100. https://doi.org/10.1038/s41577-020-00479-7.

Powell, W. 1996. "Interorganizational Collaboration in the Biotechnology Industry." *Journal of Institutional & Theoretical Economics* 152 (1): 197–215.

Prahalad, C.K., and S.L. Hart. 2002. "The Fortune at the Bottom of the Pyramid." *Strategy and Business* 26: 54–67. https://www.strategy-business.com/article/11518

Qiu, L., Z. Y. Chen, D. Y. Lu, H. Hu, and Y. Wang. 2014. "Public Funding and Private Investment for R&D: A Survey in China's Pharmaceutical Industry." *Health Research Policy & Systems* 12 (1): 27. https://doi.org/10.1186/1478-4505-12-27.

Rader, R. A., and E. S. Langer. 2019. *Biosimilars Set to Further Expand the Biopharmaceutical Market*. American Pharmaceutical Review, March 22.

Rezaie, Rahim, Anita M. McGahan, Abdallah S. Daar, and Peter A. Singer. 2012. "Innovative Drugs and Vaccines in China, India and Brazil." *Nature Biotechnology* 30 (10): 923–926. https://doi.org/10.1038/nbt.2380.

Salter, B. 2009. "China, Globalisation and Health Biotechnology Innovation: Venture Capital and the Adaptive State, East Asian Science" 3: 401–420. https://doi.org/10.1007/s12280.

Schrammel, T. 2013. "Bridging the Institutional Void: An Analytical Concept to Develop Valuable Cluster Services." *Management Revu* 24 (2): 114–132. https://doi.org/10.5771/0935-9915-2013-2-114.

Seyhan, A.A. 2019. "Lost in translation: The valley of death across preclinical and clinical divide – Identification of problems and overcoming obstacles." *Translational Medicine Communications* 4: 18.

Shaw, James, Payal Agarwal, Laura Desveaux, Daniel Cornejo Palma, Vess Stamenova, Trevor Jamieson, Rebecca Yang, R. Sacha Bhatia, and Onil Bhattacharyya. 2018. "Beyond "Implementation": Digital Health Innovation and Service Design." *NPJ Digital Medicine* 1: 48. https://doi.org/10.1038/s41746-018-0059-8.

Silvestre, B. S. 2015. "Sustainable Supply Chain Management in Emerging Economies: Environmental Turbulence, Institutional Voids and Sustainability Trajectories." *International Journal of Production Economics* 167 (C): 156–169. https://doi.org/10.1016/j.ijpe.2015.05.025.

Simula, H., M. Hossain, and M. Halme. 2015. "Frugal and Reverse Innovations Quo Vadis?." *SSRN Electronic Journal* 109 (5). https://doi.org/10.2139/ssrn.2678861.

Singh N., N.J. Madkaikar, P.M. Gokhale, and D.V. Parmar. 2020. New Drugs and Clinical Trials Rules 2019: Changes in Responsibilities of the Ethics Committee. *Perspectives in Clinical Research* 11 (1): 37–43. doi: 10.4103/picr.PICR_208_19.

Soete, L., B. Verspagen, and B. Weel. 2010. *Systems of Innovation*, CPB Discussion Paper, No. 138. CPB Netherlands Bureau for Economic Policy Analysis.

Stiglitz, Joseph E. 1999. "The World Bank at the Millennium." *The Economic Journal* 109 (459): F577–97. http://www.jstor.org/stable/2566064.

Su, L.. 2013. "Drug Development Models in China and the Impact on Multinational Pharmaceutical Companies" Sept/Oct. Update 2013, Sidely.com https://www.sidley.com/~/media/files/publications/2013/09/drug-development-models-in-china-and-the-impact-__/files/view-article/fileattachment/fdli-article--ling-su--2013.pdf

Sun, G., D. Dong, Z. Dong, Q. Zhang, H. Fang, C. Wang, S. Zhang, S. Wu, Y. Dong, and Y. Wan. 2022. "Drug repositioning: A bibliometric analysis." *Frontiers in Pharmacology* 13: 974849.

Toole, A.A.. 2012. "The impact of public basic research on industrial innovation: Evidence from the pharmaceutical industry." *Research Policy* 41 (1): 1–12.

Torsekar, M. 2018. "Technology Innovation Report. China Climbs the Global Value Chain for Medical Devices." *Journal of International Commerce & Economics* UN, Harnessing Frontier Technologies for Sustainable Development.

UNCTAD. 2021. *Technology and Innovation Report 20121, Catching Technological Waves Innovation with Equity.* UNCTAD.

Utt, E., and C. Wells. 2016. "The Global Response to the Threat of Antimicrobial Resistance and the Important Role of Vaccines." In *Pharmaceuticals Policy & Law*, edited by J. L. Valverde, E. Pisani 18 (1–4): 179–97, IFPMA ORG. https://doi.org/10.3233/PPL-160442.

WHO. 2011. *Pharmaceutical Production and Related Technology Transfer: Landscape Report.* WHO.

WHO. 2016. *"Pharmaceutical Policy in China: Challenges and Opportunities for Reform, Contributors: Elias Mossialos", Yanfeng Ge.* Jia Hu and Liejun Wang.

WHO. 2020a. *Promoting Access to Medical Technologies and Innovation.* 2nd ed., Intersections between Public Health, Intellectual Property and Trade.

WHO. 2020b. *Global Vaccine Market Report, Working Draft Dec 2020, MI4A.* WHO.

Klein Woolthuis, R. K., M. Lankhuizen, and V. Gilsing. 2005. "A System Failure Framework for Innovation Policy Design." *Technovation* 25 (6): 609–619. https://doi.org/10.1016/j.technovation.2003.11.002.

The White House. 2021. "Building Resilient Supply Chain, Revitalizing American Manufacturing and Fostering Broad Base Growth." 100-Day Reviews under Executive Order 14017.

UNCTAD. 2021a. Improving access to medical products through trade: What can regional trade agreements do in times of crisis?

UNCTAD. 2021b. Technology and Innovation Report 2021: Catching technological waves - Innovation with equity.

UNESCO. 2015: UNESCO science report: towards 2030, UNESCO Publishing: Paris, https://uis.unesco.org/sites/default/files/documents/unesco-science-report-towards-2030-part1.pdf

UNESCO. 2021. UNESCO Science Report: The Race Against Time for Smarter Development. S. Schneegans, T. Straza and J. Lewis (eds). UNESCO Publishing: Paris.

United Nations. 2018. "Technology Innovation Report: Harnessing Frontier Technologies for Sustainable Development." UNCTAD, 2018, United Nations

White, S., J. Gao, and W. Zhang. 2002. China's venture capital industry: Institutional trajectories and system structure. INSEAD R&D Working Papers 2002/122/ABA, https://flora.insead.edu/fichiersti_wp/inseadwp2002/2002-122.pdf

WHO. 2017a. Indian policies to promote local production of pharmaceutical products and protect public health, Geneva: World Health Organization.

WHO. 2017b. China policies to promote local production of pharmaceutical products and protect public health. Geneva: World Health Organization.

Xi, K. 2020. *The Rise of Chinese Biosimilars.* Pharma Boardroom, March 2.

Yes Global Institute Indian Pharma. 2017. *Solutions for Mitigating SMEs' Difficulties in Accessing Finance: Asian Experiences*, ADBI Working Paper 768. Transitioning to Specialty Generics.

Yoshino, N., Taghizadeh-Hesary, F. 2017. *The Role of SMEs in Asia and Their Difficulties in Accessing Finance.* Asian Development Bank Institute.

Zeschky, M., B. Widenmayer, and O. Gassmann. 2011. "Frugal Innovation in Emerging Markets." *Research-Technology Management* 54 (4): 38–45. https://doi.org/10.5437/08956308X5404007.

Zhang, J. 2018. *Biosimilars in China*. PharmExec.com, April 23.

Zhang, Y., L. Dawei, Y. Changyong, and D. Qiong. 2011. "On the value chain and international specialization of China's pharmaceutical industry." *Journal of International Commerce and Economics*, USITC Number 1. United States International Trade Commission.

Zhou, Laixin, Ying Li, Hayden B. Bosworth, John Ehiri, and Changkun Luo. 2013. "Challenges Facing Translational Research Organizations in China: A Qualitative Multiple Case Study." *Journal of Translational Medicine* 11: 256. https://doi.org/10.1186/1479-5876-11-256.

9 Strengthening the medical sector

Concluding remarks

The biopharmaceutical industry and medical devices are high-technology sectors that invent and develop lifesaving and life-enhancing medicines and medical technology. The industry, with its commendable record of progress in contributing to improvements in life expectancy and quality of life, its proven agility to fight deadly pandemics and eliminating communicable diseases, need to be strengthened to deliver more affordable medicines and devices across the globe and to preserve the healthy eco-environment.

The major areas that deserve priority attention include ameliorating the following concerns:

- Declining productivity in research and development
- Powering the global supply chain with more diversified supply sources of essential medical components and intermediate inputs
- Carbon emission and environmental sustainability (SDG 12)
- Inequitable and affordable access to essential medicines, vaccines, and technologies
- Impoverished health infrastructure, weak technological capability, and poor institutional capacity of developing countries to address local tropical diseases

This book has addressed the above-mentioned critical challenges and elaborated key evidenced-based measures for the sustained viable growth of the medical goods sector.

In regard to reversing the productivity slowdown and containing the high risk of attrition rates, the evidence suggests the critical role of public investment in basic scientific research, overcoming of translational research gap (from bench-side ideas to bedside safe therapeutic products), strong partnership between industry, academia and government, new design of clinical trials for expediting regulatory approval, and adequate availability of venture capital with exit mechanism. In the path of drug discovery and development, the most hazardous stage is the high attrition rates at later stages of product development. Bridging the translational gap is the most vexing challenge that needs to be tackled to prevent a high risk of failure. The complexity of

DOI: 10.4324/9781003449331-9

translational roadblocks is growing due to the exploding knowledge in biosciences, which is demystifying the underlying causes of complex diseases. In this context, research collaboration at a global scale, open access to scientific publications, and unhindered sharing of biomedical research data are proving to be of immense value for advancing technological capabilities. The rapid development of the COVID-19 vaccine is a strong testimony of scientific globalism (Lee and Haupt 2021). Advances in information and digital frontier technologies present a great promise of contributing to productivity growth by revolutionizing the drug development process. Chapter 5 has analyzed the potential of these frontier technologies (artificial intelligence, machine learning, Internet of Things, 3D printing, biotechnologies, nanotechnologies) in improving efficiency and effectiveness aspects of productivity.

Many developing countries are heavily reliant on the imports of finished medical products, with no domestic production base and trade linkages. Lack of active participation in the global supply chain deprives these countries of reaping the benefits of technology transfer and learning that trade confers to the participants. Global trade offers opportunities to countries to benefit from international cooperation, international division of labor, and sharing of global pool of knowledge. Economies can participate in GVCs by using imported inputs in their exports (the so-called backward linkages) or by supplying intermediates to third-country exports (forward linkages). The degree to which countries benefit from GVC participation ultimately depends on the absorptive capabilities of domestic actors to assimilate external knowledge and quality improvements, and to upgrade their position in the GVC. Upgrading of the position along the value chain calls for both general and industry-specific investments, including (i) increasing investment in basic science education (viz., biological and other related disciplines), (ii) formulating policies that encourage competence in conducting clinical research, (iii) developing policies that forge critical academic-industry linkages, and (iv) promulgating public policies to address institutional weaknesses and to reform regulatory standards(harmonization of technical requirements for new and existing medicines as per the International Council of Harmonization). Open science and open collaborative research models can help developing nations to upgrade their technological capabilities and technical know-how. Development of a healthy life sciences eco-system[1] at the global level would require joint working and collaboration of all stakeholders—patients, researchers, governments, manufacturers, and international multilateral organizations. The remarkable breakthrough in the COVID-19 vaccine through joint global efforts has kindled a bright hope of our collective ability to manage the future risks of pandemics with success (Li et al. 2021).

Fast-developing countries, such as China and India, are appearing as key partners in the global production and trade chain and have opportunities to specialize in new niche areas. China and India have emerged as global players in frugal and reverse innovations. Integrating China, India, Brazil, and other pharmamerging into global value chain would be more likely to strengthen the global medical industry in delivering affordable healthcare solutions for neglected tropical diseases and in fulfilling the unmet needs of the largest, but the poorest socio-economic group (the "bottom of the pyramid").

In regard to meeting SDG 12 of ensuring sustainable consumption and production patterns, it is found that the pharmaceutical industry has failed so far to adapt its development pattern to contribute to overcoming environmental challenges of protecting ecosystems. The global pharmaceutical industry has become a major global polluter, generating more global emissions per dollar of revenue than the automotive sector. Many efforts are now underway to reduce the conflict between the production and use of medical goods and sustainability of environmental quality. Some prime proposals and suggested strategies include accelerated application of green technologies, increasing thrust on using renewable resources, promoting bioeconomy, restricting illegal trade in medical goods, and intensifying global collaboration on meeting sustainable development goals. Bioeconomy is a bio-resources-based economy that supplies renewable raw materials, resources, and components along the value chain from natural resources and biological processes. Biotechnology and biomanufacturing are the pillars that are shaping the bioeconomy. Biomanufacturing applies the principles of engineering and chemical design to engineer cell-based therapies. Bionanotechnology (the convergence between biotechnology and nanotechnology) has many promising applications in environmental remediation. The above-mentioned proposals of "greening" the medical supply chain are likely to have far-reaching effects on promoting collective well-being and sustainable use of resources.

Under the current patent system, there is a conflict between pharmaceutical patent protection and drug accessibility. Evidence affirms that pharmaceutical companies, using their legal monopoly power, are able to set the price of a prescription drug at whatever level they believe the market will bear. The current patent system is found to be a very expensive way to stimulate R&D. Branded drug companies are stifling competition in several ways such as using strategic patenting to prolong the market exclusivity period, without any benefit for consumers or innovation. There is growing consensus to reform the existing patent system and supplement it with a system of "innovation" prizes for financing R&D. Critics of the patent system argue in favor of eliminating monopolies, the decoupling of R&D incentives from prices, and the creation of an evidence-based reward system linked to changes in health outcomes (Love and Hubbard 2007).

Affordable access to essential medicines ranks among the top priority issues for healthcare providers globally. To improve affordability and cost-effectiveness, value-based pricing is being used in many developed countries, since this method aligns prescription drug prices to their clinical benefits, leading to lower spending and better health outcomes. For developing countries, tiered pricing (differential pricing) approach, where prices are systematically lower than those in industrialized countries, has received widespread support from industry, policymakers, civil society, and academics. Differential pricing is, however, not a panacea to ensuring access. The differential pricing does not necessarily result in affordability or equitable access to a product (Yadav 2010). Drugs for diseases that have no market in the developed world will require additional measures at the global and national level (Danzon, Epstein and Nicholson 2007). In case of neglected diseases, developing countries can use TRIPS Article 66.2 for the transfer of technology from developed countries under the assumption that technology transfer to the world's poorest countries will help solve pressing global concerns ('t Hoen et al. 2001). The TRIPS agreement, however, needs amendments to enable the sharing of knowledge and technical know-how between developed countries and developing countries in priority areas of medicines and devices. Waiving of intellectual property rights is suggested as one of the remedial approaches for promoting the collaboration of developed countries with developing nations in the transfer of technology. Much, however, depends upon the developed countries' willingness to transfer technical know-how. The refusal of the developed countries to collaborate with IP waiver proposal put forward by India and South Africa in October 2020 has exposed the lack of an effective mechanism for the sharing of IP and technology required to respond to emergency situation like pandemic (WTO 2021; Erfani et al. 2021).[2]

The innovative initiatives of supranational organizations, such as "The Medicines Patent Pool" to end HIV/AIDS, malaria, tuberculosis, and hepatitis C, joint collaboration in product development, WIPO Re: Search consortium, TDR (for research on diseases of poverty) training program, the mRNA vaccine technology transfer hubs (share technology and technical know-how with local producers in poor countries), COVAX Facility (a joint initiative of WHO, GAVI, the vaccine Alliance, and CEPI[3]), and COVID-19 Technology Access Pool (C-TAP) are notable examples of international efforts to promote local production capabilities in poor countries. Working toward achieving SFG goal 3 requires the national governments to cooperate and coordinate with the supranational institutions (WHO, WIPO, and WTO 2020) and philanthropic organizations.

Ongoing advances in gene and cell-based therapies (which are opening a new era of personalized medicine), medical devices, increasing proliferation of open science networks, growing digitalization in pharmaceutical industry, and the emergence of bioeconomy are all set to revolutionize the health sector. It is important to stress that the common man, whether in developed or developing countries, ought to be at the center stage to benefit from the gains of new innovative treatments at affordable cost (Thimbleby 2013). Active involvement of international agencies in providing more streamlined support to countries lacking adequate health infrastructure and technological capabilities along with a strong commitment of national governments to increasingly invest in rejuvenating their health sector can progressively contribute to the UN goal of ensuring healthy lives and well-being for all at all ages (SDG 3).

Notes

1 The life science ecosystem has been defined as "an environment and infrastructure that supports pioneering researchers and clinicians to bring innovation to market earlier and more easily, making the given market the location of choice for investment" (Valverde and Pisani (eds) 2016).

2 This proposal of temporarily waiving the intellectual property rules related to COVID-19 vaccines and treatments was supported by more than 170 former heads of state and government and Nobel laureates. In a letter to President Biden, the former world leaders and Nobel Laureates, urged to put "the collective right to safety for all ahead of the commercial monopolies of the few" (UNAIDS 2021).

3 Coalition for Epidemic Prevention.

References

Erfani, P., A. Binagwaho, M.J. Jalloh, M. Yunus, P. Farmer, and V. Kerry. 2021. "Intellectual Property Waiver for COVID-19 Vaccines will Advance Global Health Equity." *BMJ* 374 https://www.bmj.com/content/374/bmj.n1837

Lee, J.J., and J.P. Haupt. 2021. "Scientific Globalism During a Global Crisis: Research Collaboration and Open Access Publications on COVID-19". *Higher Education* 81: 949–966.

Li, Y., R. Tenchov, J. Smoot, C. Liu, S. Watkins, and Q. Zhou. 2021. "A Comprehensive Review of the Global Efforts on COVID-19 Vaccine Development." *ACS Central Science*, 7 (4): 512–533.

Love, J., and T. Hubbard. 2007. "The Big Idea: Prizes to Stimulate R&D for New Medicines." *Chicago-Kent Law Review* 82 (3): 1519–1554.

Thimbleby, H. 2013. "Technology and the future of healthcare". *Journal of Public Health Research* 2 (3): e28. https://www.ncbi.nlm.nih.gov/pmc/articles/PMC4147743/

't Hoen, Ellen, Berger, Jonathan, Calmy, Alexandra, and Moon, Suerie. 2001. "Driving a Decade of Change: HIV/AIDS, Patents and Access to Medicines for All." *Journal of the International AIDS Society* 14 (1): 15.

UNAIDS. 2021. "Former heads of state and Nobel laureates call on President Biden to waive intellectual property rules for COVID vaccines." Feature Story, Focus Area COVID-19 and HIV, OXFAM April 14, 2021, https://www.oxfamamerica.org/press/former-heads-of-state-and-nobel-laureates-call-on-president-biden-to-waive-intellectual-property-rules-for-covid-vaccines/

Valverde, J.L., and E. Pisani (Eds.). 2016. The Globalization of the Pharmaceutical Industry. *Pharmaceuticals Policy and Law* 18. IFPMA ORG. IOS Press

WTO. 2021. "World Trade Report Economic Resilience and Trade." World Trade Organization, Retrieved from https://www.wto.org/english/res_e/booksp_e/wtr21_e/00_wtr21_e.pdf.

Yadav, P. 2010. "Differential pricing for pharmaceuticals: Review of current knowledge, new findings, and ideas for action." A study conducted for the U.K. Department for International Development (DFID), Govt. of UK.

Glossary and definitions

Adaptive designs The Food and Drug Administration (FDA) defines an *adaptive clinical trial* as one that allows for changes to be made to one or more elements while it is still ongoing, based on preliminary subject data analysis. Adaptive designs can make clinical trials more flexible by utilizing results accumulating in the trial to modify the trial's course in accordance with pre-specified rules. In the traditional approach of randomized controlled trials (RCTs), modifications are not allowed during the course of the trial.

ANDA (abbreviated new drug application) An abbreviated new drug application (ANDA) contains data which is submitted to the FDA for the review and potential approval of a generic drug product. Once approved, an applicant may manufacture and market the generic drug product to provide a safe, effective, lower cost alternative to the brand-name drug it references (FDA Home page, Glossary).

APIs (active pharmaceutical ingredients) Active pharmaceutical ingredients (APIs) are the active components in a pharmaceutical drug that produce the required effect on the body to treat a condition.

Assays These biological assays are analytical techniques are used in determining the potency of a drug or other substance by comparing the effects it has on animals with those of a reference standard.

Backward GVC participation Backward GVC participation involves importing foreign inputs to produce goods and services for export. It is measured as the foreign content of exports (foreign value added, or FVA).

Bioeconomy The term bioeconomy refers to the share of the economy based on products, services, and processes derived from biological resources (e.g., plants and microorganisms). The development of and transition to predominantly a bioeconomy as a means to address grand challenges such as climate change, food security, energy independence, and environmental sustainability (CRS Report 2022, The Bioeconomy: A Primer).

Blockbuster Drug Blockbuster drugs are those that generate annual sales of at least $1 billion for companies that produce them.

Biological target Biological target is anything within a living organism to which some drug is directed, resulting in a change in its behavior or function. Examples of common classes of biological targets are proteins and nucleic acids.

Biologic Biologic is a therapeutic drug or a vaccine, made from living organisms—human, animal, yeast, or microorganisms—licensed under a Biologic License Application by the FDA.

Biomarker A biological indicator, such as a genetic or molecular characteristic of a patient, which can be found in tissue, blood, urine, or other bodily fluids. Biomarkers can be measured to identify underlying pathological or physiological processes (AstraZeneca).

Biosimilar Competitors to the first-in-class biologic product that has an expired patent. These drugs are not currently considered to be identical to the original product (because of the nature of manufacturing with live products) but are considered to be therapeutic alternatives.

Biopharmaceuticals and synthetic drugs The term biopharmaceuticals refers to pharmaceuticals produced in biotechnological processes using molecular biology methods (Kesik-Brodacka 2018). Biopharmaceuticals are produced in living cells, whereas synthetic drugs are the products of chemical processes.

Biotechnology In 1973 Herb Boyer and Stanley Cohen showed it was possible to take a human gene and put it in a bacterium that could then mass-produce quantities of that gene. Modern biotechnology began when bacteria were genetically engineered to produce human insulin. Biotechnology is recognized as one of the strategic technologies of the 21st century.

The bottom of the pyramid The "bottom of the pyramid" (BOP) proposition postulates that there is a huge untapped market with significant buying power at the bottom of the world's economic pyramid (Prahalad & Hart 2002). According to Prahlad & Hart (2002), many of the innovations for the bottom can be adapted for use in markets of the developed world

BRICS It is an acronym for Brazil, Russia, India, China, and South Africa.

Cell and molecular biology Cell and molecular biology studies the structure and function of the cell, which is the basic unit of life. By understanding how cells work in healthy and diseased states, cell biologists working in animal, plant, and medical science will be able to develop new vaccines and more effective medicines.

Compulsory licensing Compulsory licensing flexibilities identified in the Doha Declaration include "the right to grant compulsory licenses." A compulsory license is issued by a government authority or a court to make certain use of a patented invention without the consent of the patent holder.

CRISPR-Cas9 It is a naturally occurring protection system found in bacteria to combat and destroy invading viruses. This system has been adapted by scientists to facilitate precise gene editing of DNA in cells (AstraZeneca).

COVAX COVAX facility, formally launched in June 2020, is a partnership between WHO, the Coalition for Epidemic Preparedness Innovations, the Global Alliance for Vaccines and Immunizations (Gavi), and UNICEF.

DNA Deoxyribonucleic acid (DNA) contains the genetic information that defines the development and function of a living organism (AstraZeneca).

Domestic value-added in exports Domestic value-added in gross exports is an estimation of value-added, by an economy, in producing goods and services for export, simply defined as the difference between gross output at basic prices and intermediate consumption at purchasers' prices.

Drug repurposing (also called repositioning) Drug repurposing involves the identification of new applications for existing drugs centered on the readily available ideas, knowledge, and technologies (Von Krogh, Kucukkeles & Ben-Menahem 2020). This type of innovation potentially allows developers to circumvent costly and time-consuming safety trials, thus greatly reducing the cost compared with novel drug discovery and development.

Efficiency-seeking FDI Efficiency-seeking motivation stems from the consideration of reaping economies of scale and economies of scope (Lanz and Miroudot 2011).

Epidemiologic transition The epidemiologic transition describes changing patterns of population age distributions, mortality, fertility, life expectancy, and causes of death (McKeown 2009, Harper & Armelagos 2010).

Epigenetic Genes play an important role in your health, but so do our behaviors (habits) and environment, such as what we eat and how physically active we are. Epigenetics is the study of how our behaviors and environment can cause changes that affect the way our genes work.

First-in-class pharmaceuticals The FDA defines a first-in-class drug as one that "uses a novel and unique mechanism of action to treat a medical condition"; therefore, they are innovative, cutting-edge, and have the potential to produce unprecedented patient outcomes.[1]

Forward GVC participation Forward GVC participation involves exporting goods and services that become inputs in the exports of other countries. It comprises transactions in which a country's exports are not consumed in the importing country but are instead reexported by that country as part of a good or service (indirect value-added) to a third country.

Gavi Gavi, The Vaccine Alliance, is a health partnership that provides immunizations to the world's poorest people. Created in 2000, Gavi works with public and private partners to provide new and underused vaccines to children living in the world's poorest countries. Gavi supports vaccines that immunize children against pneumonia, diarrhea, and meningitis, some of the world's leading killers of children.

Gene A basic unit of hereditary which passes from parent to child containing a sequence of DNA. Genes are present in every cell's nucleus and are made from strands of DNA.

Genetic Traits or processes relating to a particular gene (AstraZeneca). All inheritable traits of living organisms are determined by their genetic material, the "genome," a long nucleic acid called deoxyribonucleic acid (DNA). DNA is a chemical that has a genetic code for making proteins.

Genome: The entire DNA information contained within a cell (AstraZeneca).

Genomics Knowledge of human genes and their functions may allow effective preventive measures and change drug research strategy and drug discovery development processes.

Genomic technologies Genomic technologies are best defined as technologies used to manipulate and analyze genomic information. Genomic technologies can be used to diagnose patients who have high-risk genetic errors causing disease.

Genotype The genetic make-up of an individual organism (AstraZeneca).

Gene therapy Gene therapy involves the administration of DNA or RNA, in order to correct a genetic abnormality or modify the expression of genes.

Genome editing Genome editing uses molecular techniques to modify the genome—genome editing can add in, cut out, or replace sections of the DNA sequence. Emmanuelle Charpentier and Jennifer A. Doudna got the Nobel Prize in chemistry in 2020 for discovering one of gene technology's sharpest tools: the CRISPR/Cas9 genetic scissors.

Global value chains (GVCs) A global value chain (GVC) consists of a series of stages involved in producing a good or service, with each stage adding value and with at least two stages produced in different countries (World Bank 2020).

Globalization Globalization refers to the global movement to increase the flow of goods, services, people, real capital, and money across national borders in order to create a more integrated and interdependent world economy.

Globalization of production Trend by individual firms to disperse parts of their productive processes to different locations around the globe to take advantage of differences in cost and quality of factors of production.

Gross domestic product (GDP) GDP is a measure of the market value of goods and services produced in a nation.

Hit-to-lead Once a promising drug target has been identified, researchers aim to identify molecules that can interact with the target to produce desired biological effects. A hit compound is a molecule that shows the desired type of activity in a screening assay.

High-throughput sequencing High-throughput sequencing, also known as next-generation sequencing (NGS), is the comprehensive term used to describe technologies that sequence DNA and RNA in a rapid and cost-effective manner. Throughput is a measure of how many units of information a system can process in a given amount of time.

Human Genome Project The Human Genome Project is an international research project aimed at deciphering the chemical makeup of the entire human genetic code (i.e., the genome). Human Genome Project (HGP) was a 13-year project, completed in 2003. Project's key goals were to:

- *Identify* all the approximately 20,500 genes in human DNA
- *Determine* the sequences of the 3 billion chemical base pairs that make up human DNA
- *Store* this information in databases

Innovation Innovations are new creations of economic significance (Edquist 2005). Pharmaceutical innovation requires *novelty of effectiveness*, which means either it meets otherwise unmet or inadequately met healthcare needs. (Morgan, Lopert & Greyson 2008).

Institutions Institutions consist of both informal constraints (sanctions, taboos, customs, traditions, and codes of conduct) and formal rules (constitutions, laws, property rights) (North 1991). Institutions create order provide incentives and reduce uncertainty in exchange.

Institutional voids Institutional voids refer to lack of institutions that can help facilitate market transactions (Khanna and Palepu, 2010). Missing institutions (non-existence of specialized market intermediaries to facilitate trade among firms) impact the functioning of labor markets, product markets, and capital markets in general. Examples of such voids include weak intellectual property rights, lack of transparency, red tape, bureaucracy, administrative delays, inadequate disclosure regime, corruption, and political instability.

Intra-trade Intra-industry trade is defined as the trade of similar goods within the same product category. For example, intra-industry trade in wine (simultaneous imports and exports of wine) represents trade in different qualities of wine between two countries.

Intra-firm and inter-firm trade Intra-firm trade corresponds to international flows of goods and services between parent companies and their affiliates. Inter-firm trade, on the other hand, refers to arm's-length trade between unrelated parties (Lanz and Miroudot 2011).

In vivo vs. in vitro In vivo is Latin for "within the living." It refers to research performed on a living organism. In vitro is Latin for "within the glass." In vitro means research done in a laboratory dish or test tube—that is outside of a living organism.

Technological product innovations A considerable part of industrial R&D goes to the development of new and/or better products (rather than processes), although this figure varies between countries.

International Monetary Fund (IMF) An international organization designed to promote global economic stability and development.

Lead identification and optimization Lead identification and optimization is the process of discovering a small molecule or large molecule lead compound to a pre-clinical candidate.

Macromolecules Macromolecules are large molecules necessary for life that are built from smaller organic molecules (Britannica). There are four major classes of biological macromolecules (carbohydrates, lipids, proteins, and nucleic acids), and each is an important component of the cell and performs a wide array of functions.

Market-seeking FDI This is the main type of horizontal FDI, meaning that the subsidiary produces the same good or service as the parent country.

Medical device A medical device can be any instrument, apparatus, implement, machine, appliance, implant, reagent for in vitro use, software, material, or other similar or related article, intended by the manufacturer to be used, alone or in combination for a medical purpose (WHO 2012).

Medicines Patent Pool (MPP) The Medicines Patent Pool (MPP) is a United Nations-backed public health organization working to increase access to and facilitate the development of life-saving medicines for low- and middle-income countries.

Metabolome The metabolome represents the collection of all metabolites (glucose, lipid, amino acid, fatty acid, alkaloids, phenolic compounds, etc.) in a biological cell, tissue, organ, or organism, which are the end products of cellular processes.

Molecular level Molecular level describes the very smallest units that make up organisms or elements.

Molecular biology Molecular biology is the branch of biology dealing with the molecular basis of all living things—the study of macromolecules, such as proteins and DNA, and the mechanisms behind the way they interact within cells. With the increased knowledge of molecular biology, scientists are able to answer more complex questions about physiology, the immune system, and diseases in humans.

Molecular target In cancer, a term used to describe certain genes, proteins, and other molecules that are involved in the growth, spread, and survival of cancer cells and may be used as targets for cancer treatment. Treatments that block molecular targets or the signals they send may kill cancer cells or keep cancer cells from growing or spreading.

Monoclonal antibodies Monoclonal antibodies are immune system proteins that are created in the lab. Antibodies are produced naturally by your body and help the immune system recognize germs that cause disease (National Cancer Institute, USA).

mRNA vaccine Messenger ribonucleic acid (mRNA) vaccines are designed to produce an immune response that protects us against the virus that causes COVID-19. Our cells read the mRNA as a set of instructions, building proteins that match up with parts of the pathogen called antigens.

National System of Innovation NSI is defined as the set of organizations, institutions, and linkages for the generation, diffusion, and application of scientific and technological knowledge operating in a specific country (Edquist 2005, Riccardo Galli and Morris Teubal, Ch 15). System of innovation is about the determinants of innovation, not about their consequences (that is, not the ultimate output, innovation) (Edquist 2001).

Next-generation sequencing (high-throughput DNA sequencing) can sequence hundreds and thousands of genes or whole genome in a short period of time.

Nucleic acids Nucleic acids carry genetic information which is read in cells to make the RNA and proteins by which living things function.

New biotechnology firms Most NBFs (new biotechnology firms) were founded during the early 1980s. These firms are dedicated to researching and developing new products.

Omics An "ome" is a totality. Omics technologies are aimed at primarily four omics research fields namely, genomics, transcriptomics (mRNA), proteomics, or metabolomics (Karahalil 2016).

Patent Cliff Drugs are granted 20 years of *patent* protection. A patent cliff is a colloquialism to denote the potential sharp decline in revenues upon patent expiry of one or more leading products of a firm.

Offshore in-sourcing Lead firm sets up its own subsidiary in another country to carry out certain stages of production (internalized production done by foreign affiliates). This sometimes referred to as "captive offshoring." Offshoring is different from the concept of outsourcing, which always involves a third party, but not necessarily a transfer abroad.

Offshore outsourcing Lead firm uses overseas suppliers to supply inputs or carry out certain tasks (externalized production abroad). That is, MNCs use foreign suppliers for certain inputs and tasks.

Organization for Economic Cooperation and Development (OECD) A group of 30 countries that meets regularly to discuss global issues and make appropriate economic and social policies.

Open innovation network Open innovation network is a distributed innovation process based on purposively managed knowledge flows across organizational boundaries (Chesbrough and Bogers 2013). Pharmaceutical companies are increasingly adopting open innovation business model that uses internal and external ideas to generate value (to reduce attrition rate and improve productivity) (Gay 2014).

"Orphan drugs" An orphan drug is a medication or other medicinal product used to treat a rare disease or disorder. It is called an "orphan drug" because due to its limited market, it is unlikely to be adopted by a pharmaceutical company. Orphan drug designation qualifies sponsors for incentives including, such tax credits for qualified clinical trials, potential seven years of market exclusivity after approval (FDA.gov home page).

Outsourcing (international) A situation in which a firm's functions are performed or provided by a person or group from outside the company.

Outsourcing (domestic) Lead firm hands over some production stages to another firm in the same country (externalized production at home).

Patent A patent grants the inventor of a new product or process exclusive rights to the manufacture, use, or sale of that invention.

Precision medicine Personalized medicine describes the use of our genetic information to tailor healthcare intervention to our own individual needs. In some cases, such as cancer, we can identify the genetic drivers of disease and then give drugs which specifically target that pathway. This is known as targeted therapy.

Pharmacogenomics Pharmacogenomics is the application of genomic technologies such as gene sequencing, statistical genetics, and gene expression analysis to drugs in clinical development and on the market. It explores how DNA affects a person's response to a drug.

Phenotype Phenotype refers to an individual's observable traits, such as height, eye color, and blood type. A person's phenotype is determined by both their genomic makeup (genotype) and environmental factors (National Human Genome Research Institute, glossary).

Predictive modeling Predictive models often include multiple predictors (covariates) to estimate the probability or risk of a certain outcome or to classify *that* a certain outcome is present/absent (diagnostic prediction model) or *will happen* within a specific timeframe (prognostic prediction model) in an individual (Cichosz, Johansen & Hejlesen 2015).

Proteins Proteins are large, complex molecules that play many important roles in the body. They are critical to most of the work done by cells and are required for the structure, function, and regulation of the body's tissues and organs (NHI, National Human Genome Research Institute).

Proteomics The study of the entirety of proteins within an organism or cell (AstraZeneca). The term proteome refers to the sum of all the proteins in a cell, tissue, or organism.

Rational drug design Rational drug design is the process of finding new medications based on the knowledge of a biological target (Zhou & Zhong 2017).

Recombinant DNA technology The rDNA technology is sometimes referred to as molecular cloning or genetic engineering. Basically, it allows DNA from different sources to be combined which creates new DNA sequences that are not always found in nature. The protein products of these new sequences can then be identified and isolated (Biotech Basics, Genentech, Gene.com). Recombinant DNA technology and molecular genetics are also referred to as "biotech" revolution (Galambos & Sturchio, 1998).

R&D Research and development (R&D) consists of four types of activities: basic and applied research, and product and process development. Basic research is frequently done by universities. Applied research is original experimental work with a specific aim done by the corporations. Product development is the improvement and extension of existing products. Process development is the creation of new or improved processes.

Resource-seeking FDI (foreign direct investment) This is a vertical type of FDI (i.e., where the subsidiary is an input supplier to the parent company); the MNE tries to gain access to certain resources in a foreign country.

Reverse innovations Reverse innovation commonly refers to an innovation initially launched in a developing country and later introduced in an advanced country.

RNA biology Ribonucleic acid (RNA) biology has emerged as one of the most influential areas in modern biology and biomedicine. The discovery of numerous new classes of RNAs and their functions in a wide spectrum of biological processes has revolutionized molecular biology, with profound implications for clinical sciences.

RNA Ribonucleic acid (abbreviated RNA) is a nucleic acid present in all living cells that has structural similarities to DNA. Different types of RNA exist in cells: messenger RNA (mRNA), ribosomal RNA (rRNA), and transfer RNA (tRNA).

Sustainable Development Goal 3 (SDG 3) Goal 3: Ensure healthy lives and promote well-being for all at all ages (https://www.un.org/sustainable development/health/).

"Smile'' curve The hypothesis of a "*smile curve*" in an industry postulate that tasks at the early and late stages of the supply chains generate higher value-added, possibly due to a higher knowledge intensity,

Specialty drug A drug that is costly, requires special supply chain features (such as freezing or cold storage), typically indicated for a small group of patients, and where the patients may need special case management services.

Strategic asset-seeking FDI The objective is to acquire assets, such as knowledge, technology, or information on local market with a view to increase its competitiveness. It is neither vertical nor horizontal FD (Lanz & Miroudot 2011)

Strategic patenting Patents are granted to the originator to protect an active compound of a drug (a so-called "basic" or "primary" patent) (Gurgula 2020). These practices are used to delay or even block generic competition.

Target A target is a broad term which can be applied to a range of biological entities which may include, for example, proteins, genes, and RNA (Hughes, Rees, Kalındjian, & Philpott 2011). The idea for a target can come from a variety of sources including academic and clinical research and from the commercial sector (Hughes, Rees, Kalindjian & Philpott 2011).

Technological product innovations: A considerable part of industrial R&D goes to the development of new and/or better products (rather than processes), although this figure varies between countries.

Transcriptome Transcriptome is the set of all messenger RNA (mRNA) molecules in one cell, tissue, or organism. RNA is the intermediary biomolecule (molecule in a living organism) that transfers information stored in genomic DNA to proteins.

Technology transfer (TT) Technology transfer in biomedical research and development is the transfer of a medical technology from the originator to a secondary user, allowing that user to manufacture the technology and sell it on usually new markets. The channels of technology transfer include trade in capital goods, technology licensing, FDI (foreign direct investment), and movement of people (e.g. scientists, employees moving from one organization to another, international students, etc.).

Vaccine Technology Transfer Hub A technology transfer *hub is* a multilateral initiative that brings together in one single place all the elements needed to establish the technology (know-how, data, formula, intellectual property, and in many cases training) and then transfers the fully validated manufacturing process to multiple secondary users.

Triadic patent families Triadic patent families are a set of patents filed at three of these major patent offices: the European Patent Office (EPO), the Japan Patent Office (JPO), and the United States Patent and Trademark Office (USPTO) (OECD Library).

Vaccine A vaccine is a biological product that can be used to safely induce an immune response that confers protection against infection and/or disease on subsequent exposure to a pathogen. The essential component of most vaccines is one or more protein antigens that induce immune responses that provide protection (Pollard & Bijker 2021).

Vaccine supply chain Vaccine manufacturing is a multistage process. There are five main stages critical to getting a new vaccine from start to finish: pre-clinical stage of research and development; clinical trials; production of the drug substance and its formulation into drug product; "fill and finish," or the assembly-line process of putting a vaccine into millions of tiny vials; and then distribution (Bown & Bollyky 2022).

Value-based pricing Value-based pricing aligns prescription drug prices to their clinical benefits (expressed in terms of quality of life or efficacy).

Vectors Vectors are vehicles that ferry the genetic material into a wide variety of cells, tissues, and whole organs.

Vector-borne diseases Vectors are living organisms that can transmit infectious pathogens between humans, or from animals to humans. Vector-borne diseases include malaria, dengue, chikungunya, Zika virus, yellow fever, and others.

Vertical Integration Retaining the entire production chain within the firm rather than contracting through the marketplace.

World Bank An international organization created at Breton Woods in 1944 to help in the reconstruction and development of its member nations.

WHO (World Health Organization) The United Nations agency working to promote health, keep the world safe, and serve the vulnerable.

World Intellectual Property Organization (WIPO) Group of 188 countries that have signed international treaties designed to protect intellectual property.

World Trade Organization (WTO) A multilateral organization that promotes free and fair trade among the nations of the world. It was created in 1994 by 121 nations at the Uruguay Round of the General Agreement on Tariffs and Trade (GATT).

Zoonotic disease A zoonotic disease (or zoonoses—plural) is an infectious disease that is transmitted between species from animals to humans (or from humans to animals.

Note

1 FDA website. 2011. Novel New Drugs document.

Appendix

Table A: Sales and R&D expenditure of top 50 pharmaceutical companies

Rank	*Company [Website]*	*2022 Rx Sales USD in Billions*	*2022 R&D Spend USD in Billions*
01	**Pfizer** New York, New York [pfizer.com]	$91.303	$12.381
02	**AbbVie** North Chicago, Illinois [abbvie.com]	$56.179	$7,823
03	**Johnson & Johnson** New Brunswick, New Jersey [jnj.com]	$50.179	$14.140
04	**Novartis** Basel, Switzer land [novartis.com]	$50.079	$9.088
05	**Merck & Co.** Kenilworth, New Jersey [merck.com]	$49.627	$11.842
06	**Roche** Basel, Switzerland [roche.com]	$47.909	$14.781
07	**Bristol-Myers Squibb** New York, New York [bms.com]	$45.417	$10.016
08	**AstraZeneca** London, England [astrazeneca.com]	$42.998	$9.500
09	**Sanofi** Paris, France [sanofi.com]	$40.353	$7.156
10	**Glaxo Smith Kline (GSK)** Brentford, England [gsk.com]	$38.254	$6.337
11	**Takeda** Osaka, Japan [takeda.com]	$29.690	$4.697
12	**Gilead Sciences** Foster City, California [gilead.com]	$26.615	$4.968
13	**Eli Lilly** Indianapolis, Indiana [lilly.com]	$25.463	$7.191
14	**Novo Nordisk** Bagsvaerd, Denmark [novonordisk.com]		1848.00
15	**Amgen** Thousand Oaks, California [amgen.com]	$22.536	$4.341
16	**Boehringer Ingelheim** Ingelheim, Germany [boehringer-ingelheim.com]	$19.473	$5.386
17	**Bayer** Leverkusen, Germany [bayer.com]	$18.898	$7.013
18	**Moderna** Cambridge Massachusetts [modernatx.com]	$18.435	$2.993
19	Viatris Canonsburg, Pennsylvania [viatris.com]	$15.999	$0.698

Rank	*Company [Website]*	*2022 Rx Sales USD in Billions*	*2022 R&D Spend USD in Billions*
20	**CSL** Melbourne, Australia [csl.com.au]	$13.123	$1.347
21	**Teva Pharmaceutical Industries** Petha Tivka Israel [tevaparam.com]	$12.071	$0.838
22	**Astellas Pharma** Tokyo, Japan [astellas.com]	$10.511	$2.011
23	**Vertex Pharmaceuticals** Boston, Massachusetts [vrtx.com]	$8.607	$2.104
24	**Merck KGaA** Darmstadt, Germany [merckgroup.com]	$8.366	$2.690
25	**Biogen** Cambridge, Massachusetts [biogenidec.com]	$ 7.988	$2.146
26	**Otsuka Holdings** Tokyo, Japan [otsuka.com]	$7.357	$2.009
27	**Daiichi Sankyo** Tokyo, Japan [daiichisankyo.com]	$7.089	$2.314
28	**Regeneron Pharmaceuticals** Tarrytown, New York [regeneron.com]	$6.894	$3.831
29	**Bausch Health Companies** Laval, Quebec [bauchhealth.com]	$6.569	$0.529
30	**Organon** Jersey City, New Jersey [organon.com]	$6.038	$0.522
31	**USB** Brussels, Belgium [usb.com]	$4,518	$1,203
32	**Perrigo Company** Dublin, Ireland [perrigo.com]	$5.436	$0.125
33	**Sun Pharmaceutical** Mumbai, India [sunpharma.com]	$5.424	$0.294
34	**Les Laboratoires Servier** Suresnes, France [servier.com]	$5.193	NA
35	**Chugai Pharmaceutical** Tokyo, Japan [chugaI-pharm.co.jp]	$5.120	$1.228
36	**Abbott Laboratories** Abbott Park, Illinois [abbott.com]	$4.885	$2.606
37	**Grifols** Barcelona, Spain [grifols.com]	$4.864	$0.425
38	**Eisai** Tokyo, Japan [eisai.com]		
39	**Sino Biopharmaceuticals** Hong Kong [sinobiopharm.com]	$4.463	$0.601
40	**Fresenius** Bad Homburg, Germany [fresenius-kabi.com]	$4.463	$0.601
41	**Shanghai Pharmaceuticals Holding** Shanghai, China [sphchina.com]	$4.043	$0.261
42	**Horizon Therapeutics** Dublin, Ireland [horizontherapeutics.com]	$4.022	$0.477
43	**Jiangsu Hengrui Medicine** Lianyugang, Jiangsu province, China	$4.010	$0.893
44	**Jazz Pharmaceuticals** Dublin, Ireland [jazzpharma.com]	$3,550	$0.813
45	**Menarini** Florence, Italy [menarini.com]	$3.621	NA

Rank	*Company [Website]*	*2022 Rx Sales USD in Billions*	*2022 R&D Spend USD in Billions*
46	**Ispen** Paris, France [ispen.com]	$3,141	$0.344
47	**BioNTech** Mainz, Germany [biontech.com]	$3.339	$1.640
48	**CSPC Pharmaceutical Group** Shijiazhuang, China [cspc.com]	$3.334	$0.511
49	**Incyte** Wilmington, Delaware [incyte.com]	$2.747	$1.457
50	**NOVAVAX** Gaithersburg, Maryland [Novavax.com]	$1.555	$1.235

Source: EvaluatePharma, May 2023, Also reproduced in Michael C "2023 Pharm Exec Top 50 Companies" Pharmaceutical Executive, June 2023, Volume 43, Issue 6, https://www.pharmexec.com/view/2023-pharm-exec-top-50-companies

Author Index

Note: Page locators followed by 'n' refer to notes.

Subject Index

Note: Page locators followed by 'n' refer to tables; Locators in italics refer to figure and bold refer to tables.

Made in the USA
Las Vegas, NV
19 September 2026

c595b9f1-3365-4b22-943e-a09e65b20322R01